CREATING CURRICULUM EARLY CHILDHOOD

Creating Curriculum in Early Childhood explores the backward design model of curriculum development, equipping readers with the tools and methods they need to effectively apply backward design in the early childhood classroom.

Clear yet comprehensive chapters walk new and veteran educators through an effective method for curriculum design that promotes meeting standards through intentional teaching while engaging children in developmentally appropriate, interest-based education focused on big ideas and conceptual understanding. Featuring desired results, assessment methods, and teaching techniques specific to birth to age eight, this critical guide also includes practical tips for educators new to the method.

Designed to help students and practitioners alike, this powerful textbook combines early childhood philosophy and developmental research with highly practical descriptions, rationales, and examples for developing curricular units using backward design.

Julie Bullard is a Professor of Early Childhood Education at the University of Montana, USA.

CREATING CURRICULUM IN EARLY CHILDHOOD

Enhanced Learning through Backward Design

Julie Bullard

Routledge
Taylor & Francis Group

NEW YORK AND LONDON

First published 2020
by Routledge
52 Vanderbilt Avenue, New York, NY 10017

and by Routledge
2 Park Square, Milton Park, Abingdon, Oxon, OX14 4RN

Routledge is an imprint of the Taylor & Francis Group, an informa business

Library of Congress Cataloging-in-Publication Data
A catalog record for this title has been requested

ISBN: 978-1-138-57012-2 (hbk)
ISBN: 978-1-138-57013-9 (pbk)
ISBN: 978-0-203-70381-6 (ebk)

Typeset in Interstate
by codeMantra

To my mentors; the many children, college students, early childhood professionals, colleagues, and individuals I've learned from. While I cannot name each of you, I do want to mention a few who were especially significant, Eve Malo, Walt Oldendorf, Pat Tierney, and Randy Hitz. Each played different roles in my professional life. However, each caused me to improve my skills, question my beliefs, and to think more deeply. My wish is that this book might provide an avenue for you to engage in this type of transformative learning.

CONTENTS

PREFACE

This book addresses the backward design model of curriculum development through an early childhood lens. Through interacting with the book, early childhood students and practitioners will learn an effective method for curriculum design that promotes intentional teaching focused on big ideas and conceptual understanding, while still engaging children in developmentally appropriate, interest-based learning. The book combines early childhood philosophy and research with practical information about designing curriculum.

It is written for those teachers who will be or who are working with children from birth through age eight. There are also sections in each chapter that address early childhood adult educators who are learning this method. To increase understanding and to make the book more engaging, the text is filled with examples. Additionally, in the book, you will hear from some other voices besides mine. Throughout the text, four students make comments and ask clarification questions.

Why is this book necessary? I have been teaching the backward design model to early childhood students and professionals for many years. I've also been using the backward design model in development of curriculum and while leading curriculum development teams. While backward design is not the typical planning method used in early childhood, I have found that early childhood students and professionals embrace this method and find that it is a valuable tool to support deeper and more coherent learning. However, I have found that early childhood students and practitioners often struggle with the content. This is due to several reasons. Current books and materials on backward design typically are written for teachers who are teaching an older age level with examples often focusing on middle school and high school students. Desired results, the assessment methods, and learning experiences are different for younger children than for older children. Additionally, even terminology can vary between the early childhood field and other educational fields. Therefore, while comprehending a new approach with challenging content and ideas, learners must simultaneously be translating what they are reading into methods that are appropriate for young children and that align with early childhood philosophy. This book solves this issue by providing a book on backward design written specifically for early childhood.

ACKNOWLEDGEMENTS

A special thanks to Libby Hancock, Lisa Bullard, and Lucy Marose for reading drafts and providing thoughtful critiques, to my grandchildren Seamus Bullard for crucial assistance with graphics and for Mike and Suzi Stufflebean, Aidan and Ember Bullard-O'Dea, and Opal Bullard for providing inspiration and for keeping me grounded in the early childhood years. Thank you also to Dave Browning who survived my preoccupation, listened patiently to book updates, and brainstormed challenges while I was writing the book. I also want to acknowledge the previous Routledge Editor Alex Masulis for meeting with me repeatedly to encourage me to write the book and for Editor Misha Kydd and Editorial Assistant Olivia Powers for support and guidance through the book writing and the editorial process.

1 Setting the Stage

Every day, early childhood teachers across the world design curriculum-determining goals, planning learning experiences, and designing assessments for children birth to age eight. We become early childhood teachers because we want to make a difference in young children's lives; to capitalize on the rapid growth in brain development that occurs at this age; to ensure that children are gaining developmentally appropriate social-emotional, physical, and cognitive knowledge, dispositions, and skills; and to lay a strong foundation for children's future learning and success. Through early childhood programs, we want to assist children to become confident socializers, relationship-builders, thinkers, creators, problem-solvers, readers, and writers who know how to learn and who also love learning.

What is the best way to design curriculum so that we meet these goals? One effective way is through designing your own curriculum using backward design. This book will teach you this effective model for designing curriculum.

As you read the book, you will be hearing from some other voices besides just mine: three teachers and one teacher in training. They will be interacting with the text by asking questions and making comments. Let's meet them now.

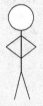

Meet Heidi—Heidi teaches in a public-school Pre-K program. The district is using a scripted curriculum that Heidi is required to implement to fidelity. This is her first year as a Pre-K teacher. However, she is an experienced teacher who has taught third and fourth grades for several years. Heidi has a K-8 grade teaching credential. Since she is teaching Pre-K, she must obtain a PreK-3 teaching endorsement, so she is taking graduate coursework in early childhood. Heidi describes herself as a very busy mom of twin toddlers.

Meet Jennifer—Jennifer is an adult educator who works for a resource and referral agency planning and implementing courses for child care providers. Previously, she was a teacher and a director of a Head Start program. Jennifer describes her life-work as advocating for increased quality in early childhood programs. She began teaching adults recently, feeling like this would allow her to have a greater impact on the field.

Meet Tony–Tony is a second-grade teacher in a charter school that uses the project approach to plan projects based on children's interests. He describes himself as a constructivist who is a non-conformist. Tony enjoys outdoor activities including hiking, fishing, and kayaking and enjoys sharing this passion with the children. Tony is currently getting his master's degree in curriculum and instruction.

Meet Tunisia–Tunisia is an early childhood major who is just entering a full-semester practicum. She also works part-time in a child care. She loves to read and wants to help children develop a love of literacy too. Tunisia is also interested in research-based practices and is concerned with what she deems "folklore teaching" or teaching based on past unproven practices.

What Is Curriculum?

What do you think of when you hear the word "curriculum?" This seems like a very simple question. However, there are numerous diverse images of curriculum. Wiggins and McTighe (2012), the authors of *Understanding by Design* (UbD), found 83 different definitions for curriculum in educational literature. Some describe curriculum in broad terms. The most traditional image is of curriculum as a subject matter such as math or science or literacy. Others view curriculum as a detailed blueprint for achieving outcomes through specific activities, defined methods, and listed materials. The focus of what is included in the term curriculum is also varied with some definitions including content only, others including content and methodology, while still others only refer to outcomes.

Regardless of our image of curriculum, when teachers begin to plan and assess "curriculum" they might think of the intended, published, enacted, or learned curriculum. The intended curriculum is what society expects children to learn. This is often embodied in the written or published curriculum. The enacted curriculum is what actually happens in the classroom or what children have the opportunity to learn. This is sometimes referred to as the "curriculum in action" or the "taught curriculum." The learned curriculum or attained curriculum is what children actually gain from the curriculum. There is often a large gap between what we intend to teach, what we actually teach, and what children ultimately learn. It is humbling to realize that teaching does not equal learning. Just because I teach something does not necessarily mean that anyone else learns what I am attempting to teach.

In addition to the explicit curriculum, children also learn through the hidden curriculum. The hidden curriculum is not written and is often unintended. These are the messages and experiences that children gain from being in the setting. Children learn from the structure, routine, and from the values and attitudes of teachers, administrators, and other children. For example, they might learn that a child that sleeps well, is quiet, or lines up quickly is a "good child." If they are bullied, they might learn that they are not worthy of being protected. They might see the star chart on the wall and absorb the message that they are not very smart if they have very few stars or they are very smart if the chart next to their name is filled with stars. It's crucial that we consider these hidden messages we are giving learners.

Curriculum specialists remind us that even the untaught curriculum provides messages about what and who is important and unimportant. This is sometimes referred to as the null curriculum. For example, the No Child Left Behind Act began by only assessing literacy and math. As a result, other subjects such as the arts, social studies, and science received far less attention, sending the potential message that these subjects are not worthy of study. Another example of null curriculum is the decision of who to study; what type of families, what cultures, and what writers, poets, and historians. Each of these decisions provides messages. For example, if we don't have materials and books that represent diversity, we may be giving children the message that you are only important if you are from the dominant culture. Since it is impossible to teach everything in school, some things are intentionally excluded (untaught) and someone is given the power and authority to make this decision. If we are using a textbook or a purchased curriculum, the authors and publishers are making this decision based upon their views.

Whether we are purchasing a curriculum or designing our own, we must be consciously aware of how we can make the curriculum inclusive for all children and families. This includes critiquing our environment for what is on our walls and on our shelves, as well as examining the music, art, guest speakers, and books we provide for children. Are we portraying a variety of cultures? Are cultures being portrayed accurately and respectfully?

We have touched on just a few of the different images of curriculum. The view we have of curriculum is important because it strongly influences the way we approach curriculum design. What is your view of curriculum?

For this book, we define curriculum as a roadmap that teachers use to assist learners in meeting desired outcomes. This roadmap includes content, teaching methods, learning experiences, and assessment. Like planning a trip, we know our end destination and can plan backwards from there. This does not exclude unplanned side trips but does help to ensure that our destination is either reached or a conscious decision is made to change direction.

Does the Choice of Curriculum Matter?

John Hattie, a professor from the New Zealand's University of Auckland, synthesized over 15 years of research, 800 meta-analyses, involving millions of children to determine what actually works to improve learning. He examined types of practices and major contributors to learning. In his

Table 1.1 Influences on Achievement

Influence	Included in the influence category	Effect size
Curriculum	Types of curriculum and how curriculum is implemented	0.45
Student	Background knowledge, self-concept, ability, motivation	0.39
Student's home	Socio-economic status, parental expectations, socio-psychological environment, intellectual stimulation, parental involvement, structural aspects	0.31
Student's school	Finances, mobility, leaders, class size, groupings, retention, classroom climate	0.23
Teaching	Goals and strategies	0.43
Impact of the teacher	Education, quality of teaching, teacher-student relationships, professional development, expectations, clarity, and communication of lesson goals	0.47

Data from Hattie (2012).

review, he found 153 meta-analyses involving 10,129 studies that examined curriculum in relationship to achievement. In examining the categories of influences on achievement, he found that the curriculum has a greater effect on children's achievement than the influences of the child, child's home, the school, or the teaching approach. The curriculum influences children's achievement nearly as much as the teacher (2012, p. 14). See Table 1.1 for the effect size for each of these variables.

What is Effect Size?

Effect size is a statistical measure used to compare the magnitude or size of an effect. Effect sizes allow you to quantify and compare across studies and so are used in meta-analysis. Hattie (2012) found that the average effect size of over 900 meta-analyses of 240 million students to be 0.40. Therefore, an effect size of over 0.40 is above the norm and indicates greater growth than normal.

How does effect size differ from statistical significance? Statistical significance is often used to describe the difference between two or more groups. If the results are found to be statistically significant, it indicates that the difference is most likely not due to chance. The larger the sample size, the more likely it is that statistical significance will be found. This does not always mean that it has practical significance. Effect size quantifies this difference.

Why Is There So Little Research about Which Curriculums Are Most Effective?

Although schools across America and the world use curriculum materials, few have been evaluated for effectiveness. Chingos and Whitehust (2012) from the Brown Center on Education Policy point out that "many instructional materials have not been evaluated at all, much less with studies that produce information of use to policymakers and practitioners" (p. 6). They further state that when the Institute of Education Sciences What Works Clearinghouse (WWC) reviewed 73 commonly used elementary school mathematics curriculum, they found that 66 had either no studies of their effectiveness or studies that didn't meet reasonable standards of evidence (p. 6).

To complete an effective curricular study, there needs to be a control or a comparison group that uses an alternate curriculum. A multi-year study is also desirable since the effects of curriculum can be enhanced or fade as time goes on. Ideally, children in the study need to be assigned randomly to either the control group or the curriculum group. But it is very expensive to conduct a randomized study of curriculum. For example, a randomized study of four math curriculums over the course of eight years cost 20 million dollars (Agodini et al., 2009; Chingos & Whitehurst, 2012; NCEE, 2016). As a result, many curriculum studies are not randomized. They do not include a control group. Without a control group, it is difficult to determine the effects of the curriculum since young children typically make gains in knowledge and skills regardless of the curriculum. It is also difficult to conduct controlled studies because schools are reluctant to have their children test a new, unproven curriculum. Further complicating the study of a specific curriculum is the difficulty in isolating the effect of curriculum versus other variables on learning. Additionally, even if a curriculum is researched, this research is quickly outdated as curriculum tends to be frequently updated.

The Preschool Curriculum Evaluation Research

In early childhood, there have not been many studies that have met these criteria. However, there was one large study that examined curriculum for preschoolers, The Preschool Curriculum Evaluation Research (PCER) study (Preschool Curriculum Evaluation Research Consortium, 2008). We often assume that if we purchase and follow a well-known curriculum to fidelity, we will be guaranteed better child outcomes. The PCER study was designed to examine whether children involved with each of 14 different curriculums had better outcomes than children who were not using the specific curriculum. Are child outcomes significantly better if teachers followed a curriculum to fidelity? Let's examine this large national study to determine if this is the case.

In 2002, the Institute of Education Sciences contracted with 12 research teams to evaluate 14 different Pre-K curriculums: Bright Beginnings; Creative Curriculum; Creative Curriculum with Ladders to Literacy; Curiosity Corner; DLM Early Childhood Express supplemented with Open Court Reading Pre-K; Doors to Discovery; Early Literacy and Learning Model; Language-Focused Curriculum; Let's Begin with the Letter People; Literacy Express; Pre-K Mathematics supplemented with DLM Early Childhood Express Math software; Project Approach; Project Construct; and Ready, Set, Leap.

Children were randomly assigned to participate in the curriculum or to continue with curriculum as usual. Children were assessed at the beginning and end of the Pre-K year and at the end of kindergarten with a battery of individually administered assessments that examined beginning reading skills, phonological awareness, oral language development, and mathematical knowledge and skills. Other assessments included teacher ratings of child behaviors, classroom observations, and teacher and parent interviews. All the teachers who were administering the intervention curriculums received professional development both before and during implementation.

Six of the intervention curriculums (Bright Beginnings, Creative Curriculum, Doors to Discovery, Project Approach, Project Construct) were compared to teacher-developed curriculum. In all six curriculum studies, there were no significant differences between child outcomes at the end of Pre-K or kindergarten on any of the measures between the children receiving the intervention curriculum and the children receiving the teacher developed curriculum. The only exception was the Project Approach where children received a lower score on behavior at the end of the kindergarten year if they were in the Project Approach group. The other intervention curriculums were compared against either currently used or provided curriculum. Four of the curriculums had significant impacts on child outcomes for at least one indicator. The results are shown in Table 1.2.

In summary, out of 14 Pre-K curriculums, only four of the curriculums had any child outcomes that were significantly better than child outcomes in the control group. Further, for each curriculum, there was a possibility for ten outcomes (five Pre-K and five kindergarten) to be significant. Three of the four curriculums that showed a significant difference had only one significant outcome out of the possible ten. The other curriculum, DLM Early Childhood Express supplemented with Open Court Reading Pre-K had six significant outcomes (Preschool Curriculum Evaluation Research Consortium, 2008).

Table 1.2 Preschool Curriculum Evaluation Research Results

Curriculum	Significant results in Pre-K	Significant results in kindergarten	No significant results in Pre-K or K
DLM Early Childhood Express supplemented with Open Court Reading Pre-K	Reading Phonological awareness Language	Reading Phonological awareness Language	Mathematics Behavior
Curiosity Corner	None	Reading	Language Phonological Awareness Mathematics Behavior
Early Literacy and Learning Model	None	Language	Reading Phonological Awareness Mathematics Behavior
Pre-K Mathematics supplemented with DLM Early Childhood Express Math Software	Mathematics	None	Reading Language Phonological Awareness Behavior
Project Approach	None	Negative impact behavior	Reading Language Phonological Awareness Mathematics
Bright Beginnings	None	None	Reading Language Phonological Awareness Mathematics Behavior
Creative Curriculum	None	None	Reading Language Phonological Awareness Mathematics Behavior
Creative Curriculum with Ladders to Literacy	None	None	Reading Language Phonological Awareness Mathematics Behavior
Doors to Discovery Language-Focused Curriculum	None	None	Reading Language Phonological Awareness Mathematics Behavior
Let's Begin with the Letter People	None	None	Reading Language Phonological Awareness Mathematics Behavior
Literacy Express	None	None	Reading Language Phonological Awareness Mathematics Behavior
Project Construct	None	None	Reading Language Phonological Awareness Mathematics Behavior
Ready, Set, Leap	None	None	Reading Language Phonological Awareness Mathematics Behavior

Data from Preschool Curriculum Evaluation Research Consortium (2008).

Why Learn about Curriculum Design?

Most teachers do develop or modify curriculum including: designing the curriculum used in in-dividual classrooms, being part of a curriculum team who develops curriculum, supplementing purchased curriculum, and/or modifying curriculum to meet the unique needs of their group of children (Kane et al., 2016; Opfer, Kaufman, & Thompson, 2017). By understanding curriculum design, you will be able to create an effective curriculum that allows children to meet standards while also honoring their unique needs, interests, and development.

Design Classroom Curriculum

Nearly all teachers are instructional designers, designing some, if not all, of their curriculum. This includes designing learning experiences, environments, and assessments that are guided by early learning standards. For example, Kane et al. (2016) who examined the practices of 1,642 teachers and administrators in five states found that 80% of English language arts teachers and 72% of math teachers used materials that they created themselves at least weekly. This study also found that 50% of the teachers either did not use a textbook at all or did not use the textbook as the primary source for their curriculum. A large study by the RAND Corporation of 2,300 schools found similar results. They discovered that 82% of elementary math teachers and 89% of elementary language arts teachers used self-developed and selected materials at least once a week. Only 57% of the districts mandated a math curriculum and only 37% of districts mandated a language arts curriculum (Opfer et al., 2017).

Since I teach in a school that mandates curriculum and requires me to teach to fidelity, I don't see why I need to learn this. It seems like a waste of time.

It is difficult when you must teach a specific curriculum to fidelity. However, even in these cases the teacher often designs some parts of the curriculum. Additionally, you may move to a new school where you are expected to design curriculum either individually or as part of a team. Finally, schools themselves change the way that curriculum is designed. Although you are required to follow a curriculum to fidelity now, this may change with a new principal.

Participate in Curriculum Teams

Even if you are not developing curriculum for your individual classroom, you may be on a team that develops curriculum. The study referenced above by Opfer et al. (2017) found that the ma-jority of the district-mandated curriculums were developed by a curriculum specialist and/or by teams of district teachers. Another national study found that in 80% of districts that adopted the common core standards, materials were developed locally, typically by the teachers (Rentner & Kober, 2014). At the time of this study, 42 states and the District of Columbia had adopted the Common Core State Standards (CCSS). The CCSS were developed for K-12 language arts and mathematics to provide more consistency across schools and to increase student achievement.

When teachers develop their own curriculum, it deepens their knowledge of the standards and allows them to create curriculum that is meaningful to the children they serve. To illustrate, in Louisiana, 75 teachers created language arts curriculum guidebooks. They designed the units to be relevant to Louisiana learners. For example, Cajun Folktales is one of the third-grade units. The units are also designed to be closely aligned with standards. Although not required, 80% of Louisiana districts are currently using the guidebooks. Since using the new curriculum, state test scores for reading have improved (Will, 2017).

Supplement Existing Curriculum

Additionally, even if you use a purchased curriculum like Heidi, you might need to supplement it to meet standards. In a review of the most commonly used math textbooks, the Center for the Study of Curriculum found that the books only covered 72% of the standards. On average, one-fourth of the grade level standards were not included. Furthermore, the focus of the books often included material that was not considered grade appropriate. On average, the books published before 2011 contained ten to fifteen weeks of off-topic material. Newer books were off-topic six to eight weeks (Cogan, Burroughs, & Schmidt, 2015).

Moreover, many curriculums only cover some of the subjects required. As a teacher, you will need to develop curriculum for the remaining areas. For example, you may be using a purchased curriculum for math and language arts; but need to design the science, social studies, and the arts curriculum.

Meet Children's Unique Needs

Finally, even if you have a purchased curriculum that covers all curricular areas, you will typically need to supplement the curriculum to meet your children's unique needs. This can include adding additional information to supplement the children's background knowledge, providing activities for children who have already mastered the content, and adding materials and activities to make the material more relevant and meaningful to the children in your group. For example, a popular Pre-K curriculum includes a unit on the ocean. If the children in your class have never visited the ocean, they will need additional opportunities to learn about the ocean and the animals that live there to grasp the unit concepts.

Planning curriculum can be very time-consuming, but I find it very rewarding. I enjoy using my creative talents to plan projects that will be engaging to the children in my classroom. It is rewarding to see their excitement and learning as a result of the time and thought that I've put into the project. I find that my projects are rarely perfect, but this allows me to learn and adapt the next time I teach a project.

What Is Backward Design?

While there are different ways to design curriculum, backward design is a popular, proven method that is used worldwide and is promoted by the Association for Supervision and Curriculum Development (ASCD). ASCD is a professional educator's association with members in 128 countries. Backward design (sometimes referred to as backward planning or backward mapping) is not a curriculum, it is instead a framework or model for designing curriculum. In the backward design model, the teacher begins by determining the desired results (what will the learner know, understand, and be able to do at the completion of the unit), then decides how to assess these results (what tasks will reveal that the learner has achieved the desired results), and lastly plans learning experiences (what activities and experiences will ensure that learners have the knowledge, understanding, and skills to pass the assessment). We will examine each of these in depth in the following chapters.

What Are the Advantages of Backward Design?

By beginning with outcomes and then planning the assessment before planning the activities, the focus remains on the desired outcomes. This emphasis on outputs rather than inputs allows a focus on deeper, content-rich curriculum, higher level thinking, transferability of learning, and increased learner understanding. The design process also assists with alignment, helping to ensure that learners will meet measurable outcomes.

Focus Is on Outputs versus Inputs

The focus of backward design is on what children will learn (output) rather than what we will teach (input). For example, let's look at two kindergarten teachers who are designing a unit on friendship. Amy plans in a traditional way, focusing on inputs rather than outputs. She plans many different activities to help children learn about their peers, searching lesson planning books and the Internet for ideas. In planning, she thinks about activities that relate to friendship, are appropriate for kindergartners, and that she thinks will be relevant to the children. However, she might not assess what children have learned or to have a clear idea herself of the specific outcomes she hopes children will achieve. Rather she simply hopes that through the unit, children will have a better understanding of friendship. Tabatha also plans a friendship unit, using backward design. She begins with what she wants children to learn, understand, and be able to do as a result of the friendship unit. Then she thinks about how she will assess whether they have achieved these desired results. Finally, she plans the learning experiences. While Tabatha might use many of the same learning experiences as Amy, she does so with an intentional focus. For example, both read several books on friendship. Since one of Tabatha's desired outcomes is that children will be able to discuss the characteristics that make someone a friend, she makes certain to choose books that highlight this. She also engages children in deep discussion about this topic as they read the books.

We've been studying intentional teaching. Is this similar?

According to Ann Epstein, the author of *The Intentional Teacher* intentional teaching is defined as:

> Planful, thoughtful, and purposeful acts teachers implement to ensure that young children acquire the knowledge and skills (content) they need to succeed in school and in life. Intentional teachers use their knowledge, judgment, and expertise to act with specific outcomes or goals in mind for children's development and learning, and they integrate and promote meaningful learning in *all* domains.
> (2014, p. 242)

Intentional teaching is at the heart of backward design. Backward design provides a structure that helps ensure that intentional teaching leads to deep, transferrable learning that is integrated, meaningful, and developmentally appropriate.

Enhances Alignment

The backward design model also enhances the alignment between goals, assessment, and learning experiences, improving the chances that the learners will achieve the desired results. Several studies have shown the significance of alignment (Blank & Smithson, 2014). For example, one study of 4,000 third graders found a statistically significant difference in achievement test scores when teachers aligned their curriculum to the assessment. Importantly, providing this opportunity to learn the content reduced the impact of other variables that often negatively affect achievement test scores such as socio-economic status (Mitchell, 1999).

Alignment is equally important when teaching adults. Studies indicate that when there is alignment, students are more successful, produce higher quality work, engage in deeper learning, and are more confident learners (Wang, Su, Cheung, Wong, & Kwong, 2013; Winkelmes, Bernacki, Butler, Zochowski, Golanics, & Weavil, 2016). Instructional alignment is so crucial that S. Alan Cohen, a specialist in research design and instructional psychology, once referred to it as the magic bullet. He stated that alignment routinely produces effect sizes of 1.2 to 3 sigma. To put this in context, most instructional techniques only result in 0.25 to 0.50 sigma effects (1987).

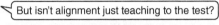

But isn't alignment just teaching to the test?

Heidi makes a good point. Alignment can be teaching to the test if we are directly teaching children the test items. For example, in traditional testing, one test item is chosen to represent a body of knowledge. If you directly teach the sample, it will not indicate whether the child understands the body of relevant knowledge. However, backward design stresses authentic assessment or using meaningful, real-world tasks to determine if children have mastered the concepts. Typically, these tasks do not lend themselves to memorization or mimicry (Mueller, 2016). For example, if you were assessing children's ability to classify, you might give the child a set of materials that he had not previously used and ask him to classify the items and to provide an explanation for the classification categories.

Promotes Higher Order Thinking and Understanding

The "ability to engage and apply higher-order thinking skills makes the difference between simply recalling information and being able to think critically, solve problems, and transfer learning to novel situations" (Varlas, 2013, p. 1).

Let's look at an example. Courtney was reading *Gooney Bird Greene* by Lois Lowry to her second-grade class. After reading the book, she asked the following questions about Gooney Bird.

1. "What was Gooney Bird wearing on her first day at Watertown Elementary School?" (This asks children to recall information, a low-level skill)
2. "Would you wear an outfit like that to school?" (This question asks for a simple yes or no and does not involve higher order thinking)

3. "In what other ways is Gooney Bird different than the other students at Watertown Elementary?" (This might have been a question that involved analysis. However, the book specifically describes this, so the children are being asked to recall the information.)
4. "What makes Gooney Bird Greene a great storyteller?" (This question requires analysis, a higher order thinking skill)

When we ask children questions that move beyond simple recall, we are asking them to use their intellectual abilities to analyze, synthesize, evaluate, interpret, make inferences, draw conclusions, and to transfer what they have learned to new situations. Since it is easier to design, assess, and to teach lower level knowledge, we must be intentional if we are to assist learners to engage in higher level thinking.

The goal of backward planning is to enhance higher order thinking and understanding. In the backward design framework, we determine enduring understandings and essential questions that engage learners in higher order thinking. "Enduring understandings represent ideas and processes we want students to integrate, refine, and keep as they move through their ... schooling and eventually into adulthood" (Stewart, 2014, p. 6). Essential questions are thought-provoking, transferable, open-ended questions that promote inquiry and aid in the transfer of learning. They are revisited over time resulting in deeper understanding.

Additionally, the framework itself helps to ensure that this occurs. For example, we begin with establishing higher order thinking skills and understanding as an important outcome. As we think about how we will know if learners can use higher level thinking and have truly developed an understanding, we ourselves engage in higher level thinking. As we think more deeply about the understandings, we want learners to gain and how we assess this understanding, the kinds of activities and experiences learners need to gain to accomplish this become clearer. On the other hand, if we begin by planning the activities first, learners may engage in higher level thinking. However, without the deep thought involved in planning the assessment first, it is less likely.

Aids in the Transfer of Learning

The Committee on Developments in the Science of Learning and the Committee on Learning and Practice, after a two-year in-depth examination of research, produced a consensus document on how people learn and how we can link the science of learning to classroom practice. After examination of the research, they state that "the ultimate goal of schooling is to help students transfer what they have learned in school to everyday settings of home, community, and workplace" (Bransford, Brown, Cocking, & National Research Council, 2000, p. 73). They further report that,

> A key finding in the learning and transfer literature is that organizing information into a conceptual framework allows for greater "transfer"; that is, it allows the student to apply what was learned in new situations and to learn related information more quickly.
>
> (Bransford et al., 2000, p. 17)

Backward design as developed in the UbD model provides the framework for conceptual learning. Through focusing on big ideas, enduring understandings, and essential questions, teachers design curriculum that allows learners to develop higher level thinking and to transfer what they have learned to new situations.

Helps Ensure Content-rich Curriculum

A content-rich curriculum typically covers fewer topics but covers these topics in more depth. Topics are thoughtfully chosen to assist students in learning about "big ideas." As mentioned earlier, big ideas are incorporated into the backward design model. According to the researchers, there are few published curriculums in the United States that are content-rich. Instead published curriculums are typically "a mile wide and an inch deep." This provides exposure to many topics, but the lack of depth often means that the knowledge gained is superficial. Therefore, learners often do not remember the information provided.

Traditional math curriculums provide an example. As a result of children in the United States consistently performing poorly on international exams such as the Trends in Science and Mathematics Study (TIMSS), researchers began to examine the difference in math education between the United States and high performing countries. They found that math curriculum in the United States covered far more topics each school year than high performing countries. In the United States, children revisited these topics throughout succeeding school years. However, rather than this spiraling curriculum leading to increased understanding, as initially intended, the same lower level skills would need to be retaught, since children had not been successful in learning them in the first place. Countries whose children did well on the international exams instead focused on fewer topics but covered these topics in-depth (Schmidt, 2012). The Common Core Math Standards were an attempt to move United States math curriculum from "a mile wide and an inch deep" to a more focused, in-depth study of fewer math topics each year (National Governors Association Center for Best Practices & Council of Chief State School Officers, 2010). Does this make a difference? Let's see what happened in one state that changed their practices. Between 1995 and 2007, Minnesota developed math content standards that were focused and coherent. Before 1995, they covered a "laundry list" of topics and nearly half of the topics were inconsistent with the international model for coherence. After the revamping, less than 5% of the topics were inconsistent with the international model for coherence (Schmidt, 2012). In 1995, Minnesota students scored in the average US range, which placed them in the lower middle of international students. However, after the new standards were implemented, they scored in the upper ranges. For example, in 1995, 70% of fourth graders met the intermediate benchmarks in math and 35% met the high benchmarks in math. By 2007, the next time that Minnesota participated in TIMSS, 85% of fourth graders met the intermediate benchmarks and 55% met the high benchmarks (Mullis, Martin, & Foy, 2008). In this era of increased attention to STEM (Science, Technology, Engineering, and Math) and global competition, increased competence in meeting international benchmarks has become increasingly important. While this example is not proof that it was the standards that resulted in this change, it is strong correlational evidence.

History of Backward Design

Backward design has a rich history beginning nearly 70 years ago. Today, the backward design framework is used throughout the world for teaching both children and adults.

Using Objectives for Planning

In 1949, Ralph Tyler introduced the concept of planning curriculum around objectives using a four-stage process that included determining educational purposes (the objectives), planning educational experiences, effectively organizing the experiences, and then assessing and evaluating to determine if the objectives were met.

In 1998, Jay McTighe and Grant Wiggins in their book *Understanding by Design* (UbD) popularized the term "backward design" and stressed using backward design as a mechanism to increase student understanding. Similar to the model proposed by Ralph Tyler, backward design begins with the outcomes (desired results). However unlike the Tyler process, in backward design, the next step is to determine how you will assess these desired results. The third step is to plan and organize the educational experiences. Thus, the term backward design.

Backward Design in Elementary and Secondary School

The UbD framework is currently being used in elementary and secondary schools throughout the country. For example, the New Jersey and Pennsylvania Departments of Education are providing units for different grade levels that were developed using UbD. Massachusetts used a Race to the Top federal grant to gather teams of teachers to develop over 100 UbD units. Utah has developed social studies units using UbD. Individual school districts have also developed UbD units including New Heights Academy Charter School in New York City, Oakland Independent School District in Michigan, and Nanue Public School District in New York. Advanced Placement (AP) courses that are developed by the College Board are also being redesigned using UbD as a framework. In 2017, over one million students took AP exams. Students who score a three or higher on the exam typically receive college credit for the high school AP course (College Board Communications, 2018).

Backward design is also used internationally. In The International Baccalaureate Primary Years Programme, taught in 109 countries around the world, teachers use backward design to plan at least six units of inquiry each year. The entire island nation of the Philippines is using the UbD framework for their national secondary curriculum (Barnachea, 2013).

Backward Design in Higher Education

Backward design is also gaining prominence in higher education. For example, backward design is highlighted on the University of Arizona Office of Instruction and Assessment, Western Washington University teaching handbook, Center for Teaching at Vanderbilt University, and on the Yale Center for Teaching and Learning.

Backward Design in Other Settings

The influence of backward design is not limited to schools. Intel, a company that manufactures computer chips, designs unit plans for teachers using UbD. "Pondwater and Pollywogs," "Are We What We Eat?" and "My Family" are some of the units available for early childhood educators.

Some national standards also emphasize backward design. For instance, The National Core Art Standards include the critical components of UbD, enduring understanding and essential questions in their standards documents.

Early Childhood Education

Is Understanding by Design the only model for backward design for adult learners?

No, another model that has gained popularity in higher education is Fink's Taxonomy. In 2003, Dr. L. Dee Fink released a book, *Creating Significant Learning Experiences: An Integrated Approach to Designing College Courses* which incorporated backward design. However, Fink's design begins with considering situational factors such as the number of students in the course, learner characteristics, course delivery method, instructional challenges, how the course fits within the larger curriculum, expectations for the course, nature of the subject, characteristics of the instructor and of the administration. Similar to UbD, Dr. Fink stresses designing learning outcomes that result in significant learning, then designing assessments, and finally planning learning experiences with an emphasis on active learning. He also provides a taxonomy of significant learning that includes foundational knowledge (key information and ideas), application (skills, managing projects, and critical, creative, and practical thinking), integration (connecting ideas within the course, connecting to other courses, connecting to own person, social, work life), human dimension (learning about self and others), caring (developing new feelings, interests, and values), and learning how to learn (becoming a better student, learning about this subject, becoming a self-directed learner) (Fink, 2005).

A study of human development that compared students in courses designed in a traditional way with students in a course designed using Fink's model found the students in the course using Finks model scored significantly higher on a test of knowledge, on case studies examining their ability to apply and to integrate the information, and on a Likert scale on increased knowledge about themselves (Fallahi, 2008).

Research on the Impact of Backward Design

Many research studies exist that examine the impact of backward design on learner outcomes. The findings reveal that learners have higher achievement when the backward design framework is used to develop the curriculum versus other ways of planning. However, most of these studies have been conducted with adult learners, including teachers-in-training.

Research on Backward Design in Preschool through Grade 12

Few studies exist in preschool through grade 12 that examines the use of curriculum developed using backward design in comparison to a control group using other curriculum designs. However, the studies that do exist find that curriculum developed using backward design results in enhanced learning. One of the more interesting studies involved 53 middle school earth science teachers in 19 schools. Teachers were randomly assigned to one of four groups: a control group, a group using the Investigating Earth Science (IES) curriculum (developed by the American Geosciences Institute), a group that designed their own units using Understanding by Design, and a hybrid group that received training in both the IES curriculum and UbD. The students in the UbD group and the hybrid group showed statistically significant gains in unit tests in comparison to the control group. Interestingly, the students in the IES curriculum were not significantly different from the control group. The authors theorize that this difference might be due to the assessment and instruction alignment as well as the opportunities for the UbD group to learn more pedagogical strategies (Penuel & Gallagher, 2009). Another study conducted in Dubai, found significant differences in science achievement in eighth-grade students with the group using UbD designed units outperforming the control group (Almasaeid, 2017).

Research on Backward Design in Teacher Education

More studies on backward design have been conducted in designing courses for adults. Again, these studies support backward design as a framework that enhances learning. For example, a study that examined elementary teachers' ability to design lessons found that the students who were taught backward design showed a statistically significant difference in their ability to plan lessons with the backward design group outperforming the control group in designing coherent instruction, planning suitable goals, and assessing student learning. Their knowledge of their students, content, pedagogy, and resources was also superior to the control group (Kelting-Gibson, 2005). Another study found that 69% of education students who were taught to use a backward design model felt prepared to plan learning experiences with most indicating that the backward design framework had assisted them by providing a process for planning, a conceptual framework with which to judge their own teaching and the curriculum materials that they were provided, and in emphasizing what students would learn as well as why that particular learning was important (Graff, 2011).

Research on Backward Design in Other Areas of Higher Education

A couple of large-scale studies have also been conducted in other areas of higher education. Winkelmes et al. (2016) completed a study involving 1,800 students, 35 professors, and seven colleges and universities throughout the country. They asked professors to use backward design to revise two assignments to make them more transparent and project-based. Students were compared with students in courses that did not have the redesigned assignments. Those students who received the redesigned courses reported statistically significant gains in academic confidence, sense of belonging, and mastery of skills. The benefits were larger for those students who were first-generation college students, low-income, and underrepresented in the university. There was also greater short-term retention of material and fewer course withdrawals in the courses with the redesigned assignments.

In another large study, The University System of Maryland revised 57 courses using backward design. When the student outcomes were compared in the redesigned courses versus traditionally designed courses, students in the redesigned courses received higher grades on final exams and withdrawals from courses and failures decreased by seven percentage points (William E. Kirwan Center for Academic Innovation, 2015).

There have been similar findings in biology and health. Biology courses for non-majors were redesigned using a backward design model. In these courses, students experienced a greater variety of teaching techniques, more active versus passive learning, more frequent feedback, and more prioritized content (Reynolds & Kearns, 2017). In a backward designed health policy course, there was increased interest in health policy as well as an increase in knowledge of health care policy in comparison to the control group (Krueger, Russell, & Bischoff, 2011).

International Research

While the previous higher education studies were conducted in the United States, studies have also been conducted in other countries. For example, Iranian students learning English as a foreign language (EFL) were taught with either a backward designed course or a forward designed course. The students in the backward designed course had significantly better reading comprehension than the group in the forward designed course (Hodaeian & Biria, 2015). Another study conducted in Turkey with ten teachers and 436 students in EFL courses found that students who received instruction with the UbD design had significantly increased foreign language learning motivation and knowledge transfer skills in comparison to the control group. The exception was a group of students who had extremely limited English skills. In this case, the UbD and the control group were similar (Yurtseven & Altum, 2016).

Why Use Backward Design for Early Childhood Curriculum?

For much of our history in early childhood, we have focused first on activities, thought secondarily about what standards could be incorporated into the activities, and often ignored assessment. Although this system of planning can work and children might achieve desired outcomes, it is somewhat by chance. Early learning standards have now become part of the fabric of early childhood. With this has come increased accountability in assessing whether learners are achieving these standards. But, along with the standards movement have been questions about how we can ensure that children receive a developmentally appropriate education that honors their individuality, development, and cultural background while still meeting these standards. Can we meet standards without standardizing curriculum? Can we honor the field's emphasis on constructivism while still meeting standards?

Relationship of Backward Design to Constructivism

There is a long history within early childhood of subscribing to the constructivist philosophy. Both Jean Piaget and Lev Vygotsky, two influential early childhood theorists promoted constructivism. Constructivists believe that learners actively construct their knowledge based on their needs, interests, motivation, background knowledge, and cultural experience and beliefs. The teacher is a guide who facilitates learning through providing rich experiences, engaging in meaningful interactions, and promoting peer interactions. To be effective, the teacher needs to know the learner so that he/she can make the content relevant and meaningful. This philosophy is in contrast to the transmission model. Paulo Freire describes this transmission model as the banking model of education. In this model, the teacher is the primary actor and the children are passive, receiving and depositing information that they "bank" for later use.

Backward design provides a framework that helps ensure that early learning standards are considered, assessed, and that learning experiences assist children to meet standards. However, unlike a scripted curriculum, that might not be relevant to the group or that might not meet the developmental level or background knowledge of the children, units can be chosen that are interesting and engaging to the children you work with. The younger the child the more important it is that the curriculum is developed around the child's interests and their background knowledge. Since hands-on investigations are a primary way that young children learn, this is also an important consideration. In choosing your own units, you can plan units that allow first-hand investigation, allow for resources such as fieldwork and visiting experts, and that help children learn about local culture. With backward design, the teacher is granted flexibility in choosing units or projects but is given a systematic way to ensure that outcomes are met and assessed.

In Summary

Backward design provides a research-based framework for developing units that assist children and adults in meeting outcomes. Backward design honors early childhood history and philosophy and allows the flexibility to meet programs serving different ages, in different settings, and with different educational philosophies and emphases. As we proceed through the book, we will be learning how to implement the backward design model in early childhood programs so that we can assist learners to achieve outcomes and to understand "big ideas" that will transfer to new learning situations.

Apply Your Knowledge

1. Write your definition of curriculum. Which image of curriculum does your definition most closely align with?
2. You are on a curriculum committee that is deciding whether to buy a curriculum or develop a curriculum using backward design. Your co-workers wonder whether there is evidence to support the backward design framework. Describe the evidence base that exists.
3. You have a coworker who believes in following the curriculum guide with fidelity. What are the advantages and disadvantages to this approach?
4. A coworker states that she works with children who face incredible challenges. In a case such as this she argues, the curriculum you use makes little difference. Is she correct? Defend your answer.
5. Explore the website of a school or a department of education using backward design. You will find several listed in this chapter. What did you learn?

References

Agodini, R., Harris, B., Thomas, M., Murphy, R., Gallagher, L., & Pendleton, A. (2010). *Achievement effects of four early elementary school math curricula: Findings for first and second graders.* Washington, DC: National Center for Education Evaluation and Regional Assistance at the Institute of Education Sciences.

Almasaeid, T. F. (2017). The impact of using Understanding by Design (UbD) model on 8th-grade student's achievement in science. *European Scientific Journal, 13*(4), 301–315. doi:10.19044/esj.2017.v13n4p301

Barnachea, A. A. (2013). *Public School Curriculum.* Retrieved from https://www.slideshare.net/TeacherAdora/curriculum-models-philippines-curriculum-models

Blank, R. K., & Smithson, J. L. (2014). Analysis of opportunity to learn for students with disabilities: Effects of standards-aligned instruction. *Journal of Research in Education, 24*(1), 135–153.

Bransford, J., Brown, A. L., Cocking, R. R., & National Research Council. (2000). *How people learn: Brain, mind, experience, and school: Expanded Edition.* Washington, DC: National Academy Press.

Chingos, M. M., & Whitehurst, G. J. (2012). *Choosing blindly: Instructional materials, teacher effectiveness, and the Common Core.* Washington, DC: Brown Center on Education Policy at the Brookings Institute.

Cogan, L. S., Burroughs, N., & Schmidt, W. H. (2015). Supporting classroom instruction: The textbook navigator/journal. *Phi Delta Kappan, 97*(1), 29–33. doi:10.1177/0031721715602233

Cohen, S. (1987). Instructional alignment: Searching for a magic bullet. *Educational Researcher, 16*(8), 16–20. doi:10.3102/0013189X016008016

College Board Communications. (2018). *More students than ever are participating and succeeding in advanced placement.* Retrieved from https://www.collegeboard.org/releases/2018/more-students-than-ever-are-participating-and-succeeding-in-advanced-placement

Fallahi, C. R. (2008). Redesign of a life span development course using Fink's taxonomy. *Teaching of Psychology, 35*(3), 169–175. doi:10.1080/00986280802289906

Fink, L. D. (2005). *Self-directed guide to designing courses for significant learning.* Retrieved from http://www.ou.edu/idp/significant/Self-DirectedGuidetoCourseDesignAug%2005.doc

Graff, N. (2011). "An effective and agonizing way to learn": Backwards design and new teachers' preparation for planning curriculum. *Teacher Education, 38*(3), 151–168.

Hattie, J. (2012). *Visible learning for teachers: Maximizing impact on learning.* New York: Routledge.

Hodaeian, M., & Biria, R. (2015). The effect of backward design on intermediate EFL learners' L2 reading comprehension: Focusing on learners' attitudes. *Journal of Applied Linguistics and Language Research, 2*(7), 80–93.

Kane, T. J., Owens, A. M., Marinell, W. H., Thal, D. R. C., & Staiger, D. O. (2016). *Teaching higher: Educators' perspectives on Common Core implementation.* Cambridge, MA: Center for Education Policy Research, Harvard University.

Kelting-Gibson, L. (2005). Comparison of curriculum development practices. *Educational Research Quarterly, 29*(1), 26–36.

Krueger, K. P., Russell, M. A., & Bischoff, J. (2011). A health policy course based on Fink's taxonomy of significant learning. *American Journal of Pharmaceutical Education, 75*(1), 1–7. doi:10.5688/ajpe75114

Mitchell, F. M. (1999). *All students can learn: Effects of curriculum alignment on the mathematics achievement of third-grade students*. Paper presented at the Annual Meeting of the American Educational Research Association, Montreal, Quebec, Canada.

Mueller, J. (2016). *Authentic assessment toolbox*. Retrieved from http://jfmueller.faculty.noctrl.edu/toolbox/whatisit.htm

Mullis, I. V. S., Martin, M. O., & Foy, P. (with Olson, J. F., Preuschoff, C., Erberber, E., Arora, A., & Galia, J.). (2008). *TIMSS 2007 international mathematics report: Findings from IEA's Trends in International Mathematics and Science Study at the fourth and eighth grades*. Chestnut Hill, MA: TIMSS & PIRLS International Study Center, Boston College.

National Center for Education Evaluation and Regional Assistance (NCEE). (2016). *NCEE study information page: Achievement effects for four early elementary math curricula: Findings for first and second graders*. Washington, DC: IES NCEE. Retrieved from https://ies.ed.gov/ncee/pubs/20114001/

National Governors Association Center for Best Practices & Council of Chief State School Officers. (2010). *Common Core State Standards for Mathematics*. National Governors Association Center for Best Practices, Council of Chief State School Officers, Washington, DC: U.S. Government Printing Office.

Opfer, V. D., Kaufman, J. H., & Thompson, L. E. (2017). *Implementation of K-12 state standards for mathematics and English language arts and literacy: Findings from the American Teacher Panel*. Santa Monica, CA: RAND Corporation https://www.rand.org/pubs/research_reports/RR1529-1.html

Penuel, W., & Gallagher, L. (2009). Preparing teachers to design instruction for deep understanding in middle school earth science. *The Journal of the Learning Sciences, 18*(4), 461–508. doi:10.1080/10508400903191904

Preschool Curriculum Evaluation Research Consortium. (2008). *Effects of Preschool Curriculum Programs on School Readiness* (NCER 2008-2009). Washington, DC: National Center for Education Research, Institute of Education Sciences, U.S. Department of Education. Washington, DC: U.S. Government Printing Office.

Rentner, D. S., & Kober, N. (2014). *Common Core State Standards in 2014: Curriculum and professional development at the district level*. Washington, DC: Center on Education Policy. Retrieved from http://www.cep-dc.org/displayDocument.cfm?DocumentID=441

Reynolds, H. L., & Kearns, K. D. (2017). A planning tool for incorporating backward design, active learning, and authentic assessment in the college classroom. *College Teaching, 65*, 17–27. doi:10.1080/87567555.2016.1222575

Schmidt, W. H. (2012). At the precipice: The story of mathematics education in the United States. *Peabody Journal of Education, 87*, 133–156. doi:10.1080/0161956X.2012.642280

Stewart, M. G. (2014). Enduring understandings, artistic processes, and the new visual arts standards: A close-up consideration for curriculum planning. *Art Education, 67*(5), 6–11. doi:10.1080/00043125.2014.11519285

Varlas, L. (2013). Developing students higher order thinking. *ASCD Express: Ideas from the Field, 8*(18). Retrieved from http://www.ascd.org/ascd-express/vol8/818-toc.aspx

Wang, X., Su, Y., Cheung, S., Wong, E., & Kwong, T. (2013). An exploration of Biggs' constructive alignment in course design and its impact on students' learning approaches. *Assessment and Evaluation in Higher Education, 38*, 477–491. doi:10.1080/02602938.2012.658018

Wiggins, G., Wiggins, G. P., & McTighe, J. (2005). *Understanding by design*. Alexandria, VA: ASCD.

Will, M. (2017). *Teacher-made lessons make inroads*. Education Week. Retrieved from https://www.edweek.org/ew/articles/2017/03/29/teacher-made-lessons-make-inroads.html

William, E. Kirwan Center for Academic Innovation. (2015). *Pushing the barriers to teaching improvement: A state system's experience with faculty-led, technology-supported course redesign*. Retrieved from http://www.usmd.edu/cai/pushing-barriers-teaching-improvement-state-systems-experience-faculty-%C2%ADled-technology%E2%80%90supported

Winkelmes, M., Bernacki, M., Butler, J., Zochowski, M., Golanics, J., & Weavil, K. (2016). A teaching intervention that increases underserved college students' success. *Peer Review, 18*(1–2), 31–36.

Yurtseven, N., & Altun, S. (2016). Understanding by Design (UbD) in EFL teaching: The investigation of students' foreign language learning motivation and views. *Journal of Education and Training Studies, 4*(3), 51–62. doi:10.11114/jets.v4i3.1204

2 Determining Desired Results

In Chapter 1, we explored the advantages and research that supports backward design as a framework for developing early childhood curriculum. In this chapter, we will explore what teachers need to consider in determining desired results, the first step in the backward design model. We will begin by examining the purpose of school, then discussing standards, and finally examining the big ideas, knowledge, skills, and approaches to learning that compose the desired results.

What Is the Purpose of School?

There are many reasons that societies establish and fund educational programs for children. The purpose has been the subject of ongoing and historical debates. As stated by Eleanor Roosevelt in 1930, "What is the purpose of education? This question agitates scholars, teachers, statesmen, every group, in fact, of thoughtful men and women" (p. 97).

While there are many purposes, we will examine three that are relevant to early childhood, to meet the needs of society, nurture the individual, or promote social change or reconstruction. What we believe is the purpose of education affects what results we hope to achieve.

To Meet the Needs of the Society

One purpose of schools is to assist students to become future productive members of society. Societies need individuals that have the knowledge and skills to be employable and able to function effectively within the society. The standards movement is aligned with this purpose. Achieve, an education reform organization formed by governors and business leaders in 1996, has been a leader in the standards movement. They promote high expectations for students; rigorous, common core grade level standards with benchmarks; and meaningful assessments as a way of ensuring that students graduate from high school and college, career ready (Achieve, 2017b).

In most educational settings in the past, meeting the needs of society was accomplished through cultural reproduction where current knowledge and values were passed on to the succeeding generations. For example, a tribal society over time may have developed an effective way to fish that fed the tribe but also preserved enough fish to continue the supply. For this society, cultural reproduction was the purpose of education, involving the technique of how to fish, the big idea of conservation, and the cultural stories and traditions that surrounded this important part of life. "For most of humanity's history, and for most of humanity, life took place in a slow-changing agrarian world where few ventured beyond their immediate community and even fewer moved beyond their social class" (DeAddareo, 2019, p. 1). Therefore, this method was successful. It was possible to teach children all the skills and the knowledge that they would need to be successful as adults.

However, as the needs of society changes so then does the education. Today our world is rapidly changing and becoming more complex. As emphasized by the P21 Partnership for 21st Century Learning, a powerful entity representing two million US school children and five million global partners, we are now globally connected, have an expanded civic life, there is information overload, and an economy driven by innovation and creativity that is constantly changing (n.d.). If we want to continue to meet the current and future needs of students, our teaching emphasis must also change. They advocate that along with strong academic, life and career, and information, media and technology skills, schools also need to focus on learning and innovation skills. Labeled the 4C's, these building blocks for learning are critical thinking, communication, collaboration, and creativity (P-21 Partnership for 21st Century Learning, 2015).

As early childhood teachers, it is impossible to know what our children's future world will be like. Unlike in the past, we cannot simply teach children the information and skills they will need in the future. Instead, we need to promote lifelong learning skills including how to find information, what information is valuable and reliable, and how to use this information to inform decisions. Children will need to be innovative problem-solvers who will most likely be communicating and collaborating with global partners. Children will need effective social skills to interact with a variety of different people and the emotional skills to cope with rapid changes.

To Nurture the Individual

Instead of focusing on society's needs for productive members, some advocate that the purpose of schooling is to nurture the individual. This includes identifying and nurturing children's passions, with the goals of assisting each child to be confident and to lead a self-fulfilling life both currently and in the future. Schools that promote this purpose, help students to identify their interests, needs, and abilities. They support children in self-cultivation, helping children set personal goals and providing support in meeting these goals. Children are involved in decision-making about their own learning and about how the classroom functions. Curriculum is designed around children's interests.

Nurturing the individual was an important component of the progressive movement in education of which John Dewey was an influential spokesperson. The progressive movement has had a profound effect on early childhood education. For example, the progressive movement encouraged child choice, self-directed activities, meeting the needs of individuals, hands-on learning, and educating "the whole child." These ways of nurturing the individual are also promoted in *Developmentally Appropriate Practice in Early Childhood Programs: Serving Children from Birth to Age 8* (Copple & Bredekamp, 2012), the book containing and elaborating upon NAEYC's (National Association for the Education of Young Children) position statement on developmentally appropriate practices. This book is considered the gold standard for early childhood education.

To Promote Social Change or Reconstruction

If the purpose of schooling is social reconstruction, the goal is to reconstruct and improve society through identifying social issues, finding solutions to these issues, and providing practice in being change agents to advocate for these solutions. Schools are set up as labs where children learn and practice these skills. For example, the purpose might be to provide a society that is more equitable. If this were the purpose, the school would be set up based on these principles. Children would not only learn about social inequities, social justice, and advocacy but would recognize it within their school setting and their community and would work together to solve these problems. A leading advocate of social reconstruction was Paulo Freire, a Brazilian educator and author of *Pedagogy of the Oppressed*. This seminal book is often required reading in teacher education programs (Steiner, 2005). In early childhood, we see the promotion of social reconstruction in Anti-Bias Education (ABE). One of the goals of ABE is that "Each child will demonstrate empowerment and the skills to act, with others or alone, against prejudice and/or discriminatory actions" (Derman-Sparks & Edwards, 2010, p. 5). For example, a mother in a wheelchair had to park a long distance from the school when attending a conference because all the parking spaces at the school were filled and there were no "handicapped" parking spaces. The children and the teachers decided that something should be done. They began by studying handicap spaces at other parking lots and then created a space in their school parking lot by painting blue lines and a blue H on the pavement and posting a handicap sign. The children also created tickets that they gave to anyone who parked "illegally" in the space (Derman-Sparks, 1989).

Each of these purposes seems important. Can't a school include all of them?

While many schools try to incorporate more than one purpose, there is typically one that predominates. The structure of the day, the curriculum that is chosen, the role of the teacher and the learner are all based upon this purpose. For example, if the goal is to nurture the individual, the school will have a variety of choices for children, a curriculum that is based upon the interests of the child, an emphasis on the whole child, and a goal that learning be joyful. The school who promotes the needs of society is often more focused on academic knowledge and skills rather than the whole child, following the purchased curriculum to fidelity rather than considering children's interests, and choice for children might be limited with the idea that all children need exactly the same experience to be competent in meeting the standards.

There is much debate about the primary purpose of school. Additionally, there is debate about how to specifically accomplish each purpose. For example, those who believe that the primary purpose of school is to help society flourish might still disagree on whether "back to the basics" is the way to accomplish this or whether we should, as the P21 Partnership for the 21st Century advocate, concentrate on a wide range of skills including thinking and learning skills.

Why Is the Purpose Important?

The teacher's, the school's, the community's, and the nation's view on the primary purpose of schooling influences the desired results we wish to achieve and the way that we determine if we have met these results. It can be difficult when the primary view of schooling across these different stakeholders does not align. Currently, the nation is embarked in a standards movement that aligns with the purpose of meeting the needs of society. The Common Core State Standards Initiative (CCSS) was established to help the United States flourish. The goal is that all children regardless of where they go to school will meet standards that will help them to be college and career ready and able to compete in a global economy. However, with this movement comes accountability to meet these standards, to score and rank children and schools based upon this acquisition. Early childhood philosophy has typically been more aligned with nurturing the individual. The early childhood teacher walks a tightrope in trying to meet the requirements of the standards movement while also nurturing the individual. Through the process of backward design, we will try to make this tightrope easier to navigate.

Our basic belief about schooling, often unwritten and unspoken, can also account for many of the differences and disagreements between teachers and administrators and between families and programs. Consider your own beliefs about the purpose of school. Examine your program's mission statement. Does it provide a clear purpose? Are educational policies and practices consistent with this purpose? To meet this purpose, what should the ideal curriculum look like? What are the desired results?

Standards Governing Early Childhood Programs

To achieve the purpose of schooling especially as it relates to the needs of society, learning standards have been written. These standards tell us what children should know, understand, and be able to do at different age and grade levels. They provide a set of expectations for children and teachers to meet.

Learning Standards

As teachers, we are typically accountable to meet learning standards. Within the United States, there are many different sets of learning standards that govern early childhood programs. These include the Head Start Early Learning Outcomes Framework, Pre-K standards, Early Learning Standards, and Elementary Education Standards.

While the Head Start Early Learning Outcomes Framework is a set of mandatory national standards that govern Head Start programs, the other sets of standards are developed or adopted by each individual state. However, many states base their Elementary Education Standards on national standards such as the CCSS, the Next Generation Science Standards (NGSS), the National Core Art Standards, and The National Standards and Grade Level Outcomes for K-12 Physical Education, which has resulted in some conformity across states.

Whereas early learning standards specifically address what young learners should know, understand, and be able to do, other standards also affect curriculum including program accreditation standards and individual school initiatives. Quality rating systems and goals related to funding sources also affect the curriculum.

Program Accreditation Standards

Program accreditation standards often impose criteria related to the curriculum. For example, the NAEYC Early Learning Program Accreditation, a voluntary nationwide accreditation for programs serving children birth through age eight, includes standards related to curriculum, teaching, the physical environment, and assessment. To meet the standards, programs need to have a written curriculum or curriculum framework. They also need a written assessment plan and to prove that the assessment is used to modify instruction and to individualize teaching.

There are also specific curricular requirements that programs are assessed on such as whether they promote early math skills for infants, toddlers, and twos by providing toys and objects that are graduated sizes and a variety of shapes, colors, and visual patterns (NAEYC, 2018).

The International Baccalaureate (IB) is another example of a program that includes specific standards. Schools that participate in a rigorous authorization process are allowed to offer the IB program. The IB Primary Years Programme for children ages 3–12, emphasizes theme-based learning that is inquiry-based.

Program-related Standards

The school or program you work in might have additional standards related to their mission and philosophy. For example, in addition to meeting the required Elementary Standards in their state, the Nature-Centered Elementary School which focuses on environmental education also meets the voluntary Excellence in Environmental Education: Guidelines for Learning (K-12) in their first- to third-grade classrooms and the Guidelines for Excellence: Early Childhood Environmental Education Programs in their Pre-K and kindergarten programs. These guidelines are designed to assist children to become environmentally responsible adults who are aware of and concerned about the environment and who can recognize environmental issues and work toward solutions and prevention (North American Association for Environmental Education, 2016). The 21st Century Learning Standards, that we discussed earlier in the chapter, are another example of supplementary standards.

Quality Rating Systems

Oklahoma started the first Quality Rating and Improvement System (QRIS) in 1998. Since then 25 states have established QRIS and most others are in the process of doing so (National Center on Child Care Quality Improvement, 2015, p. 1). QRIS are designed to assess and improve the quality of care in early childhood and after school programs. The systems also provide a way of communicating to consumers and other interested parties the level of quality of individual programs. For example, many states use a star system that is similar to what you might look for in choosing a motel or restaurant. Typically, the system will include standards, training and mentoring support, financial incentives, consumer education, and assessment and monitoring (National Center on Child Care Quality Improvement, 2015). The ECERS (Early Childhood Environmental Rating Scale) is included as one of the assessments in most of the quality rating systems. While not specifically dictating what is taught, the scale does include criteria relating to scheduling the day, classroom materials, interactions, and activities.

Funding Sources

Curriculum might also be affected by funding sources such as grants. These grants often focus on specific content such as literacy or math. For example, grants might dictate the type of curriculum used, classroom techniques, and/or the desired child outcomes.

You will want to be knowledgeable about each of the sets of standards that affect the program that you work in. In addition to reading the standards, it is also helpful to read any supporting documents. Many sets of standards include additional materials that can assist with understanding the standards. For instance, the California Preschool Learning Foundations has a set of nine DVDs that show the early childhood standards in action. Rhode Island teachers have access to online modules that provide information on integrating the Standards for Mathematical Practice and the NGSS. You might also see if there are crosswalk documents for the different sets of standards that you are required to meet. Crosswalk documents will show how these different sets of standards align with each other.

Concern about Standards

As preschool entered the age of standards, there was fear that early learning standards could cause detrimental results in children's learning. Would the standards encourage or discourage developmentally appropriate curriculum? How could children be assessed in relationship to meeting the standards? Would children, teachers, and program be held accountable to meet standards? If so, how?

Standards Being Developmentally Inappropriate

Early childhood educators and organizations were concerned that standards might not be developmentally appropriate. Specifically, there was concern that the standards might ignore the whole child and instead focus only on academics.

There was also concern that the standards would be viewed as a rigid timeline instead of recognizing that there is variability in children's acquisition of knowledge and skills. As stated in the NAEYC and NAECS/SDE position statement on standards, "The younger children are, the harder it is to create generalized expectations for their development and learning, because young children's development varies greatly and is so heavily dependent upon experience there is greater variability in younger children" (2002, p. 3).

Finally, there was concern that the standards would not consider the needs of all learners including children with special needs or children who were English Language Learners (ELL). Younger children in the United States are increasingly diverse, creating an even more urgent need to ensure that standards are relevant for all children. For example, 29% of children attending Head Start speak a language other than English at home (US Department of Health and Human Services and Administration for Children and Families, 2018, p. 5).

Inappropriate Assessments

With the standards movement, often comes assessments to determine if standards are being met. A national elementary and secondary school example was the No Child Left Behind Act (NCLB), which required that states assess children's ability to meet literacy and math standards. Almost immediately this created negative effects. Schools began to emphasize these subjects and decreased time for other subjects such as science and the arts. An inordinate amount of time was spent teaching to the test. Since it is easier to test lower level skills versus higher level skills, often teaching and learning emphasized the lower level skills that were being assessed. There was concern that this would occur in early childhood, as well.

In addition, early childhood educators were concerned about the difficulty in accurately assessing young children using a standardized assessment. In 1989, President Bush and the nation's governors set six educational goals for the United States to achieve by the year 2000. Goal number one was that all young children would start school ready to learn. However, this goal proved difficult to measure and Congress established a panel to develop guidelines on appropriate assessment of young children. These guidelines make clear that it is difficult to assess young children because their growth is "rapid, episodic, and highly influenced by environmental supports" (Shepard, Kagan, & Wurtz, 1998, p. 3). The report went on to state that since "young children's achievement at any point is a complex mix of their ability to learn and past learning opportunities, it is a mistake to interpret measures of past learning as evidence of what could be learned" (Shepard et al., 1998, p. 4).

There was also concern about who would administer the assessments. Children are highly influenced by who is administering the assessment and the environment in which the assessment is administered (Shepard et al., 1998). While some consider it best practice in assessment to have a neutral assessor, an unknown assessor can be stressful for some young children. Additionally, children often perform better for someone that they know and trust.

Finally, there was concern about how time-consuming it is to administer assessments for young children. Older children's tests are typically group administered. However, younger children often need individual assessments. There was fear that spending too much time conducting assessments would diminish the time that is spent in other important ways such as relationship building and learning curriculum.

High-stake Accountability

There was also concern about accountability based upon high-stakes tests. With the NCLB, teachers and schools were often held accountable for children meeting the standards without adequate resources or training in how to do so. There was not a recognition of the disparity between schools that existed in funding and resources or in children's prior knowledge, experiences, or skills. In some states, teachers and administrators lost jobs, children were retained in the same grade, and schools were taken over by the state based upon these high-stakes test scores.

> I taught in a school like that. I found that my only defense if children performed poorly on state tests was to show that I had followed the curriculum exactly and had covered all the content. It took some of the fun out of teaching.

Unfortunately, you are not unique. The testing movement often led to teachers having less influence over curriculum. This was often related to fear that children would perform poorly on assessments. As a result, some administrators became more authoritarian about the content and the sequencing of materials taught in individual classrooms. For example, demanding that all third-grade children in the district be covering the same math content on exactly the same day. In other cases, it was the teachers themselves who became worried about any deviation from the curriculum. However, when no deviations are permitted it is difficult to meet the needs and the varied skill levels of children.

This experience caused early childhood educators to fear the use of assessments in the preschool years. Would assessments be developmentally appropriate? Would they assess the whole child? Would teachers be given the training they needed to help children meet the standards?

Current State of Elementary and Early Learning Standards

While the debate continues about the value of standards, what should be included in standards, the level of rigor that we need in standards, and how standards should be assessed, the reality is that there are now standards for the early childhood years in all 50 states and four territories.

On the positive side, standards can offer guidance for teachers and programs about what children should learn, assist teachers to be more intentional about what they teach, provide consistency between different programs, and increase accountability. Since many state's standards include a developmental learning continuum, standards can also assist with the continuity of learning as children progress through schooling.

Elementary Standards

Since the 1980s, individual state standards have existed for elementary schools. However, these standards became more consistent across states with the adoption of the CCSS which included English Language Arts and Mathematics. Since its inception in 2009, 45 states have adopted the CCSS. Since that time, 24 states have revised their standards. However, even with revisions, an analysis by Achieve found that the CCSS still has a strong influence on the state's standards. They found that most states kept the key elements and maintained the rigor of CCSS (Achieve, 2017a).

The NGSS were completed in 2013. According to a map and information on the National Science Teachers Association website 19 states have adopted the NGSS. Another 21 states have written their own standards and have based their standards on the recommendations in the NRC Framework for K-12 Science Education. Together these states educate 69% of US elementary and secondary children (NSTA, 2019).

The National Core Art Standards have also influenced state standards. The National Core Art Standards include dance, media arts, music, theater, and visual arts. Since the publication of the standards in 2014, 15 states have updated their standards and another 19 states are in the process of doing so. While some states adopted the entire set of standards, others have used the standards as a resource in developing their own state's standards (The National Coalition for Core Arts Standards, 2017).

The National Standards and Grade Level Outcomes for K-12 Physical Education, developed by the Society of Health and Physical Educators (SHAPE), include five standards. All 50 states have standards for physical education and nearly all states include the five national standards developed by SHAPE in their state standards (Voices for Healthy Kids, National Association for Sport and Physical Education & American Heart Association, 2016).

The ISTE National Standards for Students were developed by the International Society for Technology in Education (ISTE), with input from 50 countries. They are used throughout the world and in all 50 states with 20 states and territories formally adopting the standards (Snelling, 2016). In 2016, the standards were revised. The emphasis in the revised standards is on lifelong learning including empowering learners to take control of their learning. These newly updated standards are just beginning to be adopted by states, with Connecticut, Texas, and Vermont being early adopters (Team ISTE, 2017).

Social studies include both curriculum standards that are developed by the National Council for the Social Studies (NCSS) and content standards that are developed by individual disciplines within social studies such as history, economics, geography, psychology, and civics. The NCSS curriculum standards provide principles and a framework to use in selecting and organizing content. Ten themes such as culture; people, places, and environments; and individual identity and development are used as organizers to assist with the overarching purpose of helping, "young people make informed and reasoned decisions for the public good as citizens of a culturally diverse democratic society in an interdependent world" (National Council for Social Studies, 2010, p. 4). Since standards are also developed by separate groups as stand-alone documents, there are a large number of social study standards. For example, the National Standards for History include eight content standards with 96 benchmarks and 35 historical thinking standards for K-4. The Council for Economic Education's National Content Standards in Economics includes 47 benchmarks to be achieved by grade 4. Each standard and benchmark can be extensive. To illustrate, let's examine two history standards. The history standards call for K-4 grade students to be able to, "Compare and contrast various aspects of family life, structures, and roles in different cultures and in many eras with students' own family lives" (Crabtree, Nash, & National Center for History in the Schools, 1994, p. 60). Another standard calls for K-4 students to be able to,

> Explain the importance of the basic principles of American democracy that unify us as a nation: our individual rights to life, liberty, and the pursuit of happiness; responsibility for the common good; equality of opportunity and equal protection of the law; freedom of speech and religion; majority rule with protection for minority rights; and limitations on government, with power held by the people and delegated by them to their elected officials who are responsible to those who elected them to office.
>
> (Crabtree, Nash, & National Center for History in the Schools, 1994, p. 48)

These national standards have helped to provide consistency across states, allowing families, teachers, administrators, and policy makers to know what children should know and be able to do in different content areas and across different grade levels. Additionally, they are often accompanied by supporting documents that help teachers to see how the standards can be implemented. For example, supplements for the NGSS include a resource library with sample tasks, evidence statements that provide additional information and clarification for the standards, and examples for each grade level of how standards can be bundled in a thematic or topical unit.

Early Learning Standards

Early learning standards for children ages birth through age five were more recently developed. Most state's preschool standards were developed in the last 20 years, while infant and toddler standards have just recently been completed in several states. Currently, all states have guidelines or standards for infants, toddlers, and preschool children.

Similarities and Differences in Early Learning State Standards

A review of the early learning standards in the 50 states and four territories in the United States found similarities and differences across the standards. First, early learning standards have different titles across states. A review by DeBruin-Parecki and Slutzky (2016) found 24 different titles. While they are most frequently referred to as standards or guidelines, frameworks, and foundations are also found in titles. There are also inconsistencies in what is labeled as a standard or indicator. What is considered a standard in one state, might be listed as an indicator in another.

The content that is included in the standards also varies. While all states include literacy and 94% include science, only 78% include social studies and only 30% have technology standards. Expectations about what children should learn also vary greatly between state standards (DeBruin-Parecki & Slutzky, 2016).

While public schools are required to use standards, early learning standards are still typically voluntary in programs for children birth to age five. The exception is for public school state-funded Pre-K programs. Sixty-six percent of states require that these programs use the standards. However, only 38% of state-funded, non-public school programs are required to use the standards (DeBruin-Parecki & Slutzky, 2016).

Meeting the Needs of Special Populations in Early Learning Standards

Early childhood advocates have worked hard to ensure that early learning standards are developmentally appropriate. However, states have not always been successful in addressing special populations of learners in the standards, for example, ELL. A review of 54 sets of standards from US states and territories revealed that 30 of the standard documents did not contain strategies or indicators related to ELL (DeBruin-Parecki et al., 2015). This is especially concerning given the large percentage of ELL in preschools. As mentioned earlier, 29% of children who attend Head Start are ELLs (Office of Head Start, 2017).

National Pre-K Early Learning Standards

Since nearly all states now have publicly funded Pre-K programs, there is discussion and debate about creating national standards for Pre-K education. Advocates state that this would allow for easier alignment with K-3 standards, particularly in states that adopted the CCSS. It would create more equitable expectations for all children regardless of where they live. It would encourage collaboration and forming of partnerships that could enhance and save resources in both the development of the standards and the creation of materials to support the standards (DeBruin-Parecki & Slutzky, 2016). However, those who do not support national standards argue that national standards are often not culturally and geographically appropriate.

I understand that there are standards for children, but I work with early childhood teachers. Are there also standards for them?

As with young children, there are several different sets of standards that are relevant when teaching early childhood teachers. First, each state has an Early Care and Education Knowledge Base that provides guidance on what teachers of young children should know and be able to do. Additionally, the State Board of Education may have standards for early childhood teacher education. Finally, NAEYC provides Professional Preparation Standards.

How Are Standards Developed?

Standards are often developed by a team of experts who determine what is developmentally appropriate for learners to know and be able to do at different age and grade levels. The draft is then sent out for public comment and review and changes are made based upon this feedback. This can be a time-consuming process. As an example, we'll examine how the NGSS were developed. Over a three-year period from 2010 to 2013, a rigorous process was followed in developing the Standards.

1. Under the direction of the National Research Council, a group of 18 national and international experts was convened to generate a Framework for K-12 Science Education based upon the most current research on science and science learning. The framework which included cross-cutting concepts, practices, and disciplinary core ideas, were sent out for public comment and also for a rigorous peer-review process, with changes being made based upon this feedback.
2. Next, a 40-member writing team from the 26 lead state partners used this framework to develop the NGSS.
3. During this process, critical stakeholders, both individuals and organizations, were selected to review and provide feedback to the writing team.
4. Two drafts were also released to the public for review and feedback.
5. The feedback from the critical stakeholders and the public were used to make changes to the standards.
6. Finally, to ensure fidelity to the *Framework*, the National Research Council convened a set of reviewers for a Fidelity Review to determine if the standards were consistent with the structure and the content of the framework. They determined that they were.

The standards specify outcomes, not a particular curriculum or teaching approach. We look to the standards for guidance as we determine the desired results we want learners to achieve.

Using the Standards as Our Desired Results

In determining desired results, we must think about the big transferable ideas, the knowledge, the skills, and the approaches to learning that we want children to achieve. Since teachers are required to meet standards, why can't we simply use the standards as our desired results? First, even if programs are focused on just one set of standards there are often too many standards that need to be met. If we simply try to focus on each standard separately, there is not enough time in a program day or year to address each of these standards, particularly if we want to provide for in-depth learning. For example, a study conducted by the Mid-continent Research for Education and Learning (McREL) found that it would take 22 years of schooling to address each elementary and secondary content standard separately (Marzano & Kendall, 1998). Trying to meet each individual standard can also lead to inappropriate teaching. As stated in the Developmentally Appropriate Practices Position Statement,

> Standards overload is overwhelming to teachers and children alike and can lead to potentially problematic teaching practices. At the preschool and K-3 levels particularly, practices of concern include excessive lecturing to the whole group, fragmented teaching of discrete objectives, and insistence that teachers follow rigid, tightly paced schedules.
>
> (NAEYC, 2009, p. 4)

Second, standards and benchmarks are often not written in a format that makes them useful for developing a unit. They may be too broad (engage in positive interactions with other children) or too narrow (name 15 lower case letters). Additionally, not all standards are equally important (Bailey & Jakicic, 2011). However, standards are typically provided in a list with no indication of which are more or less educationally significant.

Third, standards are typically written for a specific domain or content area. Focusing on a single standard can lead to teaching discrete knowledge and skills. Developmentally appropriate practices promote integrating content areas as a way of providing meaningful learning (Copple & Bredekamp, 2012). Integrating curriculum lets us teach in a more holistic, natural way, that makes sense to young children. After all, their real-world experiences are integrated. The integrated curriculum is more coherent and allows children to see connections across curricular areas. It can also assist in providing a unit that is relevant to children's lives and therefore a more interesting and motivating way to learn. For example, let's look at two preschool teachers and their approach to a standard that states that all children should be able to write some letters by the end of the preschool year. Lindsey approached this by isolating this specific skill and working on it throughout the year. Each day she had children spend ten minutes practicing naming and writing the letter of the week. Amy approached this by integrating the skill within her curriculum. For example, she and her four-year-old class were studying insects. Each of the children created a book, where they listed and drew pictures of the insects that they had found. Writing the letters in this context was interesting and relevant. There was a purpose for learning to name and to write the letter.

While the standards form the basis for our desired results, we must analyze them looking for the big ideas, knowledge, skills, and approaches to learning embedded within them. This includes examining the standards for both the content that children should know and also the processes they need to learn. This analysis forms the foundation for determining our desired results.

Using Big Ideas, Knowledge, Skills, and Approaches to Learning as Our Desired Results

In this section, we will examine how we determine desired results using big ideas, and the knowledge, skills, and approaches to learning found in the standards

Big Ideas

A big idea is a conceptual framework for understanding, a mental organizer, a schema, a strategy for making sense of what you are learning. Big ideas are often a concept, theme, overarching principle, or process that we revisit, gaining new and deeper understandings. For example, the concept of family is a big idea. As you think about your own learning, how has your conception of family changed? How is your concept of family affected by the society you live in and your cultural lens? Chapter 3 is devoted to understanding big ideas and the essential questions and enduring understandings that are based upon the big ideas.

In addition to big ideas, our desired outcomes need to include knowledge, skills, and approaches to learning. While it is important to consider each of these categories when planning curriculum, the differences between the categories can be subtle.

Knowledge (To Know)

Knowledge includes factual information, concepts, principles, and theories. Knowledge is typically based upon justifiable claims. In schools, we often talk about content knowledge that is derived from different disciplines. For example, the NGSS expects kindergarten children to have knowledge of each of the following; force and motion, the relationship between energy and force, the impact of humans on earth systems, and conservation of energy (Bybee & NGSS Lead States, 2013).

Do Children Need Factual Knowledge?

In this day of the Internet, you might wonder if it is still necessary for children to gain factual knowledge. Would it be better to instead only focus on learning how to learn? Despite the easy availability of the Internet, it is still necessary to have a foundation of factual information. Children need factual knowledge to understand what they read or hear. All authors and speakers assume that the audience has a certain degree of background knowledge. Without adequate knowledge, the information what is read or heard does not make sense. Factual knowledge is also essential for problem-solving and critical thinking (Saaris, 2016). As stressed in the seminal work, *How People Learn: Brain, Mind, Experience, and School*, "attempts to teach thinking skills without a strong base of factual knowledge do not promote problem solving ability or support transfer to new situations" (National Research Council, 2000, p. 23). Most experts agree that both knowledge and thinking skills are important. It is equally important that teachers have content knowledge.

How Do Teachers Enhance Their Own Content Knowledge?

We once believed that it was enough to simply know how to answer children's questions by researching questions as they arose, that it was not necessary for teachers to have strong background information. However, it is now recognized that content knowledge is important to be able to recognize children's misconceptions. This helps to prevent inadvertently teaching misconceptions and allows us to take advantage of teachable moments. For example, you might be taking a walk and children become very interested in a tree that is beginning to flower. You are better prepared to take advantage of this teachable moment if you have background knowledge about the type of tree, what kind of fruit the tree bears, and the difference between this tree and others in the area. Specific required coursework such as a geology course, a history course, or a literature course are designed to increase our background knowledge. We can also increase our knowledge through independent study and research. For example, one helpful site designed specifically to provide background knowledge for teachers is the Annenberg Learner website. This site includes a variety of resources for teaching different subjects and different age levels including "essential science for teachers." The essential science videos provide teachers information on a wide variety of topics. It is especially important that teachers prepare themselves for any new topic by researching the topic, gaining knowledge and a deeper understanding of the information related to this topic of study.

Designing Units to Promote Knowledge Acquisition

As we design units, it is important to consider the knowledge that you want children to gain. For example, Clarice, a second-grade teacher was conducting a cooking unit. As part of this unit, she wanted children to gain knowledge of:

- the five food groups and suggested serving amounts on MyPlate (a nutrition guide published by the USDA Center for Nutrition Policy and Promotion).

- the importance of good nutrition especially in maintaining a healthy weight.
- food labels.
- measurements such as the difference between a teaspoon and tablespoon and equivalencies such as three teaspoons equals one tablespoon.
- cooking terminology such as cutting butter.

In schools, we sometimes assume that because someone has knowledge, they have the skill to use the knowledge. For example, you might learn about conflict resolution in an early childhood guidance class. You know the rationale for using conflict resolution, the steps in the process, and the pitfalls to avoid when using this method. However, knowledge alone is not enough, you need the skill to be able to apply what you have learned. This often takes practice. For example, as you practice you will become better at using reflective listening to determine the problem. You will learn when you have spent enough time problem-solving solutions. You will learn when to offer solutions and when it is best to continue to encourage children to come up with their own solutions. In most situations, we need both knowledge and skills.

Skills (Be Able to Do)

Skills are the application of knowledge and theories. The development of skills typically takes practice, with increased competency occurring over time. For example, during the cooking unit that Clarice developed, children gained skills in choosing the most nutritious snacks, designing menus that conform to MyPlate, and using cooking techniques such as measuring accurately, beating an egg to a froth, and cutting butter into flour to make a biscuit.

In the early childhood years, children learn physical skills such as throwing and kicking a ball, cutting out a shape, skipping, tying a shoe, and manipulating an object such as a microscope or magnifying glass. They practice communication skills such as listening attentively, understanding nonverbal cues, engaging in turn-taking, and effectively joining a conversation. They engage in social-emotional skills such as identifying their own' and others' feelings, showing empathy, and using conflict resolution skills, and they learn cognitive skills such as problem-solving, analyzing, comparing, and determining cause and effect. These skills form the foundation for future learning. For example, in the early years, children are gaining fundamental movement skills (FMS). Researchers from Australia conducted a systematic review of published studies to determine if there was a relationship between children's FMS and potential health benefits. The researchers located 21 studies that addressed these issues from a variety of countries; Australia, the United States, Canada, Scotland, Belgium, and Germany. Their findings revealed a strong relationship between FMS and both physical activity and cardio-respiratory fitness. They found an inverse relationship between FMS and weight (Lubans, Morgan, Cliff, Barnett, & Okely, 2010). These studies highlight the importance of FMS to children's current and future well-being. Additionally, children who develop greater proficiency in these skills in the early years, are more likely to feel competent and therefore to continue to practice and use these skills creating even greater proficiency. On the other hand, those with limited skills are more likely to try to avoid them, creating even greater deficiencies in comparison to peers.

While knowledge and skills are critical, the way we approach learning tasks also has a profound influence on how much we learn. We will discuss this next.

Approaches to Learning

"Approaches to Learning includes children's motivation, habits, inclinations, dispositions, and general behaviors displayed as they involve themselves in learning or orient themselves to new situations" (Office of Early Childhood Development and the Kentucky Department of Education, 2013, p. 7). These are the processes that children engage in as they learn and upon which academic and social skills depend. They are also sometimes referred to as learning behaviors, habits of minds, dispositions, or executive functions.

Seventy-two percent of states include approaches to learning in their early learning standards (DeBruin-Parecki & Slutzky, 2016) and some states such as New Jersey and Ohio also include approaches to learning in their standards for elementary-age children. The approaches to learning behaviors listed vary between state documents but typically include such things as curiosity, initiative, independence, engagement, persistence, organization, attentiveness, risk-taking, and creativity.

Children who display these approaches are intrinsically motivated to learn, experience joy in learning, can focus and control attention, show persistence even when frustrated, demonstrate creativity and inventiveness, are planful and organized, and are able to engage in flexible problem-solving. When children's approach to learning more closely matches the expectations of teachers and schools, they are more successful. For example, Teri, a second-grade teacher expects children to ask a peer or her if they need assistance understanding an assignment, negotiating a social interaction, or if they need any type of information. A child who displays independence and initiative is more likely to be successful in class versus a child who does not display these dispositions.

Why Are "Approaches to Learning" Important?

Approaches to learning are highly correlated with children's academic outcomes. A nationwide study of kindergarten children found that children who demonstrated the most positive approach to learning behaviors started kindergarten with higher scores in math, reading, and science than their peers with lower scores in approaches to learning behaviors. They also made gains more rapidly than those children with lower scores. In fact, children who were rated as having the most positive approaches to learning behaviors had scores in reading at the end of first grade that were higher than the children with the lowest approach to learning scores at the end of second grade. This gap in academic outcomes between the children with high skills versus those with low skills continued to widen with each year of schooling (National Center for Education Statistics, 2016).

As teachers, we need to be intentional about our teaching and to consider whether we are nurturing or undermining a child's positive approach to learning. While children's temperament and cultural values and beliefs influence their approach to learning so does their environment. Children's approaches to learning are dynamic (McDermott, Rikoon, & Fantuzzo, 2014). As with knowledge and skills, we can assist children to develop greater competency through:

- using approaches that strengthen self-regulation skills such as developing effective routines and assisting children to plan for their learning.
- making activities enjoyable.

- establishing positive relationships and providing emotional support to each child.
- modeling enthusiasm, persistence, and self-regulation.
- allowing children to make choices.
- acknowledging children's efforts (Hyson, n.d., pp. 7–8).

We can also ensure that we don't use techniques that negatively affect children's approaches to learning. For instance, most teachers of young children want children to experience joy when reading books, to persist as they are learning to read, to be intrinsically motivated to read, and to voluntarily read books at home and school. However, we might destroy these dispositions if we engage in boring, repetitive drills of letters, letter sounds, and words. Another way we might negatively affect children's approaches to learning reading is if we make children feel like failures as they are learning to read. For example, Terrance is in a classroom where the teacher gives children a sticker for each sight word they can identify. The sticker chart is displayed on the classroom wall for all to see. Terrence has very few stickers, he is embarrassed and feels like a failure. The teacher stresses that you need to know the sight words to be able to read and will ask Terrance, "Don't you want to learn to read?" The teacher is under the mistaken belief that Terrance could identify the words if he tried harder. Instead of providing motivation, the teacher is destroying Terrance's desire to read. Since he feels like a failure, he avoids books. He experiences dread rather than joy when being read to since he is fearful that he will be asked to identify a word. He feels nervous when it is time for silent sustained reading. These feelings continue even the following year when he has a new teacher with a new approach to reading. Some other teaching practices that undermine children's engagement in learning include stressing ability rather than effort, emphasizing winning over collaboration, providing non-challenging activities, teaching isolated lessons that do not connect to other concepts or experiences, and not providing support for children who are struggling with a concept or skill (Hyson, 2008, p. 49).

I hadn't thought about approaches to learning in relationship to our routines and curriculum decisions. One of the approaches to learning that we emphasize at our school is persistence. As I was reading this, I thought about how we recently began to rotate children through learning centers every 15 minutes. We started this because we wanted to ensure that each child got the opportunity to learn from each center. But as I reflect on this, I see how it might negatively affect initiative and persistence.

Yes, rushed schedules can undermine children's positive approach to learning. If we want children to learn to persist, focus attention, and develop initiative we must provide time for them to do so.

It is also important to develop supportive relationships with children and to develop a community of caring in the classroom. The teacher's supportive relationships with children can assist them to be engaged and motivated to learn. Conversely, the lack of a supportive relationship with the teacher can hinder the child's positive approach to learning, causing the child to be less persistent when facing challenging tasks (Hyson, 2008). A caring community allows children to take risks and increases motivation to learn.

In Summary

As we consider the purpose of school, we need to consider how this purpose helps to determine our desired results. We must also consider how we cope when the primary purpose of school is not aligned between major stakeholders. In this book, we will be exploring how we can meet standards that are set by outside entities with a focus on the good of society while still honoring early childhood's mission, philosophy, and past and current practice of nurturing the individual.

Regardless of our individual or the early childhood field's belief in the purpose of school, we now live in a world dominated by standards. How do standards relate to desired results? The standards provide the foundation for our unit. However, we cannot simply use the standards for our unit outcomes. Instead, we must find the big ideas, knowledge, skills, and approaches to learning that are embedded within the standards. In the next chapter, we will learn a technique involving bundling, unpacking, and prioritizing as a way of using the standards as the anchor for our desired results.

Apply Your Knowledge

1. Review the mission statement for a school that you are visiting or teaching in. What is the purpose of schooling? Is this purpose evident in the classroom where you are visiting or teaching?
2. Review the standards that apply to the age level and program where you are teaching or plan to teach. If there are more than one set of standards that you must meet, look for similarities and differences within the standards.
3. Choose one or more of the standards. What knowledge, skills, and approaches to learning are implied by the standard/s?
4. Review at least one set of national standards. Read the standards for the early childhood years and explore the supplementary materials that enhance your understanding of the standards. Share what you have learned with your classmates.
5. Think of a unit that you hope to teach (perhaps a unit that you will implement as a result of this course). Search for ways that you can enhance your background knowledge on this topic. Develop a topic background sheet that lists major points related to this topic along with a list of helpful resources. Share your topic background sheet with your classmates.

References

Achieve. (2017a). *Strong standards: A review of changes to state standards since the common core*. Retrieved from https://www.achieve.org/strong-standards

Achieve. (2017b). *Twenty years of driving student success*. Retrieved from https://www.achieve.org/publications/twenty-years-driving-student-success

Bailey, K., & Jakicic, C. (2012). *Common formative assessment: A toolkit for professional learning communities at work*. Bloomington, IN: Solution Tree Press.

Bybee, R. W., & NGSS Lead States. (2013). *Next Generation Science Standards: For states, by states*. Washington, DC: National Academies Press.

Copple, C., & Bredekamp, S. (2012). *Developmentally appropriate practice in early childhood programs serving children from birth through age 8*. Washington, DC: National Association for the Education of Young Children.

Crabtree, C., Nash, G., & National Center for History in the Schools. (1994). *National standards for history for grades K-4: Expanding children's world in time and space (Expanded ed.)*. Los Angeles, CA: National Center for History in the Schools.

DeAddareo, J. (2019). *History of education*. Retrieved from https://edureach101.com/history-of-education/

DeBruin-Parecki, A., & Slutzky, C. (2016). *Exploring Pre-K age 4 learning standards and their role in early childhood education: Research and policy implications* (Policy Information Report; Research Report No. RR-16-14). Princeton, NJ: Educational Testing Service. doi:10.1002/ets2.12099

DeBruin-Parecki, A., Slutzky, C., & Shine, T. (2015). *National portrait of Pre-K learning standards and kindergarten readiness: A comprehensive study*. Paper presented at the meeting of the International Literacy Association, St. Louis, MO.

Derman-Sparks, L. (1989). *Anti-bias curriculum: Tools for empowering young children*. Washington, DC: National Association for the Education of Young Children.

Derman-Sparks, L., & Edwards, O. J. (2010). *Anti-bias education for young children and ourselves*. Washington, DC: National Association for the Education of Young Children.

Hyson, M. (2008). *Enthusiastic and engaged learners: Approaches to learning in the early childhood classroom*. New York: Teachers College Press.

Hyson, M. (n.d.). *Approaches to learning: Kindergarten to grade 3 guide*. Retrieved April 22, 2019, from https://www.state.nj.us/education/ece/rttt/k3/guide.pdf

Lubans, D. R., Morgan, P. J., Cliff, D. P., Barnett, L. M., & Okely, A. D. (2010). *Fundamental movement skills in children and adolescents: Review of associated health benefits*. ADIS Press. doi:10.2165/11536850-000000000-00000

Marzano, R. J., & Kendall, J. S. (1998). *Awash in a sea of standards*. Aurora, CO: Mid-continent Research for Education and Learning.

McDermott, P. A., Rikoon, S. H., & Fantuzzo, J. W. (2014). Tracing children's approaches to learning through Head Start, kindergarten, and first grade: Different pathways to different outcomes. *Journal of Educational Psychology, 106*(1), 200–213. doi:10.1037/a0033547

National Association for the Education of Young Children (NAEYC). (2009). *Developmentally appropriate practice in early childhood programs serving children from birth through age 8 position statement*. Washington, DC: National Association for the Education of Young Children.

National Association for the Education of Young Children (NAEYC). (2018). *NAEYC early learning program accreditation standards and assessment items*. Retrieved from https://www.naeyc.org/sites/default/files/globally-shared/downloads/PDFs/accreditation/early-learning/standards_and_assessment_web_0.pdf

National Association for the Education of Young Children (NAEYC) and the National Association of Early Childhood Specialists in State Departments of Education (NAECS/SDE). (2002). *Early learning standards: Creating the conditions for success*. Retrieved from https://www.naeyc.org/sites/default/files/globally-shared/downloads/PDFs/resources/position-statements/position_statement.pdf

National Center for Education Statistics. (2016). *Kindergartners' approaches to learning, family socioeconomic status, and early academic gains*. Retrieved from https://nces.ed.gov/programs/coe/indicator_tgc.asp

National Center on Child Care Quality Improvement. (2015). *QRIS resource guide*. Retrieved from https://qrisguide.acf.hhs.gov/files/QRIS_Resource_Guide_2015.pdf

National Council for Social Studies. (2010). *Executive summary. Expectations of excellence: Curriculum standards for social studies*. Retrieved from https://www.learner.org/workshops/socialstudies/pdf/session4/4.NCSSThemes.pdf

National Research Council. (2000). *How people learn: Brain, mind, experience, and school: Expanded edition*. Washington, DC: The National Academies Press.

National Science Teachers Association (NSTA). (2019). *K-12 science standards adoption*. Retrieved from http://ngss.nsta.org/About.aspx

North American Association for Environmental Education (NAAEE). (2016). *The guidelines for excellence: Early childhood environmental education programs*. Retrieved from https://cdn.naaee.org/sites/default/files/final_ecee_guidelines_from_chromographics_lo_res.pdf

Office of Early Childhood Development and the Kentucky Department of Education. (2013). *Building a strong foundation for school success: Kentucky's early childhood standards*. Retrieved from https://kidsnow.ky.gov/families/readiness/Documents/early-childhood-standards.pdf

Office of Head Start. (2017). *Head Start program facts fiscal year 2017*. https://eclkc.ohs.acf.hhs.gov/about-us/article/head-start-program-facts-fiscal-year-2017

P-21 Partnership for 21st Century Learning. (2015). *P-21 frameworks definition document*. Retrieved from http://www.p21.org/our-work/p21-framework

P-21 Partnership for 21st Century Learning and the Parent Teacher Association. (n.d.). *What is 21st Century Learning and Citizenship all about? Education for a changing world – A parents' guide for 21st Century Learning and Citizenship*. Retrieved from http://www.p21.org/storage/documents/citizenship/P21_Citizenship_Overview.pdf

Roosevelt, A. E. (1930). Good citizenship: The purpose of education. *Pictorial Review, 4*(94) 97.

Saaris, N. (2016). *The content comeback: Why knowledge matters to thinking and learning*. Retrieved from https://www.activelylearn.com/post/the-content-comeback-why-knowledge-matters-to-thinking-and-learning

Shepard, L. A., Kagan, S. L., & Wurtz, E. (1998). *Principles and recommendations for early childhood assessments*. Darby, PA: Diane Publishing Company.

Snelling, J. (2016). *New ISTE standards aim to develop lifelong learners*. Retrieved from https://www.iste.org/explore/articleDetail?articleid=751

Steiner, D. (2005). Skewed Perspective. *Education Next, 5*(1), 54–59.

Team ISTE. (2017). *Vermont State Board of Education adopts updated ISTE Standards for Students*. Retrieved from https://www.iste.org/explore/articleDetail?articleid=2116

The National Coalition for Core Arts Standards. (2017). *The status of arts standards revision in the United States since 2014*. Retrieved from http://www.nationalartsstandards.org/sites/default/files/The%20Status%20of%20Arts%20Standards%20Revisions%20in%20the%20United%20States%20Since%202014%20FINAL.pdf

US Department of Health and Human Services and Administration for Children and Families. (2018). *Head Start program facts fiscal year 2017*. Retrieved from https://eclkc.ohs.acf.hhs.gov/about-us/article/head-start-program-facts-fiscal-year-2017

Voices for Healthy Kids, National Association for Sport and Physical Education, & American Heart Association. (2016). *2016 Shape of the nation report: Status of physical education in the USA*. Reston, VA: National Association for Sport and Physical Education.

3 Big Ideas, Enduring Understandings, and Essential Questions

There are four elements we need to consider when determining our desired results—knowledge, skills, approaches to learning, and big ideas. In Chapter 2, we reviewed knowledge, skills, and approaches to learning. In this chapter, we will be exploring big ideas and the enduring understandings and essential questions that are based upon the big ideas.

One of the issues with teaching subject matter is that there is always an endless amount to know and understand contrasted by a limited amount of time. We are continually called upon to make choices. How do we prioritize what is most important? How do we know that we are preparing learners for what they need today and also what they need in the future? How can we ensure that what learners gain is not quickly forgotten as we move to the next chapter, unit, or topic? How can we ensure that what we teach is intellectually stimulating rather than a series of endless facts? One way to approach these dilemmas is to consider the big ideas and the enduring understandings that we want learners to leave with. What essential questions do we want learners to be able to answer? What concepts must they master? We will explore these questions in this chapter.

Big Ideas

In this section, we will explore several questions about big ideas including what they are, why we use them, and how we can help learners to understand them. We'll also examine whether young children are capable of exploring big ideas.

What Are Big Ideas?

A big idea is a conceptual framework for understanding, a mental organizer, a schema, a strategy for making sense of what you are learning. It is a "linchpin" idea that is central to understanding a subject and that helps to make sense of other pieces of isolated information (Wiggins & McTighe, 2005, p. 66). Without understanding the "big idea" information can become a series of unrelated ideas, facts, and terms that are quickly forgotten. The big idea is like a clothesline to which the ideas, facts, and terms are pinned. A big idea might be a/an:

- concept such as friendship or pattern.
- overarching principle or a core assumption such as price is a function of supply and demand or all people are created equal.
- process such as problem-solving, resolving conflict, or decision-making.
- theme such as overcoming adversity or achieving equity.

Big ideas are broad and abstract, stated concisely often in one or two words, universal in application, timeless, and can be represented by different examples that share common attributes (Erickson, 2008, pp. 35-36).

Big Ideas Require Uncoverage

You must "uncover" a big idea. You can't teach it simply as a definition or a fact instead it is an inference to be explored, contemplated, and validated (Wiggins & McTighe, 2005). For example, "family" is a concept. When I taught an early childhood college course on working with families, one of the first activities was for students to write their views of, "What is a family?" This would be an essential question based upon the concept of family. Many of the students gave a dictionary-type definition of family such as parents and children who live together and felt very certain that this was accurate. However, as we began to discuss our concept of family, we began to realize that it is not that simplistic. The concept of family is embedded within culture, with different cultures having different ideas about who is part of the family and what the structure looks like. Additionally, the concept of family is based upon personal experience. There are many questions to explore in relationship to the concept of family. Are families those people who live together? Are they people who are biologically or legally related? Are they a group of people who take responsibility for each other? Do you need to be living in the same household to be family? Does family include nuclear and extended relatives? This becomes even more complex when we consider the role of the family.

I once observed a teacher who was teaching a unit on families. One of the activities was to have children draw a picture of their family. Most of the children drew their immediate family (parents and siblings), some included their pets. However, one child drew a picture that contained her parents, sister, and her cousin. The teacher had a preconceived idea of family and told the child that the cousin did not belong in the picture. She was treating the word family as a definition, her definition, rather than as a concept. Instead, she could have explored why the child added the cousin to her picture. This would allow her to understand and honor the child's concept of family. When we treat concepts as definitions to be memorized, we lose valuable learning opportunities.

Big Ideas Bring Focus to a Unit

Big ideas are a lens that helps us to determine what is important to understand. Imagine that you are taking an American history course focused on the Colonial, Revolutionary and 19th-century America through 1877. There is a plethora of social, economic, and political information about this period, with numerous topics, major events, devastating wars, and significant dates. You wonder what is important to understand and why. Without an emphasis on big ideas, you might just learn a series of disconnected facts without understanding broader ideas, how these ideas link together, or how these ideas influence today's life. Big ideas can bring focus to a study. They provide the prioritizing filter that can lead to challenging, interesting inquiry and in-depth rather than superficial learning. For example, in studying this period of time in our history, we could use cause and effect or power, authority, and governance as the lens. For a list of possible big ideas for early childhood, see Box 3.1.

Box 3.1 Big Ideas for the Early Childhood Years

Conflict, family, community, friendship, wants and needs, love, persuasion, culture, human rights, change, power, cause and effect, equilibrium, communication, audience, perspectives, perceptions, transformation, pattern, theme, stereotypes, bias, collaboration, adaptability, adaptation, systems, probability, identity, wellness, interdependence, justice, movement, diversity, measurement, balance and symmetry, spatial relationships, number sense, relationship elements (art, dance, story) rights versus responsibilities, life cycle, reading as inquiry

---

Is a Topic or Theme a Big Idea?

Many early childhood programs base their curriculum on themes as a way to provide an integrated learning experience that is interesting to the children. It's possible that the topic or theme is based on a big idea. However, unless it is intentionally designed to incorporate a big idea, it most likely does not. Teachers may have favorite themes that they have taught for many years and that have led to successful learning outcomes. By determining big ideas behind the themes, teachers can provide even more in-depth, transferrable learning opportunities.

> Every year the second-grade teachers plan a fall project. This year the children are very interested in learning about pumpkins. We have been measuring, weighing, and exploring pumpkins. We've also been cooking with pumpkins. Are pumpkins a big idea?

Pumpkins is a topic, but it is not a big idea. While one can think of many different examples of activities related to pumpkins, the project as described does not transcend this particular topic. What might be a big idea related to the study of pumpkins? There are several that one might pursue such as life cycles, ecosystems, needs of living things, properties of an object, credible evidence, or change. Your unit focus would be influenced by which of these big ideas you choose to concentrate on. Each would provide a lens for exploring more deeply. For example, if the "properties of an object" is the big idea, you might measure, weigh, cut open the pumpkin and explore the inside. But you would also have children describe the properties, compare the properties to other objects, discuss how all objects have properties, objects take up space, and that objects have mass. You might let the pumpkin rot to illustrate that properties change. You would discuss how knowing the properties of an object helps us to understand the object.

What if the big idea you wanted to concentrate on was "credible evidence." In this case, you might weigh and measure the pumpkin and also discuss and debate what types of tools and data would provide the best credible evidence. You would discuss what evidence you would need to state that "my pumpkin is the biggest pumpkin" or that "my pumpkin is the prettiest pumpkin." You might relate the credible evidence to your unit on informational texts.

Choosing a big idea is difficult. First, there is not a definitive list of "big ideas." Further, whether something is a big idea is related to the age, experience level, and interests of the learner. Big ideas need to evoke curiosity in the learner, be able to be understood by the learner, and also provide for future learning. Finally, the intention of the teacher is an important key in determining whether something is a "big idea." For example, stereotypes can be a big idea. However, if the teacher simply asks children to memorize a definition of stereotypes it would not meet the criteria of a big idea. Conversely, wrestling with how stereotypes affect us and others or examining how we can diminish the negative effects of stereotypes in ourselves, our communities, and our country is a big idea.

As mentioned earlier, there are no definitive lists of big ideas. Therefore, the teacher needs to engage in the hard work of determining big ideas. For many teachers, this is a new way to approach curriculum. As with any new approach, implementation involves a learning curve. However, as one engages in this type of thinking and practices this approach it does become easier.

Shauna is a preschool teacher who has been teaching using weekly themes for most of her teaching career. She is obtaining a graduate degree and is taking a course on developing units using backward design. After learning about the advantages for children's learning, she decided that she wanted to explore using this approach. She decided that she would begin by planning two units using backward design, one in the fall and one in the spring. However, as she developed her units, she soon discovered that she wanted more time than one week so that the unit could be more in-depth and lead to deeper learning. She decided each unit would last a month. This involved a lot of planning, especially since she typically had to do little planning. She had lesson plans and a tote filled with materials from preceding years for each weekly theme that she taught. In addition to being time-consuming, the planning was at times frustrating and she sometimes felt that she wasn't very competent. However, as she continued to develop units, it became easier, she began to enjoy the creative process and began to feel more competent, but best of all, the children seemed more engaged and assessments demonstrated that they were learning more. As you develop big ideas for your unit, it may be helpful to use the checklist found in Box 3.2.

Box 3.2 Is It a Big Idea?

- Is it a linchpin idea or an umbrella term that is central to understanding disparate information?
- Can you think of several examples of the big idea?
- Is the idea transferable, connecting learning across topics and/or curricular areas?
- Can you visit this idea over and over to gain a deeper understanding?
- Is the idea "timeless"?
- Is the idea complex, requiring uncoverage rather than direct teaching?

Information from Erickson (2008) and Wiggins and McTighe (2005).

Why Use Big Ideas When Teaching?

The primary reason for identifying and teaching to big ideas is to assist learners to transfer information and to gain deeper conceptual understanding. A study by The National Academies of Science (Bransford & National Research Council, 2004) investigated the research on how people learn or develop expertise in an area. To explore this, they examined the differences between novices and experts. Some of these findings are very interesting. For example, it is not just the amount of information but also the ability to develop and access conceptual structures, or schemas that distinguish the expert from the novice. Experts' knowledge is organized around underlying concepts and principles or "the big ideas." When learners understand the big ideas, they are more likely to be able to see and tie new information they learn to this schema, examine a problem using a conceptual lens, and know when this information is applicable. They can more easily retrieve the information and transfer this information to new learning situations. For example, David studies rights and responsibilities as a preschooler as he helps to create and follow classroom rules. Later in kindergarten, he revisits this concept in a study of communities. In third grade, he studies the rights and responsibilities of citizens in the United States. If the teachers have made the concept of rights and responsibilities explicit in each of these units and engaged in discussions and activities about this, David will be able to link the learning in these units and be continuing to create a more in-depth schema.

The need for teaching to big ideas is also recognized in national standards. For example, the Next Generation Science Standards emphasize unit coherence with lessons that build upon previous lessons and the integration of crosscutting concepts and core ideas from different disciplines and subjects. The performance expectations are even written to communicate the big ideas (NGSS Lead States, 2013). For example, some of the crosscutting concepts listed in the standards are cause and effect, patterns, and structure and function (National Research Council, 2011). As another example, the National Curriculum for Social Studies includes ten major themes that are developed around big ideas and concepts such as the interaction among individuals, groups, and institutions and the study of culture and cultural diversity (Adler & NCSS, 2013).

How Can We Help Learners Understand the Big Ideas?

To help learners understand big ideas we need to:

- identify the big ideas or conceptual understandings that we want learners to gain. Identifying big ideas also helps us as teachers to focus on important learning and to provide more coherence and articulation across topics and subject areas. As mentioned earlier, we can frame a unit in many ways. The big ideas can help us be intentional about how we frame the learning experience.
- organize learning to stress conceptual understanding such as providing deep, hands-on, minds-on experiences; discover and build upon learners' background knowledge; and provide learners with several examples over time. For example, if we want children to understand the life cycle, we might study it in relationship to a unit on butterflies, again when we study plants, and also when we have a topic on hamsters.
- be aware of children's conceptual development and understand children's common misconceptions. Once we are aware of this, we can intentionally design curriculum to provide experiences that counter the misconceptions. For example, children often believe that heavy

things sink and light things float, regardless of size, material, or shape. If we are aware of this, we can provide counter-examples. We can have children start with two balls of clay that weigh the same amount. They will soon discover that the clay sinks. Then you can provide them with the challenge of figuring out a way to make the clay float by changing its shape.

- provide vocabulary. Words can help the learner to organize, store, and share conceptual understandings. Academic vocabulary can also help children to communicate and to share their learning with others who have a common vocabulary. Children learn vocabulary during both incidental teaching and also while actively engaged in rich experiences and conversations.

- provide many opportunities to revisit big ideas and concepts in different contexts. Your teaching can be the bridge that helps children to see how new things that they are learning fit within the structure of what they have already learned. Promote a more complex, more sophisticated level of understanding each time you revisit the concept.

We will be exploring additional teaching techniques that aid in conceptual understanding in future chapters.

Are Young Children Capable of Conceptual Understanding?

I thought that children were not ready to gain conceptual understanding until they were around age seven or had reached the stage of concrete operations. Are young children really capable of learning concepts?

It is a common misconception that conceptual development is so intellectually challenging that young children are incapable of achieving it. One of the dangers to this belief is that it is often accompanied by the belief that children must memorize discrete facts before they can begin to gain higher level skills or conceptual understanding. For example, we might believe that children need to be able to identify all the names of the letters before they can begin to read. However, research demonstrates that children from birth are beginning to develop concepts. We now know that children's conceptual understanding is more advanced than we were previously aware.

Children are very capable of developing conceptual understanding. In examining children's ability to develop conceptual understanding, we need to examine how children learn. We know from our own observations and from research that children even from birth develop concepts to help organize and to make sense of their experiences. They do this through developing categories or schemas. Research shows that these early schemas or categories such as faces, objects, and animals are similar to categories formed by adults and are based not only on observable features but are theory-based including non-observable features (Gelman, 1996; Gelman & Koenig, 2003). As stated by Gelman who studies children's conceptual development, "If children were *unable* to categorize, their experiences would be chaotic—filled with objects, properties, sensations, and events too numerous to hold in memory" (1999, p. 50).

In the past 30 years, more than 7,000 papers have been written that explore concept development in young children. This research has revealed four major themes regarding young children's conceptual development.

- Concepts are tools and as such have powerful implications for children's reasoning–both positive and negative.
- Children's early concepts are not necessarily concrete or perceptually based. Even preschool children are capable of reasoning about non-obvious, subtle, and abstract concepts.
- Children's concepts are not uniform across content areas, across individuals, or across tasks.
- Children's concepts reflect their emerging "theories" about the world. To the extent that children's theories are inaccurate, their conceptions are also biased (Gelman, 1999, p. 50).

Children's conceptual development is aided by experience and grows and changes over time. For example, Anna, a two-year-old child initially believed that one of the characteristics of animals is that they bark. She believed this because when she first heard the word "animal" it was in relationship to Harriet, the family's black lab. Her mother frequently said, "Get that animal out of the kitchen" in an exasperated voice. However, as she gained more experience with different kinds of animals, her concept of animal changed. As this example illustrates, since concepts are often based upon our experiences, we can form erroneous concepts, especially when we have a limited knowledge base. As children try to figure out how the world works, it is common that they form inaccurate concepts. For example, children might believe that rain comes from holes in the clouds. As teachers, it is important that we try to understand the learner's current thinking and concepts since this is the basis upon which new knowledge is built.

What Are Enduring Understandings and How Do They Relate to Big Ideas?

"Enduring understandings represent ideas and processes we want students to integrate, refine, and keep as they move through their schooling and eventually into adulthood" (Stewart, 2014, p. 6). They have, "Endured over time and across cultures because it has proven so important and useful ... it will help the student make sense of the content *and* it will enable transfer of the key ideas" (Wiggins & McTighe, 2005, p. 136). Enduring understandings relate to one or two big ideas, require uncoverage rather than memorization, and include critical concepts, principles, or processes. They are written in a sentence format. The learner will understand that....

Although it seems at first glance that it is easy to determine whether something is simply a fact that can be memorized or an understanding, it often is not. This is because we must consider two additional factors, the learner's development and the intent of the teacher. Something that we, as adults, now accept as fact, is often based upon a lifetime of experiences and learning that have helped us with this understanding. We must think from the learners' point of view about whether this is a fact or an understanding for them. After a learner has read about or been taught this information, can they effectively use it? Is the information obvious to a novice learner? If so, it is a fact. An understanding requires that the problem, concept, or idea be wrestled with and be uncovered. We comprehend this concept or idea better if we discover the proof ourselves. Learners are likely to have misconceptions about this idea or concept. If this is the case, it is likely to be an understanding. In the book, *Understanding by Design*, Wiggins and McTighe (2005) use the example of the Pythagorean theorem ($A^2+B^2=C^2$) to illustrate this. This theorem lets us know that the square of the long side of a right triangle is equal to the sum of the square of the other two sides. Although the theorem is regarded as a fact having been proven in multiple ways for over 2,000 years, simply memorizing it is unhelpful. It is also not obvious to the novice. Instead, we must understand that the theorem is indeed true regardless of the size or shape of the right triangle. We must also understand how and when the theorem is applicable in our everyday lives. This calls for understanding versus memorizing. However, if the intent of the teacher is that children only memorize the formula, the Pythagorean theorem would simply be a fact not an understanding.

Therefore, as you think about enduring understandings you must consider the developmental level of the learner and the intent of the teacher. In writing enduring understanding statements, it is helpful to think about these questions. When learners have forgotten the details of what they have learned, what understanding do you hope that they are still left with? What is the essence or the "so what" for exploring and learning about this topic? You will want to include overarching understandings that you will revisit in other units, in other grades, often even into adulthood. Additionally, you will write topical understandings that relate more specifically to the specific topic. These are often a subset of the overarching understandings.

For example, every year, Tessa completes a unit on community helpers. As she thinks about enduring understandings, she realizes that she has never framed her unit in this way or considered how she might make connections between this unit and others she is teaching. She has never thought about the larger concepts that might be tied to this unit. As she contemplates this, she considers the concepts she wants children to begin to understand. She decides on two concepts: interdependence and rights and responsibilities. For overarching understandings, she decides on the following:

- There are different types of communities such as communities based on place classrooms/ schools/neighborhoods/towns, communities based on interest, and communities based on circumstances.
- Individuals have rights and responsibilities within communities.
- Within a community, relationships and interdependence are developed.

As she thinks about the topical understandings for the community helper unit she decides on the following:

- People assume different roles to meet the community's needs.
- Community helpers assist in the well-being of the community.

Tessa also thinks about other units she has taught where the overarching understandings could be reinforced. Toward the beginning of each year, Tessa has a unit on getting to know our classroom. She realizes that a classroom is a community with needs. It is composed of individuals who have rights and responsibilities and that members develop interdependencies. She could introduce these understandings during this unit and then continue to explore these understandings during her unit on community helpers.

What If My Unit Focus Is Primarily On Skills Rather Than Concepts?

McTighe and Wiggins point out that the purpose of skills is their transfer, "to produce fluent, flexible, and effective performance in varying contexts" (2013, p. 37). Even if learners have mastered skills, they must still be able to determine what skill to use, when to use it, how to use it, and why to make the choice. Learners need to understand the key concepts related to the skills, the purpose and value, the strategy and tactics, and the context of use. These then can become the basis for essential questions (2013, p. 36). For example, a skill that children learn in the early childhood years is running. Some essential questions related to running are: What conditions make it easier to run? What strategies can I use to run a long distance without getting too exhausted? What is the best body position for efficient running? What is the value in running?

Another skill is to write legibly. Some essential questions related to the skill of writing legibly are: How does handwriting affect communication? How does (the mechanics) the way I hold my pencil affect the ease of writing? What are the different forms of writing and why am I using this particular one? What is the purpose of handwriting?

Using conflict resolution is another skill. Some essential questions related to this skill are: Is conflict inevitable, why or why not? Is conflict desirable, why or why not? Under what conditions would I want to use conflict resolution?

Do Children Need a Basic Level of Skills Before They Can Begin to Gain Enduring Understandings?

Often skills and understandings can be taught concurrently. The understandings often provide the justification for learning the skill. For example, many early childhood classrooms emphasize the knowledge of identifying and naming colors. Some conceptual understandings that can be emphasized as we teach color are that color is an attribute that helps us to describe an object, colors can affect emotions, and colors can be categorized in different ways.

As you develop your unit, you need to think deeply about the most important enduring understandings you want learners to gain from this unit. As you write the enduring understandings, it is a balancing act to determine how specific to make the statement. The more specific you make the statement, the more limiting. However, greater specificity provides more direction. See Box 3.3 for a checklist on enduring understandings.

To see some examples of enduring understandings you might examine the National Core Art Standards. The 195 art standards have been organized into 15 enduring understandings across and within the areas of art; music, visual arts, dance, media arts, and theater. They have also included essential questions based upon these enduring understandings. We will examine essential questions next.

Box 3.3 Is It an Enduring Understanding?

- Does your enduring understanding include one or more big ideas?
- Does it focus on understanding rather than on what the learner will know (knowledge) or do (skills)?
- Does the enduring understanding summarize important overarching concepts, principles, and processes?
- Does the enduring understanding require "uncoverage"?
- Is the enduring understanding written in a sentence format? For example, you might begin with "I want the children in my classroom to understand that...."

Information from Wiggins and McTighe (2005).

Essential Questions

In this section, we will examine what essential questions are, who they are written for, and how many questions are typical within a unit. We'll also examine how essential questions relate to skill-based units.

What Are Essential Questions?

Essential questions are designed to promote inquiry and to aid in the transfer of learning. The essential questions provide the focus for the unit. The questions invite children to use inquiry as they seek answers. As they use inquiry, learners engage their curiosity, actively explore and grapple with ideas, and as a result construct meaning and an increasing understanding of the topic. As such, essential questions are always open-ended. However, not all open-ended questions are essential questions. Essential questions are those that are important or timeless such as, "How do we balance individual and societal rights?" For a young child, this might become, "What is a fair way to share toys and materials in the classroom?" Essential questions might also relate to ongoing debates within a discipline such as, "What killed the dinosaurs?" Or, essential questions might help learners make sense of isolated facts in core content such as, "What makes a great story?" (McTighe and Wiggins, 2013). These questions are thought-provoking and encourage the learner to gain content as they begin to investigate and to answer the question.

Essential questions will vary based upon the age of the child. For example, a toddler classroom and a second-grade classroom are both studying worms. While the topic of study is the same, the big ideas, essential questions, enduring understandings and acceptable evidence of learning will vary. In the toddler classroom, the enduring understandings might be, "We can learn through observation" and "tools can help us to learn more." Essential questions could be, "What can we observe using our eyes, a magnifying glass, and a digital microscope?" "What do we learn about the worms by watching them closely?" The second-grade classroom is also studying worms. However, they are focusing on the characteristics of living things and creating effective habitats for living things.

Essential questions also aid in the transfer of learning. Transfer of learning allows the learner to apply what they have learned to a new situation or setting. One of the primary goals of education is that learners will be able to use what they have learned in new contexts. This includes applying this learning in school settings as children study new topics, engage in learning in different disciplines, and proceed to the next grade. It also includes applying their learning to everyday life. For example, the child uses the vocabulary word they learned for a spelling test in their everyday speech and in their writing. While it is one of the most important goals of education, research demonstrates that transfer of learning is often not achieved (Mestre, 2002).

It is impossible to teach everything that a learner needs to know, so as teachers we must continually decide what is essential to know and how we can teach in a way that what is learned is transferable to new situations. Lee Shulman, who was the President of the Carnegie Foundation for the Advancement of Teaching sums it up in this way.

> What's the least amount of material we can teach really well that will, in turn, make it possible for those whom we teach to use that knowledge in the widest possible range of situations—including not only situations that we can anticipate but also situations that no one can anticipate. And that's abstractly the problem with transfer. How can you learn less, and make much more of it?
>
> (2002, p. 1)

Designing curriculum around essential questions is one way that we can accomplish this. Essential questions:

- provide a focus for the unit. The unit will be based upon answering these questions.
- are connected to the big ideas and enduring understandings. There is a strong correlation between the enduring understandings and the essential questions. Often there is a direct relationship with the enduring understanding being placed in a question format to form the essential question.
- are broad in scope and open-ended. They cannot be answered with a simple yes or no or even in a brief sentence but instead, require justification.
- are intellectually engaging, involving higher order thinking, discussion, and debate.
- involve ongoing thought and inquiry to answer, often raising additional questions as the investigation continues.
- are recurring. They can be revisited over time to gain deeper insights.
- include valuable ideas that can be transferred across topics and disciplines (McTighe & Wiggins, 2013).

In thinking about essential questions, Jeffrey Wilhelm, a professor at Boise State University and the author of many books states that essential questions should:

- be interesting and compelling to your students right now.
- invite the learner into the ongoing disciplinary debates and conversations that create knowledge in the first place.
- require students to learn—and to use—the same understandings and strategies as the real experts in the field (2012, p. 26).

Let's look at an example. Let's say that the big ideas you are working on are our rights and responsibilities. An example of an enduring understanding is, "Rights are balanced by responsibilities." Essential questions could be, "What are my rights? What responsibilities go with my rights?"

While some essential questions relate more specifically to particular curricular areas, many relate across curriculum areas. For example, an essential question such as "Where is meaning made?" can be examined through many different subjects. This could be a question examined in a language, literature, art, music, drama, or science course. For example, is what the speaker says the true meaning or is what the listener hears the true meaning? Is it the artist's interpretation of their artwork the "correct" interpretation or is the meaning based upon each individual's interpretation?

Overarching and Topical Essential Questions

Additionally, similar to the enduring understandings, in designing units one typically includes both overarching questions and topical questions. Overarching essential questions are more general, requiring us to revisit them again and again to achieve a deep understanding. The overarching question does not typically mention the particular topic of study. Topical essential questions are more focused on the particular area we are studying. The topical questions may be a subset of the overarching questions. For example, Tom, a Pre-K teacher is planning a unit on gardens. An overarching essential question might be, "What are the needs of living things?" A topical question might be, "What do our garden plants need to survive and grow?" Note that both the overarching and topical questions are open-ended, provide opportunities for inquiry and deep-learning, and are important critical questions for understanding living things and gardens.

Although the topical question is the focus of the unit, the teacher will also tie the learning to the overarching question. As learners revisit the overarching question over time, their understanding deepens. For example, Tom revisits the question, "What are the needs of living things?" when they complete a unit on bugs. Later in the year, when several of the children in his class have baby brothers and sisters, they have a unit on babies where they again revisit the needs of living things.

Who Are Essential Questions Written for?

When teaching young children, you might first write the question for the teacher. Then you can translate this into language that will be understandable to the learner.

How Many Essential Questions Would a Unit Typically Have?

It was common in the past to design a project or unit and then to think about the learning standards that related to this project or unit. The belief was that the more standards that were listed, the more justification for offering the unit. However, this often resulted in superficial coverage of the standard. The belief with backward design is that we should explore fewer questions but cover them in-depth. The length of the unit helps determine the number of enduring understandings and essential questions. Generally, for a month-long unit, we would only have two or three overarching enduring understandings, two or three topical understandings, two or three overarching essential questions, and two or three topical questions for each unit.

As you create your backward design unit, you will include both overarching and topical essential questions. In the next section, we will examine several examples. These can be used as a starting point for developing your unit. After you develop your essential questions, you can use Box 3.4 to critique them.

Box 3.4 Is It an Essential Question?

- Is the question clearly connected to the big ideas and enduring understandings?
- Is the question interesting and compelling to students?
- Is the question broad in scope and open-ended?
- Is the question intellectually engaging, involving ongoing higher order thinking, inquiry, discussion, and debate?
- Can the question be revisited over time to gain deeper insights?
- Does the question invite learners into ongoing disciplinary debates and conversations that create knowledge in the first place?
- Does the question explore ideas that can be transferred across topics and disciplines?

Information from McTighe and Wiggins (2013) and Wilhelm (2012).

Examples of Early Childhood Enduring Understandings and Overarching Essential Questions in Different Curricular Areas

In this section, there are many samples of enduring understandings and essential questions (see Tables 3.1-3.7). To help illustrate these, they are divided by curricular areas. However, when teaching, you could use many of these to transcend a specific curricular area.

Table 3.1 Sample Enduring Understandings and Essential Questions Related to Science

Enduring understanding	Essential question
Living things have unique characteristics that are different from non-living things	How are living and non-living things alike and different?
Every organism and every system has a cycle. Every living thing has a life cycle. Living things change throughout their life cycle	What are some of the cycles that occur in nature?
	How do plants change as they go through their life cycle?
	What cycles are we part of?
	What and how are cycles related to one another?
	How are life cycles of plants, animals, and humans the same and different?
People, animals, and plants are influenced by the environment and they also influence the environment	How does what I do affect the environment? How does the environment I live in affect me?
	How do animals affect the environment?
	How does the environment affect animals?
	How do plants affect the environment?
	How does the environment affect plants?
All organisms, places, and systems are constantly changing. Some things change very quickly while others change very slowly. Daily and seasonal changes affect plants, animals, and people	What changes do we see around us?
	How do living things adapt to change in their environment?
	How have you changed over time?
Recognizing patterns helps us to make predictions and to understand and make generalizations. Patterns have rules and relationships. We can see patterns, hear patterns, describe patterns, and show patterns numerically, graphically, and symbolically	Where do we find patterns?
	How do I identify a pattern and use it to predict what occurs next?
	How can I express a pattern mathematically?

Table 3.2 Sample Enduring Understandings and Essential Questions Related to Literacy

Universal truths can be found in stories. Literature can help us to understand ourselves and others. Stories are told from a point of view	What can I learn from stories?
	How does point of view affect a story?
We write for many reasons. What we are writing influences how we write	How does writing assist me in my everyday life?
	How does what we are writing affect the form of writing?
Writing changes based upon the audience. Effective writers use a variety of strategies to make the writing clear and engaging for the audience	How do I consider the audience when I write?
	What are the strategies I can use to make my writing clear to the audience?
	What are the strategies I can use to make my writing engaging?
The correct way of speaking depends on the context you are in	What are the ways that "school talk" (academic talk) is different than "home talk" (social talk)?

Table 3.3 Sample Enduring Understandings and Essential Questions Related to Math

Numbers tell us how much and how many and can be represented in many forms. Numbers can help us to make sense of the world	What are all the different ways that I can represent numbers? How can numbers help us to make sense of the world?
Geometric shapes are humanly constructed and also exist in nature. Shapes can be analyzed, sorted, and compared based on attributes. The shape of an item determines its use	Where do we find geometric shapes in our world? How can we describe shapes? How does the shape of an item determine how it is used?
Information can be collected, organized, and represented in different ways. Data can help us to understand information, solve problems, and make predictions	What kinds of problems can we solve with data? What are ways we can organize data so that it helps us to best understand the information?
Measurement can help us to describe our world. Measurement can help us to solve problems. What we measure influences how we measure. Using the appropriate tools helps us to measure more precisely	What can be measured? What type of problems can we solve by measurement? How can we choose the right tool for measuring? How accurately do we need to measure?
There are many ways to solve problems. Some problem-solving techniques are more effective than others based upon the situation	What do good problem solvers do, especially if they are having trouble solving a problem?

Table 3.4 Sample Enduring Understandings and Essential Questions Related to Social Studies

We have wants and needs. We make choices based on our wants and needs and our available resources. Our choices can affect others, especially when there are limited resources	What is the difference between wants and needs? How do our wants and needs affect others?
We can study the past to help us understand the world today. The person writing or telling the history tells it from their perspective	How do stories from the past help us today? How can we really know what happened in the past? Whose story is it?
We each have our own culture. Our culture affects our values, beliefs, behaviors, and traditions	What is my culture? How does my culture affect me? What traditions are part of my culture?
Being a citizen includes rights and responsibilities	What are my rights and responsibilities in the classroom?
One's place is made up of both human and natural communities. Place affects the way we live and how we meet our needs	What human and natural communities make up our place? How does the environment we live in shape us? How does where we live affect how we meet our needs?
There are many different types of communities. A community is made of individuals with rights and responsibilities. People within a community develop relationships and depend upon each other	What makes a community? Who lives in our community? What is your responsibility to the community? What is the community's responsibility to you? What does a community need to survive?

Table 3.5 Sample Enduring Understandings and Essential Questions Related to Social and Emotional Development

Healthy self-esteem can help us to be more motivated, effective, and to make better choices	How do I develop positive feelings about myself?
We can use a variety of different methods to express and manage emotions	How can I express my emotions? How can I manage my emotions?
My behaviors affect me and my relationships. There are many ways to manage my behavior	How do my behaviors affect me? How do my behaviors affect others? How do I manage my behavior? Why do I behave the way I do?

(Continued)

Friends can provide companionship, offer support, and bring joy to life. It is sometimes hard to recognize true friends. Conflicts may occur between friends. We can use a variety of different skills, strategies, and approaches to make and keep friendships	What are the benefits of friendship to me and to my friend? What is a true friend? How do I solve conflicts with friends? How do I make friends? How do I keep friends?

Table 3.6 Sample Enduring Understandings and Essential Questions Related to Physical Skills, Health, and Wellness

We can make healthy or unhealthy choices. The choices we make affect ourselves, our family, and our community	What are the choices I make that are healthy? What are the choices I make that are unhealthy? How do our healthy and unhealthy choices affect ourselves, our family, and our community?
Developing and maintaining an active lifestyle improves health, well-being, and your quality of life and it reduces stress, obesity, and disease. There are many ways to be physically active	How does being physically active help us now and in the future? What are ways that I can stay physically active?
We can help ourselves to stay healthy through preventing the spread of germs, getting enough sleep, engaging in healthy eating, and avoiding unsafe situations	How do I stay healthy? What is healthy eating? What are unsafe situations and how do I avoid them?

Table 3.7 Sample Enduring Understandings and Essential Questions Related to the Arts

Dramatic play can help us to express our thoughts, feelings, and ideas	How can I express my thoughts, feelings, and ideas through dramatic play?
Art can help us to express and clarify our thoughts, feelings, ideas, and knowledge	How can I express my thoughts, feelings, and ideas through art?
We can learn about others' thoughts, feelings, and ideas by examining their music	How does a song communicate with us?
Studying the art and music of another culture can help us to understand the culture	What can works of art tell us about a culture and about ourselves? What can music and dance tell us about a culture?
Studying art and music from another time period can help us understand that time period better	What can works of art tell us about a period-of-time?
Creativity can help us to generate new ideas, find unique ways to solve problems, and allow us to make original contributions. Creativity is needed to make the world better. We can restrict or nurture creativity	How does creativity enhance my world? What are ways that I can enhance my own and others' creativity?

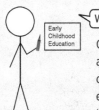

When I teach adults, do I write the questions for them or the children they teach?

Early Childhood Education

Generally, we write the essential questions for the learner that we are working with. In this case, for the early childhood teachers in our class. For example, if you were teaching a course on early childhood environments, what is a crucial concept or idea that you would want to ensure that learners grapple with? What is an idea that they will continue to explore as time goes on? One enduring understanding relating to the environment might be, "Environments give learners intended or unintended messages about expected behavior." The question might then be, "What messages, both intended and unintended, do early childhood environments give to children?" If we were teaching a workshop on culture to teachers, an enduring understanding might be, "Our cultural background provides a lens that affects our interactions, expectations, communication, attitudes, and values." An essential question could be, "How does my cultural lens affect my beliefs and practices in working with children and their families?" See Table 3.8 for more examples.

Table 3.8 Sample Enduring Understandings and Essential Questions Related to Teaching Early Childhood Educators

A reflective approach to teaching involves self-examination, observation, and ongoing commitment and practice. Reflection needs to be intentional, deliberate, and ongoing. Reflection assists with meaningful change and growth in practice	What does a reflective approach to teaching look like? How do I build systematic reflection into my practice? How do I use reflection to change my practice?
The early childhood environment can assist children to meet early learning standards, especially when the environment is intentionally designed to meet specific standards. The environment is "the third teacher"	How do I design environments to meet specific learning standards? In what way does my environment act as "the third teacher?"
Children's behavior is affected by the classrooms' transitions, environment, curriculum, and interactions	How do my transitions, environment, curriculum, and interactions affect children's behavior in my classroom?
Teachers can build resilience in young children through forming strong positive relationships; intentionally teaching social, emotional, and problem-solving skills; and by providing opportunities to develop self-efficacy and competence	How do I build resilience in each child in my classroom?
Building reciprocal relationships with families and colleagues involves effective communication, collaboration, conflict resolution, and assertiveness skills, and knowledge of one's own and others' cultural beliefs and values	What effective strategies do I use to build collaborative relationships with each family? What effective strategies do I use to prevent and resolve conflicts with families and coworkers?
Effective teachers base their practice on evidence-based practice and current research	What is evidence-based practice? How can I stay informed about evidence-based practice and current research and use this information to enhance my teaching?

As mentioned in Chapter 2, you will want to thoroughly study the state and national standards that affect your program. Some national and state standards include big ideas, enduring understandings, and essential questions. For example, Pennsylvania has created Learning Standards for Early Childhood for infants/toddlers, Pre-K, kindergarten, first grade, and second grade. Each of these sets of standards includes big ideas and essential questions. The big ideas are written as an enduring understanding (Office of Child Development and Early Learning, 2016). However, unlike Pennsylvania, most state standards do not explicitly list big ideas, enduring understandings, and essential questions. Therefore, you will need to examine the standards to determine the implicit messages.

Is it really necessary to think about any of this if we have a curriculum that we must follow to fidelity? For example, can't we just assume that the standards have been covered?

Many curriculums will produce alignment documents that show the alignment between the curriculum and the state standards. However, you will want to explore how in-depth this alignment is. For example, the most superficial alignment is to determine if the content knowledge, skills, and dispositions in the standards are covered in the curriculum. This can be done by examining a list of curriculum objectives and comparing them with the standards. However, more time-consuming is to determine how in-depth the standards are covered and whether the rigor listed in the standard aligns with the rigor in the curriculum.

The Ohio Department of Job and Family Services (2014) provides a strategy to examine alignment. Early childhood educators complete a chart that includes each standard topic. For each topic, the early childhood program gives the page numbers where the standard is addressed in the curriculum; shows how the standard is evident in classroom environments, routines, and activities; describes how the skills and knowledge are assessed; and how progress is documented. By completing this type of alignment activity, you can determine the depth of coverage of topics.

You will also want to ensure that the curriculum provides the appropriate level of rigor. For example, the standard states that the child will be able to, "use a range of strategies to manage emotions." To meet this standard, you will want to ensure that the curriculum provides opportunities for the child to not only learn about the strategies but also to practice them. To assess this standard, the child would need to demonstrate over time that they were using a variety of strategies to manage their emotions. It would not be sufficient evidence for the child to simply state what strategies they might use in a given situation. Being able to describe a strategy is not the same as being able to use a strategy, especially when one is experiencing a strong emotion.

As we discussed in Chapter 2, it is not possible to simply use early childhood standards as our desired results. Instead, we want to develop desired results based upon knowledge, skills, approaches to learning, and big ideas. The big ideas are translated into essential questions and enduring understandings. However, we are still required to base our teaching on standards. How can we accomplish this? One technique is to bundle the standards, unpack them, and then to prioritize the learning.

Bundling, Unpacking, Prioritizing: A Technique for Meeting Standards

Rather than devoting units to individual standards, we will want to bundle common standards. Bundling can assist students to see connections between content areas. It can assist teachers to create integrated units that are more coherent, and it can save instructional time. Remember, the standards are the anchor for our unit.

Once bundling is completed, you will want to unpack the standards determining what big ideas, enduring understandings, essential questions, knowledge, skills, and approaches to learning that children must demonstrate to show that they meet the standards. Finally, you will need to prioritize the knowledge, skills, and approaches to learning that you will focus on. Let's look at an example of how this can be accomplished by exploring the Montana Early Learning Standards.

Bundling Standards

Teresa, a teacher of four and five-year-old children, is planning a unit with a focus on engineering. Most of the children in her classroom have a high interest in creating and building. They've been highly engaged in the tinker boxes she has established and they have been building elaborate buildings and ramps in the block area. Teresa feels that they are ready for a more formalized design approach. Teresa feels this is a worthwhile study not only because the children demonstrate an interest, but because she can address several Montana Early Learning Standards during the study, and research demonstrates the importance of engineering in the early years.

As one of her pre-assessments, she asks the children in her classroom to draw an engineer. She finds results similar to a study by Pantoya, Aguirre-Munoz, and Hunt (2015). Either the children don't know what an engineer is, or they draw a picture of a train conductor.

She examines the standards and decides to bundle the following Montana Early Learning Standards (O'Dell & Montana Early Childhood Project, 2014).

- Use a formalized design process of investigation, invention, implementation, and evaluation with guidance (engineering standard)
- Compare, contrast, and describe objects based upon their characteristics (physical science standard)
- Develop procedures and thinking skills for investigating the world, solving problems, and making decisions (approaches to learning-curiosity standard)
- Describe a sequence of events (mathematics–algebraic thinking standard)
- Create representations of locations and space (geography standard)

When we prioritize the standards, Reeves (2002) suggests we look at three criteria, longevity (important in more than one curriculum area), endurance (important for subsequent units and years of schooling), and importance for the current and next level of learning (prerequisite skill or knowledge). As you bundle standards, you will also want to consider which standards are logical to bundle together. For example, it is often logical to bundle reading and writing standards. If we are working on the standard of writing an informative report, it is helpful to also be working on the reading standard related to informational text.

Why did Teresa bundle these particular standards? When Teresa thought about the engineering design process, she realized that solving problems using engineering design involved using objects based upon their characteristics, problem-solving, making decisions, following and describing a sequence of events, and creating and using representations.

Next, Teresa needed to consider the following questions. What are the big ideas related to these standards? What are enduring understandings and essential questions inherent in these standards? What knowledge would a child need to successfully achieve these standards? What skills would they need? What approaches to learning?

Unpacking the Standards

Next Teresa examines the bundle of standards and unpacks the standards to determine the big ideas, essential questions, enduring understandings, knowledge, skills, and approaches to learning needed to meet the standards.

In unpacking the bundled standards, she looks for the keywords in the standards. As you unpack standards, you will need to use your own knowledge, experience, and expertise to reflect upon the content and skills that are needed. In some cases, you might be able to look at guidance documents that will assist you. For example, many standards have descriptions and examples that are helpful.

Teresa decides that the big ideas she wants to concentrate on are:

- Problem-solving
- Properties of materials

For enduring understanding, she decides on the following.

- Overarching: Knowing the properties of materials helps us to use the materials effectively.
- Overarching: Using a systematic process can assist us to solve everyday problems.
- Topical: Engineers study the properties of materials to determine how to use them effectively.
- Topical: We can use an engineering design process to solve problems in our lives.

Her essential questions are:

- Overarching: How can problem-solving be used in our everyday life?
- Overarching: How does the property of an object affect its use?
- Topical: How can the engineering design process help us solve problems in our everyday life?
- Topical: How does the property of the object affect my engineering design?

Knowledge of:

- engineering design procedures
- properties of materials
- sequences of events
- ways to represent location and space
- strategies for problem-solving, observing, comparing and contrasting, investigating, and evaluating

Skills:

- problem-solving
- observation
- comparing
- contrasting
- describing

- representational drawing
- investigating
- evaluating
- inventing

Approaches to learning:

- persistence
- attention
- creativity
- reflection
- interpretation

Prioritizing

After unpacking the standards, we need to determine our unit priorities based upon the importance of the standards and the children's competence in regard to the standard. This will include considering children's background knowledge and skills. In thinking about the priorities, you will consider two categories of questions. First, how important are the understandings, knowledge, skill, and approach to learning? Second, what is the children's current level of understanding, knowledge, skill, and approach to learning? In determining the importance, answer the following questions.

- How important is this understanding, knowledge, skill, or approach to learning?
- Do the learners need this understanding, knowledge, skills, or desired approach to learning at this time?
- Is the understanding, knowledge, skill, or desired approach to learning a critical foundation for future learning?

After reflecting on these questions, you will choose one of the following criteria:

- The understanding, knowledge, skill, or desired approach to learning is not important at this time.
- The learner needs to be familiar with this knowledge, have a rudimentary level or skill, or are beginning to display the desired approach to learning.
- The learner needs some understanding and knowledge, to have an intermediate skill level, or developing approach to learning.
- The learner needs an in-depth understanding, knowledge, proficient skill, or well-developed approach to learning.

In determining children's competence, answer the following questions.

- How competent are the learners in regard to this knowledge, skill, or desired approach to learning?
- What is the learners' background knowledge?
- What have they learned from previous units or topics that you have studied?

After reflecting on these questions, you will choose one of the following criteria:

- The understanding, skill, knowledge, or approach to learning is undeveloped. The children do not yet have the understanding, knowledge, skills, or desired approach to learning.
- The understanding, skill, knowledge, or approach to learning is emerging. The children are just beginning to understand, just beginning to gain the knowledge or skill, or just beginning to adopt the approach to learning.
- The understanding, skill, knowledge, or desired approach to learning is developing. The children have some understanding, knowledge, skills, or are exhibiting this approach to learning.
- The understanding, skill, knowledge, or desired approach to learning is well developed. The children are proficient in their understanding, knowledge, skill, and in their approach for learning for their age and development.

After reviewing your list, your priorities may be apparent. If not, you might find it helpful to use Table 3.9. This table shows the intersection between the importance of the standard and the children's knowledge of the standard. Where these two intersect, you will find the amount of time and emphasis needed to develop the knowledge, gain the skill, or enhance the approach to learning. For example, if the children's skill was developing and they needed some knowledge of the skill, the teacher would need to plan a limited emphasis when designing the curriculum. You will notice that the amount of time and emphasis is; none, limited, moderate, or extensive. In addition, there is a category for reinforcing the skill. In this case, the teacher might reinforce children's knowledge, encourage skills and promote the positive approaches to learning.

While Teresa will address each of the standards she has identified at some level, the amount of time devoted will be dependent upon how she answers the above questions. Teresa quickly goes through the list of knowledge, skills, and approaches to learning she has listed to determine her priorities. For example, she determines that the children have used the engineering steps informally but have not been exposed to a more formalized process. Since this is an engineering unit and based upon their age and development, she believes that they need some knowledge of this, and their knowledge currently is undeveloped. Based on Table 3.9, she will need to spend a moderate amount of time teaching, providing opportunity for skill development, and assessing children's knowledge of this. However, Teresa and the children have been working on observation skills as children have completed representational drawings for other units. While she feels that children need some knowledge and some skills in regard to this, she feels that most of the children already have a fairly well-developed knowledge and sufficient skills in this area so she will remind children of what they have learned and provide opportunities to practice the skills, but she will not make this a priority in the unit. On her unit plan, Teresa will only list the desired results that she plans to assess.

Table 3.9 Determining Unit Priorities

Standard	Unimportant at this time	Needs some familiarity	Needs some knowledge	Needs to be proficient
Undeveloped competence	None	Limited	Moderate	Extensive
Emerging competence	None	Limited	Moderate	Moderate
Developing competence	None	None	Limited	Limited
Well-developed competence	None	None	Reinforce	Reinforce

It is tempting to list every standard that relates in any way to your unit as a way of justifying the importance of the unit. However, this makes it impossible to assess every outcome and to provide relevant activities. It ultimately hurts the learning experience since there is not a clear, targeted focus. Therefore, only list the desired results that you will assess and that you will provide activities for.

Resources for Developing Big Ideas, Enduring Understanding Statements, and Essential Questions?

Determining the concepts, enduring understandings, and essential questions can be difficult because this has often not been stressed within early childhood. In developing these, it is helpful to work with a curriculum team, to think about the questions you continue to grapple with as an adult and as an early childhood educator, and to look at others' units and lists for inspiration. Additionally, throughout this book, there will be numerous examples and strategies that will assist you.

Colleagues

Meeting with other early childhood educators including colleagues and coworkers to determine what standards to bundle and to then discuss the big ideas, enduring understandings, and essential questions to focus on can generate additional ideas and garnish support. Remember, that we are always making choices. We need to be aware that our philosophy, our values and beliefs, and our cultural context often strongly influence our choices. It is also helpful to have family and community members on curriculum development teams to provide additional insights and to ensure we are meeting their needs. For example, several years ago, the State of Massachusetts used their Race to the Top grant to bring teams of teachers together to design units based on backward design. Together these teams created over 100 units that are used throughout Massachusetts and beyond (Massachusetts Department of Elementary and Secondary Education, 2014). While this was a formalized process sponsored by the Massachusetts Department of Elementary and Secondary Education, you can also rely on a less formalized structure including teachers who are in your professional learning teams or other educators that are in a curriculum course.

Reflection

Thinking about the big ideas that you are still exploring is another way to identify big ideas, enduring understandings, and essential questions. As you begin to explore big ideas, you will often find that there are questions that you have pondered over time. For example,

> Who is a true friend? What is credible evidence and how do I find it? What does it really mean to have a democracy? or What are my responsibilities to my family, community, and my profession and how do I balance these with my rights?

These are the type of questions that you might contemplate using in units you are teaching.

You will also want to reflect on the topic you are teaching. What is important about this topic? Why are you teaching this topic? What is the heart of it? (Wilhelm, 2012). Reflecting on these questions, may help you to determine the big ideas.

Sample Units and Lists

You might also look at other's units such as those developed by Massachusetts or examine sample lists like those included in this book. However, you will want to ensure that the enduring understandings and essential questions are relevant to your setting and meaningful and appropriate for your learners. It is also important to remember that there are numerous possibilities for enduring understandings and essential questions, so it is not possible for any one list to be comprehensive.

In Summary

If we wish to teach in a way that focuses on big ideas, we must abandon or at least alter typical ways of curriculum planning where we engage in learning activities that are unrelated to context, rush through a parade of discrete tasks and activities, and/or dutifully follow the curriculum guide or textbook. Instead, we must think about the big ideas, use texts and curriculum guides as resources, and use our knowledge of our students, the community, and the cultural context as a filter for our curriculum choices. By bundling the standards, then unpacking the standards, and finally prioritizing the knowledge, skills, and approaches to learning we can be efficient and provide for more in-depth learning based upon the needs of the children.

There are common errors that teachers make as they develop enduring understandings and essential questions. To prevent these:

- choose essential questions and enduring understandings that relate to the big ideas.
- plan essential questions and enduring understandings that closely relate to each other.
- limit the number of essential questions and enduring understandings so that you can provide in-depth learning.
- list only the desired results that are assessed and taught.
- if teaching a unit on skills, also teach the concepts associated with the skills.

Although developing big ideas, enduring understandings, and essential questions is time-consuming and intellectually challenging, doing so assists us to identify the most important concepts we want learners to grasp. This then provides a lens that brings focus to our curriculum which provides learners the opportunity to gain a deeper conceptual understanding that is transferable to new settings.

Apply Your Knowledge

1. Think of a unit that you would like to teach and then explore ways that you can enhance your background knowledge.
2. Take a unit or project that you have taught in the past and develop enduring understandings and essential questions for the unit or project. How does developing the enduring understandings and essential questions change the way that you will redesign your unit or project?
3. Check your understanding of enduring understandings by critiquing the following word and statements. Determine if the word or statement is an enduring understanding. If it is not, describe why.
   - Friendship
   - A triangle always has three angles.
   - Children learn what they live.

4. Check your understanding of the essential questions by critiquing the following questions. Determine if the question is an essential question. If it is not, describe why.
   o What are the parts of a plant?
   o How many sides does a triangle have?
   o Are friends always loyal?
   o What is your favorite animal?
5. Lisa, a teacher of first grade, is planning a unit on ponds. The school is located near a pond that is filled with frogs and water snakes. What are three different big ideas that Lisa can focus on? How does the focus change the enduring understandings and essential questions?
6. Think of a unit that you would like to teach and an age group that you wish to develop the unit for. Find the standards related to this age group in your state. Then bundle, unpack, and prioritize the standards for this topic. Make sure to list the concepts, enduring understandings, and essential questions that you will emphasize in your unit.

References

Adler, S. A., & National Council for the Social Studies. (2013). *National curriculum standards for social studies: A framework for teaching, learning and assessment*. Silver Springs, MD: NCSS.

Bransford, J. D., & National Research Council. (2004). *How people learn: Brain, mind, experience, and school*. Washington, DC: National Academy Press.

Erickson, H. L. (2008). *Stirring the head, heart, and soul: Redefining curriculum, instruction, and concept-based learning* (3rd edition). Thousand Oaks, CA: Corwin Press.

Gelman, S. A. (1996). Concepts and theories. In R. Gelman & T. K. Au (Eds.), *Perceptual and cognitive development* (pp. 117–150). New York: Academic Press. doi:10.1016/B978-012279660-9/50022-1

Gelman, S. A. (1999). Concept development in preschool children. In American Association for the Advancement of Science (Ed.), *Dialogue on early childhood science, mathematics, and technology education* (pp. 50–61). Washington, DC: American Association for the Advancement of Science.

Gelman, S. A., & Koenig, M. A. (2003). Theory-based categorization in early childhood. In D. H. Rakison & L. M. Oakes (Eds.) *Early category and concept development: Making sense of the blooming, buzzing confusion* (pp. 330–359). Oxford: Oxford University Press.

Massachusetts Department of Elementary and Secondary Education. (2014). *MCU update: Model curriculum units for Massachusetts educators*. Retrieved from http://www.doe.mass.edu/candi/model/newsletter/

McTighe, J., & Wiggins, G. (2013). *Essential questions: Opening doors to student understanding*. Alexandria, VA: Association for Supervision and Curriculum Development (ASCD).

Mestre, J. (2002). *Transfer of learning: Issues and research agenda*. National Science Foundation. Retrieved from https://www.nsf.gov/pubs/2003/nsf03212/nsf03212_1.pdf

National Research Council. (2011). *A framework for k-12 science education: Practices, crosscutting concepts, and core ideas*. Committee on a Conceptual Framework for New K-12 Science Education Standards. Board on Science Education, Division of Behavioral and Social Sciences and Education. Washington, DC: The National Academy Press.

NGSS Lead States. (2013). *Next generation science standards: For states, by states*. Washington, DC: The National Academies Press.

O'Dell, C., & Montana Early Childhood Project. (2014). *Montana early learning standards*. Retrieved from https://opi.mt.gov/Portals/182/Page%20Files/Early%20Childhood/Docs/14EarlyLearningStandards.pdf

Office of Child Development and Early Learning. (2016). *Pennsylvania learning standards for early childhood*. Retrieved from http://www.education.pa.gov/Early%20Learning/Early%20Learning%20Standards/Pages/Infant-Toddler-Pre-K-Learning-Standards.aspx

Ohio Department of Job and Family Services. (2014). *Curriculum standards assessment alignment tool: Pre-kindergarten strand for step up to quality*. Retrieved from http://www.odjfs.state.oh.us/forms/num/JFS01591/pdf/

Pantoya, M. L., Aguirre-Munoz, Z., & Hunt, E. M. (2015). Developing an engineering identity in early childhood. *American Journal of Engineering Education, 6*(2), 61–68. doi:10.19030/ajee.v6i2.9502

Reeves, D. B. (2002). *The leader's guide to standards: A blueprint for educational equity and excellence*. Hoboken, NJ: John Wiley & Sons.

Stewart, M. G. (2014). Enduring understandings, artistic processes, and the new visual arts standards: A close-up consideration for curriculum planning. *Art Education, 67*(5), 6-11. doi:10.1080/00043125.2014.11519285

Wiggins, G., & McTighe, J. (2005). *Understanding by design: Expanded 2nd edition*. Alexandria, VA: Association for Supervision and Curriculum Development (ASCD).

Wilhelm, Jeffrey D. (2012). Essential questions. *Instructor, 122*(3), 24-27.

4 Determining Acceptable Evidence

After determining your outcomes (essential questions, enduring understandings, knowledge, skills, and approaches to learning), you will complete Step 2. In Step 2, you determine how you will assess these outcomes. What evidence will allow you to know that children have met the outcomes? This is an iterative process, as you develop assessments it is common that it results in further clarification of your outcomes.

As you design your assessment, you will want to ensure that the assessment relates directly to your outcomes. The assessment needs to align in both depth and breadth. Ask yourself the question, "How will I know that (child)_____ has mastered_____?" What type of assessment method will provide this information? To be clear about what children have learned, you will develop assessments for individual children rather than for groups and the assessment will reflect what children can do independently. This will be a summative assessment that will let you know if children have mastered the desired outcomes.

Group Assessment versus Individual Assessment

Let's look at an example. One of the errors that teachers sometimes make with assessment is to conduct group assessments and assume because some of the children learned the content, they all did. For example, Amanda was conducting a unit on firefighters and their tools, including fire trucks. She focused on the essential questions, "How does a community keep itself safe?" and "How do tools assist firefighters?" As she conducted the unit, she used a variety of forms of formative assessment. She:

- conducted a class web where children brainstormed what they knew about firefighters and their role in keeping communities safe
- completed a class KWHL–what I know, what I want to know, how I will learn it
- had each child make a drawing of firefighter' tools including a fire truck.

For summative assessments

- The class completed another web at the end of the unit
- The class brainstormed and completed the "what I learned" section of the KWHL chart
- Each child completed another picture of firefighter' tools including a fire truck

Amanda and the children completed the first three parts of the KWHL at the beginning of the unit. At the end of the unit, they reflected upon what they had learned, and they completed the L section of the KWHL chart. Both the web and the KWHL chart demonstrated the amount that the group of children had learned. The drawings were completed by individual children. However, Amanda had not determined how she could analyze these. At the end of the unit, Amanda had conferences with families and showed them the comparisons from the beginning of the unit to the end of the unit. As she reflected on what each child had learned, she realized that she wasn't certain, since most of her assessments were with groups of children. How could Amanda change her assessments to provide information about individual learners?

> In our program, we conduct group documentation of projects. Is this important? How does this fit with backward design?

Group assessments are sometimes used for pre-assessments and to document a unit or project. Both individual and group documentation demonstrate that we take children's ideas and work seriously, allows the children and teachers to "revisit" their and others ideas, guides teacher's planning, provides for teacher research, sustains communication with parents, provides evidence of learning and makes children's learning visible, and is a powerful tool for advocacy (Helm & Katz, 2016; Katz & Chard, 1996). Group documentation can also provide a history of the school. Group documentation has many benefits. However, you will also want individual documentation so that you can assess what each child has learned and so that you can use this information to determine their future learning needs.

Can I Provide Options in Assessment Tasks?

Wiggins and McTighe (2012) point out that you might give children options within assessment tasks. However, to determine if children have achieved the outcomes, the criteria and the rubrics must be the same regardless of the task. For example, you might be assessing children's understanding of the water cycle, this might be done by drawing a diagram, acting out the process, writing about the cycle, or demonstrating the cycle using objects. In each of these tasks, the teacher would be able to gauge the child's understanding of the water cycle.

What Is the Difference between an Assessment and an Activity?

There is sometimes confusion about the difference between assessments and activities. The assessment, referred to as a performance task in UbD, is the final assessment or key assessment or summative assessment. Summative assessments are conducted at the end of the unit and let you know if individual children have achieved the desired outcomes. Assessments provide information that you can use to determine the next steps in curriculum development. On the other hand, activities allow children or adults to gain the knowledge and skills to demonstrate the final assessment. It is confusing because they can look the same. One of the key differences is why they are being used. Are they being used to teach or reinforce or are they being used to assess?

As you develop your summative or final assessment you will also develop rubrics based upon your desired outcomes. This will allow you to determine the degree of proficiency each child has in meeting the outcomes. The rubric usually has multiple distinct criteria (typically 3-6) (Wiggins & McTighe, 2012). Finally, you will develop summaries or data tables to make it easier to analyze your data. Aggregating or combining the data provides information about what the class has learned and about the effectiveness of the unit and the teaching methods.

While Step 2 involves designing summative assessments, you will also be using assessments in other ways throughout your unit including designing and implementing pre-assessments and formative assessments. Pre-assessments occur at the beginning of a lesson or your unit. Formative assessments occur during the course of implementing your unit, providing ongoing information that allows you to tailor the unit for individual children and for the group of children. Several studies have found that using formative assessment can increase children's achievement scores (Riley-Ayers, 2014). In a classic study, Black and Wiliam (1998) synthesized the results from 250 studies that examined formative assessment and learning. They state that the research shows conclusively that:

- formative assessment improves learning with low achievers demonstrating the greatest gains.
- gains in achievement are among the largest ever reported for educational interventions with an effect size of 0.7 (p. 7).

A more recent meta-analysis that examined 13 studies on formative assessment found a much smaller effect size that varied by curriculum area with effect sizes for English language arts at 0.32, math at 0.17, and science at 0.09. However, the authors stressed that "while the weighted mean effect sizes found in this study are smaller than commonly reported in the literature, they have great practical significance in today's accountability climate" (Kingston & Nash, 2011, p. 34). Another meta-analysis of research that focused on formative assessment and teacher and parent feedback on children's writing found an effect size of 0.87 (Graham, Hebert, & Harris, 2015).

However, for formative assessment to be effective, teachers need to use the information that they gain to adapt instruction and to provide effective feedback. In addition to teachers assessing children, formative assessment often involves children engaging in self-assessment and peer-assessment.

To be effective assessors, whether designing pre-assessments, formative assessments, or summative assessments, we must understand the challenges of assessing young children, the purpose of assessments, the advantages and disadvantages of different types of assessments, how to conduct different types of assessments, and how to analyze assessment results so that we can use this information in curriculum planning and implementation. We will be examining each of these in this chapter.

Assessments and Young Children

It is important that we assess young children for a variety of reasons, including determining children's developmental level, establishing learning goals, planning an effective curriculum, and deciding whether children are progressing. However, assessing young children's development and learning is challenging for several reasons. Young children are unreliable test takers. They are greatly influenced by their surroundings, their physical and emotional needs, and even their comfort with the test administrator. Developmentally, they may lack the attention span or the verbal skills to successfully participate in the assessment. Additionally, they might not understand the need for the assessment, so they might not cooperate or might not exert the needed effort to accurately complete the assessment. Further, even if the assessor does obtain an accurate assessment of the child's development and learning, children's development is uneven, rapid, and episodic so the information that is obtained might be outdated very soon (Shepard, Kagan, & Wurtz, 1998).

To obtain accurate assessment information and to lessen the negative aspects of assessment, we can look to national organizations for guidance. The National Association for the Education of Young Children (NAEYC) and the National Association of Early Childhood Specialists in State Departments of Education (NAECS/SDE) in a joint position statement on curriculum, assessment and program evaluation stress that assessments need to be developmentally and culturally appropriate and educationally significant. Assessments should be ongoing, used to improve learning, and include multiple sources of evidence. To accomplish this, both staff and families need to be knowledgeable about assessment. The organizations also warn that the use of formal standardized testing should be limited and only used when potentially beneficial, such as when determining if children have special needs (NAEYC & NAECS/SDE, 2003, pp. 2-3).

What Is the Purpose of Early Childhood Assessment?

We conduct early childhood assessments for many different reasons; to determine program effectiveness and impact, to screen for possible disabilities and to determine if the child needs additional assessment, to provide a diagnosis of a disability, and to provide instructional support. To provide background on early childhood assessment, we will briefly examine each of these purposes. There will be a special emphasis on instructional support since this is an integral focus of curriculum planning and backward design.

Program Effectiveness and Impact

One reason we conduct assessments is to determine program effectiveness and impact. This allows us to examine the overall quality of a program. This information can be used for continuous program improvement and to provide data to funders that their investment is producing desired results. As families, the government, and private donors invest in early childhood they want to ensure that children are receiving the highest quality care and education.

Assessment data for program effectiveness often include child outcomes such as aggregated child assessment data that provide information about overall group performance. Assessments are also often included that examine variables related to quality such as classroom environments, teacher qualifications and interactions, and family and community engagement. Some examples of program accountability assessments related to classroom environments include the Early Childhood Environment Rating Scale, Third Edition (ECERS-3), Infant-Toddler Environmental Rating Scale Revised Edition (ITERS-R), School Age Care Environmental Rating Scale (SACERS), Early Childhood Classroom Observation Measure (ECCOM), and the Early Language and Literacy Classroom Observation Tool (ELLCO). The Classroom Assessment Scoring System (CLASS) is an example of a common program accountability assessment that examines teacher-child interactions. Survey instruments are often used to gauge family and community engagement.

While program-level outcomes and information on groups of children are used for assessing program effectiveness and impact; screening, diagnosis, and developmental and learning assessments focus on the individual child. We will examine these next.

Screening

Health, developmental, and early academic screenings are conducted to determine if a child is at risk of having a disability. If there are concerns, the child can be referred for a more extensive assessment and receive early intervention, if needed. A screening assessment is brief and can be administered quickly. Unlike diagnostic tests, screenings can be conducted by someone with a limited amount of training.

About 1 in 6 children in the United States have a developmental disability ranging from mild to severe (Boyle et al., 2011). For example, by age eight, 1 out of 59 children in the United States are diagnosed with autism spectrum disorder (ASD) (Baio et al., 2018). ASD is a developmental disorder characterized by communication and social impairments and repetitive behaviors that affect children from all racial, ethnic, and socio-economic backgrounds. Many children with ASD also have an intellectual disability (Ganz, 2007). ASD can be very expensive. The lifetime per capita cost for a child with ASD is 3.2 million dollars, mainly due to the loss of wages and the need for adult care (Ganz, 2007). Imagine the benefits to the individual, the family, and society if we could change the outcomes for children with ASD? Effective early intervention has been found to alter the course of ASD and enhance the child's lifetime ability to function in society. This is but one example of why screening is so critical.

Some examples of screening assessments are the Ages and Stages Questionnaire Third Edition (ASQ-3), BRIGANCE Early Childhood Screens III, Developmental Indicators for the Assessment of Learning™, Fourth Edition (DIAL™-4), and the Early Screening Inventory-Revised (ESI-R).

I didn't realize that it was that important to intervene so early. Are there research-supported interventions that make a difference for really young children?

One example is the early start Denver model (ESDM). It is a treatment designed for children as young as 12 months who have been diagnosed with ASD. A study that compared children receiving community-based services with children receiving ESDM for two years found that IQ increased 17.6 points in the ESDM group and only seven points in the community-based group. The rate of growth in adaptive behavior for the group who received the ESDM was similar to typically developing children, while the comparison group showed greater delays in adaptive behavior than when they were first tested. With the ESDM group, 30% of the children no longer qualified as ASD, but instead were labeled as having pervasive developmental disorder not otherwise specified versus 5% in the control group (Dawson et al., 2010). The ESDM treatment was expensive. Over the two-year period, the cost was $28,000 more per child for the ESDM treatment than the community-based services. However, after the intervention, the children who received ESDM needed less applied behavior analysis, intensive behavior intervention, and occupational, physical, and speech therapy services. Compared to the control group, this resulted in a cost saving of $19,000 a year per child (Cidav et al., 2017). This is but one example of the power of early intervention.

When choosing a screening instrument, you will want to ensure that it is culturally and linguistically relevant and that it is reliable and valid. Reliability means that the assessment will produce the same scores in different situations, regardless of where it is administered or who is administering it. Validity means that the instrument measures what you intend to measure (Halle, Zaslow, Wessel, Moodie, & Darling-Churchill, 2011). For example, Monique was assessing children on their ability to match uppercase and lowercase letters using a computer program. To complete the assessment, children needed to use their finger to move the letters on the laptop's touchpad. Several children struggled with this. So, in this case, it wasn't possible to know if the assessment was measuring the children's knowledge of letters or their knowledge and physical skills in using the touchpad.

Diagnosis

Diagnosis involves a comprehensive evaluation of children whose development or learning is delayed for the purpose of determining eligibility for support services, early intervention, or special education services (Slentz, Early, & McKenna, 2008, p. 15). This process is in-depth and is typically time-consuming and expensive. However, it is very important since early diagnosis and intervention has been linked to improved outcomes for children including changing a child's developmental trajectory and reducing the need for later expensive remediation (Goode, Diefendorf, & Colgan, 2011). The diagnostic assessment is a systematic and formal procedure typically conducted by a multidisciplinary team. The team reviews records, observes the child, interviews families and teachers, and conducts standardized tests and assessments.

What Are Standardized Assessments?

Standardized assessments use a prescribed method of assessment and a predetermined set of assessment items that are presented and scored in a consistent manner. This allows the scores of individual children or groups of children to be compared. The assessments can be criteria referenced or norm-referenced.

A criteria-based test (CRT) compares the child's score to a predetermined standard or criteria. This allows us to determine if the child has acquired a specific body of knowledge or skill set such as multiplying two-digit numbers or reading a passage and answering comprehension questions. Most states use standardized CRTs in elementary and secondary schools to assess whether children are meeting the state standards (U.S. Department of Education, Institute of Education Sciences, National Center for Education Statistics, 2016).

Alternatively, a norm-referenced test compares and ranks a child's score in relationship to a norm-referenced group. The score is typically reported as a percentile ranking. For example, if a child scored in the sixtieth percentile, she scored as good or better than 60% of the norming group and more poorly than 40%. Screening tools such as the Developmental Indicators for the Assessment of Learning™, Fourth Edition (DIAL™-4) are an example of norm-referenced tests.

If you use a norm-referenced test you will want to closely examine the metrics for the norming group. Since you are comparing the children's score to the norm-referenced group, it is critical that the norm-referenced group share similar characteristics to your group. "Such a comparison is only meaningful if the norm group includes children who share the language, culture, and/or (dis)abilities of those being assessed" (Slentz et al., 2008, p. 30).

Effective instruments are critical since the lack of effective instruments can lead to misdiagnosis. This can include overdiagnosis leading to inaccurately labeling children or underdiagnosis and not providing the help or services children need. This is a special concern for young children who do not speak English. Concern with the lack of effective instruments to assess young English Language Learners (ELL), led NAEYC to issue a special amendment to their *Position Statement on Curriculum, Assessment, And Program Evaluation (2003)*. In the statement, *Screening and Assessment of Young English-Language Learners* (NAEYC, 2005) they stress that young ELL have the right to be assessed. However, all screenings and assessments need to be culturally and linguistically appropriate, developmentally appropriate, and age-appropriate. Before administering assessments, it is important to learn about the child's language history and current proficiency so that after reviewing the purpose for the assessment you can choose whether the assessment is best conducted in the child's home language or in English. Those assessing young children should be culturally and linguistically aware, bilingual and bicultural, aware of children's acquisition of a second language, and knowledgeable about the assessment of young children.

Instructional Assessment

The purpose of instructional assessment, sometimes referred to as classroom assessment, is to support early learning. Classroom assessments are used to:

- determine children's current level of understanding, knowledge, and skills as a way of developing and implementing targeted instruction. This could be at the beginning of the year or at the beginning of a unit.
- adjust instruction for the group and for individuals as the year progresses or the unit progresses.
- monitor children's progress toward meeting goals.
- provide a record of children's growth over time.

Within a school year, you will administer assessments at the macro level (yearly or bi-yearly), the unit level, and the micro level (a specific lesson). Macro level assessments are broad-based, assessing physical, social and emotional, cognitive, and language development. Unit and lesson assessments are more specifically related to what is currently being studied.

The results of instructional assessments are immediately relevant. Unlike screening and diagnosis, instructional assessments are typically administered by the teacher within the classroom and are often embedded within the children's activities or routines.

The yearly and bi-yearly assessment might be purchased. Some commonly purchased assessment systems include the HighScope COR Advantage, Teaching Strategies GOLD, and the *Work Sampling System* (WSS) 5th Edition. However, you will typically need to design your own formative and summative assessments for units and individual lessons. The primary purpose of formative assessment is to provide feedback to teachers and children about academic progress. The assessment information then can be used to alter the curriculum or learning process. For example, Maria taught several lessons to children on using introductory and concluding paragraphs when writing essays. However, she found when assessing their writing that while most of the children were successfully using introductory paragraphs, few were using concluding paragraphs. With this knowledge, Maria continued to work on this aspect of writing with the children.

What Are the Different Types of Assessment Methods?

In this section, we will learn about different types of classroom or instructional assessments. Instructional assessments, particularly those at the unit and lesson level have the advantage of occurring in the child's natural learning environment and can be designed to mirror real life. They can be repeated over time. The results can be used to extend learning in the moment, as well as to plan ongoing changes to the environment and to the curriculum. Assessment results can also provide information so that tiered levels of support and instruction can be provided to children.

There are many types of assessment methods, we will focus on observations, checklists and rating scales, interviews, work samples, and performance tasks. Each of these assessment methods could also be used for other categories of assessments. For example, ECERS-R is a standardized rating scale that is used for program improvement. The Childhood Autism Rating Scale™, Second Edition (CARS™-2) is a standardized rating scale used to diagnose autism and to determine the severity of symptoms. The Teaching Pyramid Infant–Toddler Observation Scale (TPITOS™) is an observation used for program improvement. However, for the purpose of this book, we will be examining these assessment types in relation to teacher-created classroom assessments. While assessments are most typically conducted by the teacher, self-assessments, and peer-assessments can also provide valuable information. We will also explore these assessment options.

Observations

Observations are a time-honored method of assessment within early childhood. They are typically unobtrusive and are a method of assessment that is effective even with non-verbal children. Observations can provide rich and detailed information especially if taken over time. However, observations can be time-consuming to collect, organize, and interpret. Without taking the time to organize and interpret observations, they lose their value.

When we observe children, we can learn about their development, goals and strategies, strengths and areas of difficulty, approaches to learning, and interests. Let's look at each of these through the lens of a teacher Kelly and what she learned about Thomas, a four-year-old child that she was observing. Kelly examined Thomas's:

- social, emotional, cognitive, physical, and artistic development. Kelly observed that Thomas hopped on one foot for a distance of five feet while he was playing on the playground.
- learning and social-emotional goals and the strategies he used to accomplish his goals. Kelly observed Thomas watching a group of boys who were building a structure in the block area. He used a variety of strategies to join the group, including building another structure near the one that the boys were building and suggesting ways that they might join their two buildings.
- strengths and areas of difficulty. Kelly noted that while Thomas had gross motor skills that were developmentally advanced as measured by their classroom assessment, he struggled with some fine motor tasks such as cutting, drawing, and putting puzzles together.
- approaches to learning. Kelly observed that Thomas persisted for 15 minutes by building a tower on his structure even though the tower continued to fall.

- interests. Kelly noted that Thomas was especially interested in activities that involved physical skills such as building with blocks, woodworking, and participating in gross motor activities on the playground.

Through observation, Kelly was able to learn about Thomas. She used this information when interacting with Thomas, planning curriculum, and making environmental changes. For example, she added Legos to the manipulative area. This was a way to combine Thomas's interest in building with his need to engage in more fine motor activities.

Sometimes through observing we can glimpse a window into a child's thinking and are able to determine the theories they believe or are testing. For example, Julie observed Tsea taking a magnet around the room and touching all the silver items that she could find. She had a puzzled look on her face when not all the items were attracted to the magnet. Tsea's theory was that silver items are attracted to magnets.

Observing can assist us in designing more relevant environments and curriculum, assist us in planning tiered instruction, and provide an opportunity to engage in more meaningful conversations leading to in-depth learning. There are many different types of observation strategies including anecdotal records, running or narrative records, event and time sampling, and learning stories.

Anecdotal Records

Anecdotal records are a brief but detailed snapshot of an incident that can provide information about children's development in all domains, their approaches to learning, and their interests. As you write anecdotal records include details such as what is happening, when is it happening, and where is it happening. Let's look at an anecdotal record.

> Aidan, who is two, is playing in the block area during center time. He collects 6 cars and places them in a parallel row. He arranges the cars from smallest to largest. Several times he places a car in the row, compares the car to the car beside it and then moves it to place it in the correct location to maintain the smallest to the largest arrangement. As he places each car in the row, he describes it. "This is a yellow race car. It goes very fast." "This is a dump truck. It hauls sand." He says, "I like cars and trucks." He continues to place the cars and talk about them for 15 minutes.

Notice that the anecdotal record only contains factual information. The details in the anecdotal record provide a snapshot of what Aidan is doing. The quotes from him provide additional information. Through this anecdotal record, we can learn about Aidan's interests, his language and cognitive development, and his attention span.

Narrative or Running Records

Narrative records or running records are similar to recording a video in that you attempt to capture everything that is occurring. This allows you to capture a range of behavior and the context in which the behavior is occurring. Running records might focus on children's interactions, their interests, or on academic skills such as reading or math. While narrative records can provide a wealth of detailed and specific information, they are time-consuming to write. Because they are so open-ended and often lengthy, they can also be more difficult to analyze than other observation methods.

> Are you sure these are running records? This doesn't sound like the kind of running record I used when I was teaching third and fourth graders. The process I used had a very defined, specific way of observing.

The terms narrative and running records are often used interchangeably in early childhood literature. However, in other fields, a running record may describe a specific process that is more focused. Let's look at a running record process that is often used in reading.

When using a running record in reading, the teacher uses a very specific process. She begins by having the child read a text to her and uses a scoring sheet to record such things as omissions, substitutions, appeals for help, and self-corrections. She then determines the error rate, accuracy rate, and the number of self-corrections. Then the errors are analyzed. But while doing this the teacher also notes the child's attitudes, body language, and strategies used. The assessment is usually followed immediately with a conference where the teacher can review the errors with the child, reinforce the child's strategies, and provide helpful information. Most importantly, the information is used in guiding future reading curriculum for the child.

> That sounds very time-consuming. Is there any evidence that it increases learning?

Yes, John Ross conducted a study where 2,800 third-grade children in 73 Ontario schools were randomly assigned to a running records treatment or an action research treatment. He found that the children in schools that used running records outperformed children in the schools using action research. After accounting for other variables, the use of running records accounted for 12% of the variance in reading and 7% of the variance in writing between the schools. Additionally, before the intervention 39 schools in the running records group and 34 schools in the action research group were below the provincial average in the percentage of children who reached the expected standards. However, after the intervention, all the schools in the running records group surpassed the provincial average while those in the action research group fell further behind (Ross, 2004). A similar process is used in mathematics where teachers assess children's automaticity, flexibility and efficiency, and mathematical dispositions (Newton, 2016).

Event and Time Sampling

Event and time sampling are developed around a specific focus. They often lead to new discoveries and are quick and easy to administer.

Event samples—One type of event sample is the ABC sample. To conduct the ABC event sample, you divide your paper into three vertical columns. The first column is labeled A for the antecedent event, what occurred right before the incident. The second column is labeled B for the specific behavior that occurred. The third column is labeled C for the consequent event or what occurred after the behavior. Some teachers add additional columns such as the names of other children involved or the area of the room the behavior occurred in.

I used event sampling recently with a kid in my classroom. It really worked. Tera was hitting the other kids several times a day. We had tried several things including talking to her, having other kids tell her how it felt, removing her from areas when she started to hit, and keeping a close watch on her. Nothing seemed to be working. We were all getting frustrated. Our director recommended we use event sampling to gather information on the context for the hitting. She said that when we discover patterns in behavior, we can use this information as we work on changing the behavior. After we completed the observation and analyzed it, we discovered that the hitting typically occurs when other children are in Tera's personal space and that she seems to need a larger than normal personal space. Once we discovered this, we began to use some preventative measures such as providing a defined space at circle time and having Tera sit at the end of the table for lunch and snack where she had additional space. We also had circle times where we talked about personal space and did some exercises where we determined where each child's personal space limits are. At the same time, we continued to work with Tera on strategies she could use rather than hitting. Since the observation, we are able to give her some specific words she might use such as "Please move out of my space." Because of our discussions and activities, the other children understand what this means, and they also understand that Tera needs more space than most of the other children. I can't say that all the hitting is gone but it is so much better.

In timed samples, rather than an event triggering the observation a specific time schedule is the trigger. For example, Dave wanted to see what centers children were using during center time. Every five minutes, he recorded the number of children in each center. Through conducting this assessment, he found that the book area was seldomly being used. He added some eBooks that children could listen to on the class iPad. After the change, he conducted another timed sample and found that the area was being used as frequently as other centers.

Learning Stories

Learning stories feature multi-media documentation including written and computer-generated narratives, photos, videos, and work samples along with the analysis of the work (Lee & Carr, 2002). One thing that makes this a unique form of assessment is how the information is presented. The learning stories are typically written in letter form, addressed to the child, and signed by the teacher creating the assessment. They are usually written in the first person. Reflections from the child and the family might also be included. The learning stories tend to have emotional appeal, being interesting and engaging to develop and to read (Lee & Carr, 2002). A primary purpose of the learning stories is to support learning and to create a dialogue with the child, families, and teaching team.

Margaret Carr, from New Zealand, developed the concept of learning stories in the 1990s as a way to address the following criteria:

- enhance children's sense of themselves as capable people and competent learners.
- reflect the holistic way that people learn.

- reflect the reciprocal relationships between the child, people, and learning environment.
- involve parents/guardians, and where appropriate Whānau (extended family) (Lee & Carr, 2002, p. 3).

The stories describe children's strengths rather than deficits. Proponents of learning stories emphasize that as teachers focus on and write about strengths, this strength-based attitude begins to permeate all aspects of the learning atmosphere. While learning stories can be about knowledge, skills or dispositions, learning dispositions are typically the focus of the stories. In New Zealand these are tied to the Te Whāriki curriculum with a focus on the dispositions; "taking an interest, being involved, persisting with difficulty or uncertainty, communicating with others, and taking responsibility" (Carr & Lee, 2012, p. 98).

Learning stories are now being used throughout the world (Knauf, 2018). While there is widespread use of learning stories, there are some critics who are concerned that learning stories are time-consuming to write and interpret (Zhang, 2013), that they do not capture the knowledge and skills that children are learning and that the dispositions they claim to capture are not clearly defined (Blaiklock, 2013), that they may not be aligned to the standards and curriculum in countries outside of New Zealand (Müller & Zipperle, 2012), and that the stories might not be written in ways that achieve the objectives. For example, a study by Knauf (2018) conducted in Germany found that many of the stories were written in a format that were inaccessible to children and families, did not stress the subjective nature of the assessment, and compared children's development to "typical development" rather than focusing on children's strengths. However, Knauf advocates rather than abandoning this method of assessment, teachers more closely align learning stories with the original intent.

Conducting Observations

When conducting observations ensure that you have permission, if needed, from families. Written permission from families is typically required if you are administering an assessment on an individual child that is not being given to the entire group of children. You will want to check your center policies and state and federal regulations regarding permissions needed.

To effectively conduct an observation, the preparation is as important as the actual observation. Planning allows you to choose the best observational method and observational focus based on the purpose and the audience. Determining ahead of time how you will organize and interpret the information also helps you to determine the best observational strategy and the amount of information to collect. Planning strategies to use for observing ensures that observation occurs. Before beginning your observation determine:

- the purpose of your assessment. Why are you collecting the information? Are you assessing to document children's skills and knowledge in relation to standards; documenting children's skills in relation to developmental milestones; determining children's interests; examining approaches to learning; or demonstrating growth in skills, knowledge, or approaches to learning?
- who you will share the information with.
- when and how you will collect the information. For example, teachers might use
  o sticky notes.
  o clipboards in different areas of the classroom.

- o   recording devices.
- o   note-taking apps such as Evernote, Notability, or PaperDesk. Note-taking apps have the advantage of allowing photos and digital recordings to be embedded in the observation. Additionally, keywords can be embedded such as adding on, when observing math. The keywords can make it easier to analyze the data (Bates, 2013).

- how you will organize the information and interpret it.

As you observe keep these guidelines in mind to ensure that the observations you collect are helpful for later analysis, decision-making, and sharing with others.

- Provide the context for your observation including the date, time, setting, names of children and the teacher, and any information that will assist in interpreting the observation. It is also important to include your name as the observer.
- Be unobtrusive. You want to capture the children's typical interactions and experiences. To be unobtrusive, it is helpful to sit at the same level as the children rather than hovering above them. If children ask what you are doing, give them a short explanation such as, "I am writing down what you are doing as you play."
- Make the observation factual. Avoid assumptions and judgmental words such as aggressive, passive, angry, or sad. It is helpful to write down what the children say and do verbatim. Record what you are seeing not what you are thinking. One strategy that some teachers use to remain factual is to divide a sheet of paper with a vertical line. On one side, they record what they see, on the other side of the line they record what they believe it means.
- Be specific, detailed, and descriptive. Compare the information you gain from the following anecdotal records. Example one—Seamus cries when his mother leaves him at child care. He hides in the corner of the room. Example two—Seamus cries for 20 minutes when his mother leaves him at child care. He clings to her legs as she leaves the room. The teacher asks Seamus if he would like to read a story, but he runs to the manipulative corner and continues to cry. After 20 minutes, Seamus stops crying and goes to the block area and begins to build with the blocks. Both anecdotal records are factual but the lack of detail in example one makes it difficult for others who read the record to understand what is occurring. It also makes it difficult to determine any strategies that might be helpful.
- Write the incidents in the order that they occur.
- Write in the present tense.

Analyzing Observations

At the end of your observations, you have collected objective raw data. When you visit a doctor, she collects blood pressure, heart rate, temperature, and a list of symptoms. However, this is not helpful for the patient unless an analysis is performed. What does this data tell us? The same is true for data collected by teachers. You must translate this data into information that is useful for meeting children's needs. During this phase of assessment, you will be analyzing the data you have collected. The analysis is based upon the evidence you have collected, your knowledge of children's development, your theoretical knowledge and experience, your knowledge of developmentally appropriate content and methods, and your knowledge of the latest early childhood research. According to Mary Johnson (2014), early childhood teachers typically engage in one of three types of analysis; infer, summarize, or assess.

- When inferring, teachers use the evidence from the observations, as well as background knowledge, to arrive at an explanation or a conclusion. For example, Michael, a first-grade teacher, had requested that Mary, a practicum student, complete a series of anecdotal records on Chris, stating that he was frequently non-compliant and off-task. After collecting anecdotal records over several days, Chris and Mary began to analyze them. They found that Chris became more non-compliant with teacher requests during the later morning. They speculated on the cause. Could it be that he was hungry? Could it be related to what was happening in the classroom at that time of day? Since Chris was on medication for ADHD, could it be that the effect of his medication was decreasing? After discussing each of these and visiting with his mother to obtain additional information, they inferred that it was the effect of the medication no longer being in his system.

- When summarizing, teachers look at what data or other information can be combined to create a more inclusive picture. They examine the data for patterns and try to determine the most essential information. When examining a narrative record, Allysa created a summary of what she had observed that included the child's attention span, her interactions with other children, and her interactions with the teacher.

- When assessing, teachers examine the information for evidence of children's developmental levels and their interests, strengths, and difficulties. Emily observed Sally for evidence in relation to the classroom assessment. For example, she observed that Sally could cut on a line but was unable to cut simple shapes. She did not seem to have a preferred hand when completing fine motor tasks, sometimes using the left and sometimes the right. To analyze this information, Emily needs to know the developmental progression of cutting and the typical ages that children progress through these stages. She also needs to know the age that children typically choose a dominant hand.

When analyzing observations, we begin with the purpose of the observation. Why were we observing? For example, Stephanie completed ten anecdotal records on Orem, a 20-month-old boy, as a way of examining his development. She then analyzed her records looking for examples of development in the different developmental domains and comparing what she found with developmental milestones. For example, she noted that Oren was able to successfully stack two blocks. She also observed that Orem used a palmer grasp when picking up small objects. These are both examples of Orem's fine motor development. Since most children this age can stack four blocks and are using a pincher grasp, Stephanie made herself a note to continue to observe Orem's fine motor development. She had also observed that Orem was very interested in the large toy cars. She decided to also add small matchbox cars to the block area to encourage more fine motor play in an area of high interest.

I'm not that familiar with children's developmental progressions, where can I learn more?

You will want to begin by checking if the program you are working with provides this information. For example, many programs use the WSS (Meisels, Marsden, Jablon, & Dichtelmiller, 2013) which provides information in seven domains (language and literacy, science, math, social studies, arts, personal and social development, and physical development, health and safety) indicating what children should know at different ages. This assessment is available for children ages three through grade three. The Ounce Scale (Meisels, Dombro, Marsden, Weston, & Jewkes, 2003) provides developmental information for infants and toddlers in the areas of personal connections, feeling about self, relationships with other children, understanding and communicating, exploration and problem-solving, and movement and coordination.

If your program does not provide this information, there are several online sources that provide information on developmental progressions. PBS Child Development Tracker is an online resource providing developmental information for children age one through age nine in the areas of approaches to learning, creative arts, language, literacy, mathematics, physical health, science, and social and emotional growth.

If you are working with preschool children, you might look to the following for information: the North Carolina Early Learning and Development Progressions; CDC Learn the Signs: Act Early; or the Head Start Early Learning Outcomes Framework: Ages Birth to Five. If you are a teacher of elementary-age children you can find learning progressions for English and math at the National Center for the Improvement of Educational Assessments (NCIEA), also known as the Center for Assessment. You might also conduct a search for a specific area of development such as developmental milestones in children's art.

It is helpful to review your observation multiple times. Often through multiple readings or viewings, you will be able to gain new insights and be able to focus on additional details. As you review, look for patterns of behaviors. Examine your observations using different lenses such as children's development, their milestones, typical misconceptions in the knowledge domain that you are reviewing, and early learning standards. In determining how many observations to complete before analyzing your data, consider the purpose, how and when the data will be used, and the richness of the data.

With the advent of cell phones and other recording devices, video observations have become more common. There are several advantages to video recording including allowing the observation to be shared easily with children, families, and other colleagues and capturing more information than can typically be captured in written observations. However, because of the additional information, analyzing can sometimes be more time-consuming. When reviewing a video, Forman and Hall, experts in using instant video recording (IVR) with young children, suggest you look for the following. Look for:

- laughter which may mean that the child has encountered something unexpected.
- a change in direction in the play. This often means that a child is trying out a new theory.
- children co-constructing knowledge.
- representation of knowledge through such things as drawing, building, dancing, or dramatic play. This may reveal the child's thinking.
- meta-cognition where a child thinks about his or another's thinking. For example, a child might state, "I am not very good at drawing, will you draw it for me?" (Forman & Hall, 2013, pp. 195-199).

After you have analyzed your observations, it is helpful to create a chart that summarizes your information. The chart can include your observations, your analysis, and the learning possibilities based upon this information (Johnson, 2014).

Checklists and Scales

A checklist is a list of skills or behaviors that can be checked off as met or not met. A scale is used to examine a progression of skills or behaviors, to determine the degree that the child demonstrates the skill or behaviors. The scale lists the performance with the different degrees stipulated. These degrees might be listed as numbers or descriptors (consistently, often, sometimes, rarely).

Checklists and scales provide a clear focus and can be repeated to show growth. They are quick and easy to complete and can be posted near a center or completed during an activity. For example, Becky developed a series of math games in pizza boxes. Each game was focused on a specific skill such as one to one correspondence. If Becky observed the child demonstrating the skill as they engaged in the math game, she checked off the skill on a checklist that she kept posted in the area. Teresa, who worked with toddlers, wanted to assess the children's gross motor skills. She developed a checklist (see Box 4.1) and brought the checklist with her to the playground where she had set up an obstacle course focused on these skills. She was able to complete the checklist as children went through the obstacle course.

However, checklists and scales limit the assessment scope to what is included in the checklist or the rating scale. The detail, supporting evidence, or context regarding the skill or behavior is not included. For example, if you are assessing social-emotional skills with a checklist, there might be an indicator such as engages in reciprocal play with peers. Even if the child does demonstrate this skill, it might be helpful to know how often, with whom, and under what conditions. The checklist also doesn't allow for ambiguity such as a child who demonstrates the skills only under certain situations. For example, Teresa made a check besides walks up and downs steps one at a time for both Amy and Ember. However, Amy is just learning this skill and only demonstrates it occasionally while Ember is consistently using the skill.

Box 4.1 Example of a Teacher-Created Checklist

Toddlers gross motor checklist (check the box for those skills that the child has demonstrated)

Name of child_____ Date_____

- Walks up steps with one foot on each step when holding the rail
- Walks down steps with one foot on each step when holding the rail
- Walks on tiptoes
- Kicks a small ball forward
- Throws a ball overhand
- Jumps in place with feet together
- Hops on one foot for three or more hops

In many cases, you will be using checklists and scales that have been developed by others. However, if you are creating your own, you will want to use early learning standards or developmental milestones as a reference point. It is critical that the items placed on the checklist are developmentally appropriate, since assessments often drive the curriculum. Your items should be specific and observable. One way to assess this is to think about whether someone else witnessing the same event would score the child in the same way. The number of items on the checklist should be reasonable, allowing you to complete an observation of the skills in an allotted amount of time.

Analyzing Checklists and Scales

When analyzing checklists and scales it is helpful to create a data table or class grid to quickly be able to examine and summarize the data. After summarizing the data, look for data that is either higher or lower than the norm. To conduct further analysis, determine if there are commonalities in the areas that are high and low. For example, as a Head Start teacher, I assessed children's physical skills using a checklist. When I placed the information from individual children's skills in a data table, I found that there were several commonalities among the children. With further analysis, I became aware that the children were much lower in physical skills that involved any type of object manipulation such as kicking a ball and riding a trike, than in skills such as running and jumping that did not involve object manipulation. Through home visits, I knew that most of the children lived in apartments with little access to outdoor play. I inferred that this was the reason that they scored so low in these areas. As a result of this, I began to provide more object manipulation activities at Head Start. I also visited with our director to see if we could make our playground and materials available on weekends for families to use or if we could develop a check out system where families could check out materials to use at local parks. In addition to examining the data at the class level, I also examined the data at the individual child's level to determine ways to help each child to continue on their developmental path.

Children's Oral Responses

Interviews are one method we use to assess children's oral responses. Interviews can be structured with the questions and order of questions determined ahead of time or unstructured, more like a guided discussion. While the questions might be planned ahead of time in the unstructured interview, the teacher has the freedom to vary the order of the questions, probe the answers, or ask additional unplanned questions during the interview. An example of an unstructured interview is the clinical interview developed by Piaget. In the clinical interview, the interviewer begins with a very general question that explores a child's thinking such as "How did you do it?" "How did you figure that out?" "What do you think caused it to change?" "Why do you think that?" The child's answers to the questions then guide the rest of the interview (National Research Council, 2000). Meaningful conversations can also be a form of interviewing, where the teacher skillfully probes to determine a child's theories, reasoning, and thinking. Interviews can be quick such as asking pre-assessment questions at the beginning of a lesson or more structured and in-depth such as determining children's learning at the end of a unit.

Interviews can provide information that is difficult to determine through other forms of assessment. They are especially useful in capturing children's thoughts, theories, attitudes, and beliefs. It is also helpful in determining a child's goals (what is he trying to accomplish) and what strategies the child believes will help him accomplish the goals. They can also help teachers become aware of common misconceptions and strategies used by children (Clarke, Mitchell, & Roche, 2005). However, individual interviews can be time-consuming.

A strategy when interviewing children is to begin by closely observing a child as a way to speculate on the child's thinking and to begin a high-level conversation that will lead to deeper understanding and learning. For example, in an earlier scenario, we discussed how Julie, the teacher, observed that Tsea might believe that all silver items are attracted to magnets. After observing this, the teacher might interview Tsea about this theory. She might begin by stating what she observed. "I saw that you were touching all the silver items in the room with the magnet. But you looked puzzled when they didn't all stick to the magnet. Tell me about that."

Sharing key aspects of a video of the child can be another way to enhance interviews. This can assist children to recall and revisit experiences. By separating the child's actions from his thinking and removing the emotional aspects, we can uncover children's perceptions, feelings, and thinking about the event. Children might also develop new awareness as they revisit. For example, in a conflict situation, they might be able to more easily take the perspective of the other child. In addition to the increased knowledge, we gain about the child's thinking through interviewing the child we help them to construct a deeper knowledge, determine new solutions, and revise thinking and ideas. In addition to video, teachers might also revisit photos with children.

Analyzing Oral Responses

How you analyze children's oral responses will be based upon the purpose for the oral interviews. For example, if the purpose was to discover misconceptions and preconceptions before starting a unit, you would carefully choose questions to probe for this. During analysis, you would aggregate the information you had collected and use this information to plan group and individual experiences. For example, Chloe was going to be starting a unit on plants and wanted to determine children's misconceptions and preconceptions. She began by asking, "What do plants need to survive?" One of the common responses was water. When Chloe asked children how plants get water many of the children believed that plants absorb water through their leaves rather than through their roots. Children also typically stated that plants need sunlight. When Chloe asked how the sunlight helped the plants, many of the children said that the light kept the plant warm. By probing beyond her initial question, Chloe was able to uncover the children's misconceptions. She could then design activities that would challenge the misconceptions. As with observations, analysis is a critical part of the process when assessing children's responses. This might be done quickly as when leading a group discussion and determining what question to ask next based upon children's responses or it might involve a deeper look. For example, recording the discussion so that you can take your time for analysis.

We will next examine work samples and performance assessments. Although work samples are sometimes considered a performance assessment (Meisels, 1996), in this book, they are separated with work samples being products and performance tasks being observable performances.

Work Samples

A work sample is a product such as a drawing, a piece of three-dimensional art, a written or tran-
scribed story, a worksheet where a child circles the objects that sink and makes a square around
the objects that float, a photo of a block structure built by a child, or a child developed graphic
organizer. We will spend time examining Venn diagrams, KWHL's, webs, and concept maps, graphic
organizers that can be used to assess children's understanding in the early childhood years.

Venn Diagrams

Venn diagrams are typically two or three overlapping circles that are used to compare and contrast attributes. To create a Venn diagram, draw two or three overlapping circles and label each
circle. Put the characteristics of objects in the correct circle. When the characteristics are the
same between the two sets, you place the information in the intersection of the two circles. Venn
diagrams were popularized by John Venn to show relationships between sets (1881). They are
now used in classrooms in a variety of curricular areas including math, science, and literacy. For
example, Bradon's class had been studying the characteristics of animals. As a final assessment,
Bradon gave the children photos of unfamiliar water animals and land animals and had them
classify them as water, land, or both. He also interviewed children to determine why they had
classified the animals that way that they had. This allowed Bradon to assess children's ability
to classify and also to determine what they knew about the characteristics of land and water animals. For young children, you might create Venn diagrams using hula hoops with actual items.
For example, a toddler teacher was having children categorize shoes. The toddlers looked at the
closures on their shoes. Some were Velcro, some were slip-on, some were laced, and some had
more than one type of closure. They placed the shoes in the proper place in the overlapping hula
hoops. See an example of a Venn diagram in Figure 4.1. Since one of the goals for a second-grade
unit on worms was to examine living versus non-living, the teacher designed a pre-assessment
where children used a Venn diagram to compare a plastic worm with a living worm.

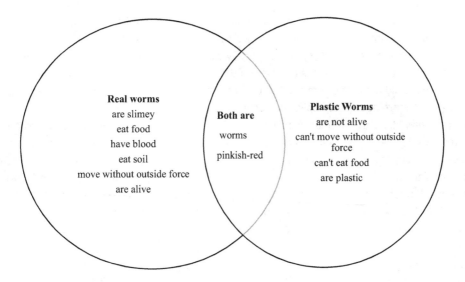

Figure 4.1 Example of a Venn Diagram

What you know	What you want to know	How you will find out	What you learned
Worms are pinkish red	Why don't worms have legs?	Ask biologist	
Worms eat soil	Why do people get scared when worms poop on them?	Interview children in class	
Worms come out of the ground when it is raining	Why do worms come out of the ground when it rains?	Watch video on worms	
Worms move by stretching out and then squishing together			
Worms don't have legs			

Figure 4.2 Example of a KWHL Chart

KWHL Charts

KWHL'S are a chart that a child fills out stating what they know about a topic, what they want to know, how they will find out, and at the end of the project what they have learned. KWHL's can be used to elicit student's prior knowledge, to document learning, for curriculum planning, and as a pre- and post-assessment. See the KWHL chart created by Ember in Figure 4.2 as part of the worm study.

Webs

Webs can be used as a pre-assessment to capture children's knowledge including their misconceptions, to record and organize children's questions, and to document and assess children's learning at the conclusion of a unit. To create a web, you will begin by generating ideas about a topic and then you will group these ideas into subtopics. Many teachers find it helpful to write each idea on a sticky note that can then be moved to the correct subtopic. Webs are often completed with the entire class during a class meeting. However, they can also be completed by individual children or small groups of children. If you are completing the web with the entire class, it is helpful to keep track of what child made the comment so that you can see if there are changes to their thinking as they learn more about the topic. As a project progresses, webs are often added to with new questions, new ideas of how to answer the questions, or with what the children have learned. It is helpful to designate this new information with a different color ink so that the progress of the project can be easily tracked. See an example of a web in Figures 4.3 and 4.4. The webs were created at the beginning of a project focused on Thumper, the class rabbit. Notice the web in Figure 4.3 contains information about what children know about Thumper while the web in Figure 4.4 is a web of the children's questions. At the conclusion of the project, children can create an individual web of what they know about Thumper as a way of assessing their knowledge.

Concept Maps

A concept map is similar to a web. However, the concept map shows relationships between concepts with a line that includes linking words that specify the relationship (see an example

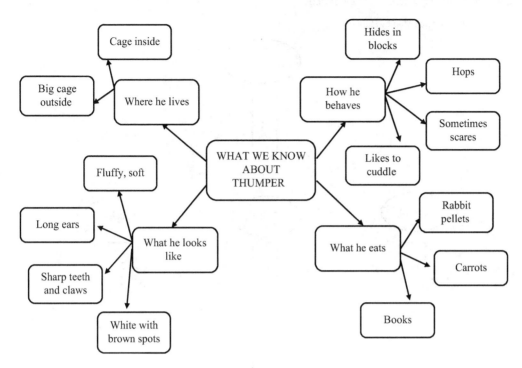

Figure 4.3 Example of a Web: What Children Know About Thumper

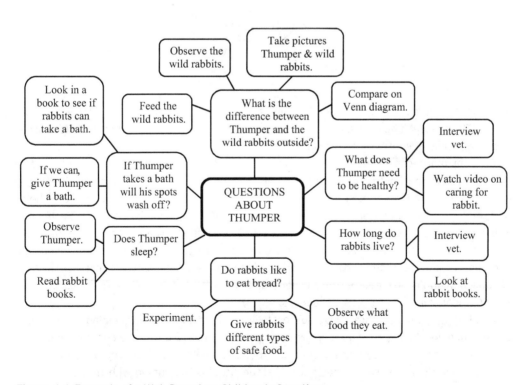

Figure 4.4 Example of a Web Based on Children's Questions

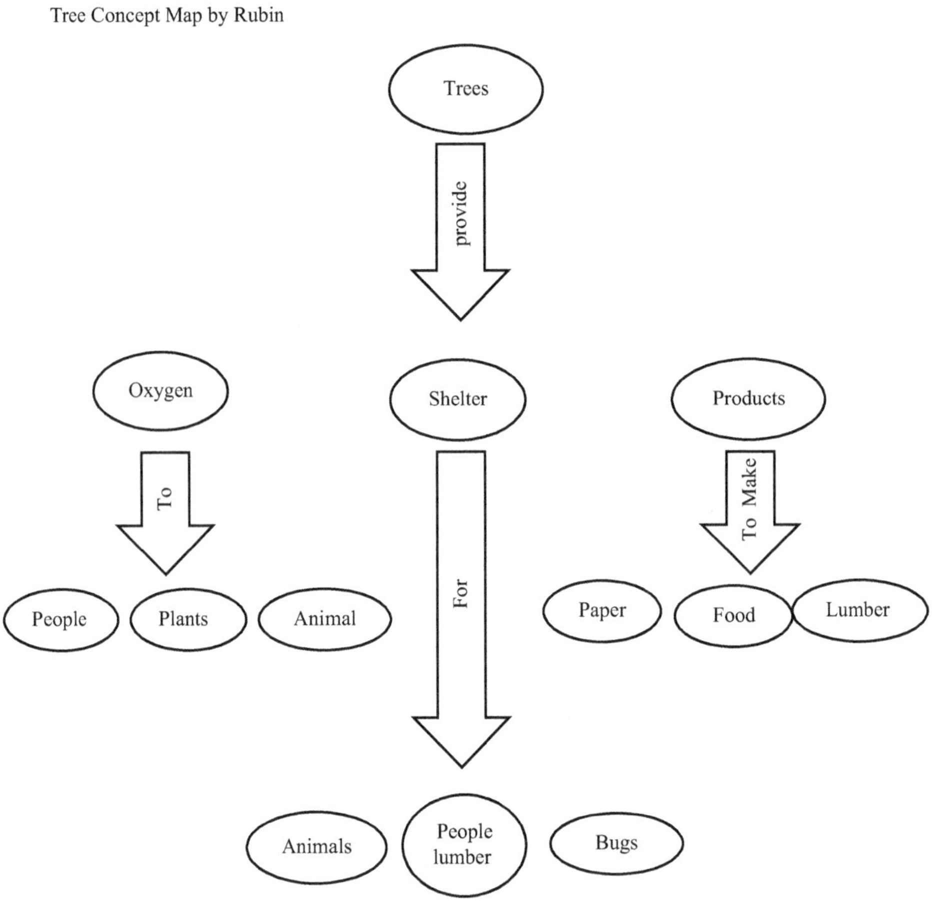

Tree Concept Map by Rubin

Figure 4.5 Example of Concept Map

in Figure 4.5). It is an "external visualization of a person's internal schema" (McAleese, 1999, p.352). The concept map connects ideas and determines the relationship between ideas to assist in making sense of information (Schwendimann, 2015).

Concept maps can be used as an assessment and as a learning tool. As discussed in Chapter 3, as young children form concepts, misconceptions are often also formed. These misconceptions can be very resistant to change. However, concept maps are a tool that helps to reveal misconceptions and also to change them (Kellough, Carin, Seefeldt, Barbour, & Souviney, 1996). Creating concept maps can assist children to organize their thoughts, connect new knowledge to prior knowledge, and engage in critical thinking, problem-solving, and decision-making (Gallenstein, 2013). This can lead to increased learning. For instance, a study of concept mapping in kindergarten showed significant increases in children's critical thinking skills (Sundararajan, Adesope, & Cavagnetto, 2018).

Children as young as three have successfully engaged in concept mapping (Gallenstein, 2013). When developing concept maps with young children, begin with the concrete and move to more abstraction. Children need concrete experiences with real objects before understanding concepts. Charlesworth suggests a five-stage process, beginning with the real objects, then objects with pictures, then cutouts, then pictures, and finally paper and pencil (2016). To link the concepts, you might use laminated arrows, yarn, or pipe cleaners. The child can then dictate the linking word to the teacher. There are also software programs such as Kidspiration 3 that allow children to make concept maps using either pictures or words (Gallenstein, 2013). Some other techniques for beginning to use concept maps with young children include having:

- the teacher model using concept maps many times before having the children complete their own concept maps.
- the teacher provides the concepts and the linking words and having the children arrange them.
- the children begin by brainstorming the concepts as a group before they individually create the concept map.

In developing concept maps, you will want to ensure that children have many hands-on experiences (Birbili, 2006). Therefore, it is better to use concept mapping with a project or unit of study rather than an individual activity. Comparing beginning concept maps with concept maps developed at the end of a unit of study can be a powerful assessment of what children have learned.

Analysis of Work Samples

Since children create many work samples in early childhood settings, it is very important that you are purposeful about what you will collect. You will want to think about the following questions.

- What will you collect?
- Why are you collecting this sample?
- What does this sample demonstrate?
- How will you analyze the sample?

For example, Samantha decided to collect photos of children's block structures to determine their stage of block building and also to analyze conditions that might lead to a more in-depth building. She analyzed the block building photos using Harriet Johnson's seven stages of block building (Johnson, 1933). She was also careful to collect information on the context including whether the child built the structure alone or with others, how much time the child spent on the structure, and how many children were in the block area at the time of the building. As Samantha analyzed the photos, she was able to determine the level of each child's block building. Additionally, because she kept such detailed notes on the context, she also was able to discover that children built less elaborate structures when there were more children in the block area. Further, the most elaborate and detailed structures occurred on days when children were allowed more time for building. As a result of this knowledge, Samantha made the block area larger and examined and changed her schedule to allow a longer center time.

Performance Tasks

During a performance task, children show evidence of their learning by applying their knowledge, skills, or approach to learning in a real-world demonstration. In early childhood, we have a rich history of using performance tasks in assessing children. Teachers often assess a child while they are engaging in an activity such as playing an instrument, completing a physical skill, demonstrating the ability to use conflict resolution, reading a short book, participating in dramatic play, or playing a math game. The advantage of this type of assessment is that it is embedded within children's daily activities and curriculum. Performance tasks can be either naturally occurring or teacher-designed. For example, a teacher might set up an obstacle course on the playground as a way of assessing multiple gross motor skills. In performance assessments children might also use what they have learned to solve a real-world problem.

The latest national standards call for skills that are best assessed using performance tasks. For example, Tina Cheuk examined the practice standards for the Common Core State Standards (CCSS) in English Language Arts and Mathematics and the Next Generation Science Standards (NGSS). She found that all the standards included students being able to use evidence when we read, write, or speak; to be able to construct viable arguments and assess others reasoning; and to engage in arguments from evidence (Cheuk, 2012). These are skills that are best assessed using a performance task. As a result of the shifting emphasis in standards, two national assessment consortiums Smarter Balanced (SBAC) and the Partnership for Assessment and Readiness for College and Careers (PARCC), have stated that they intend to include performance assessment as part of their assessment procedures (McTighe, 2015).

Performance assessments are also supported by research. For example, child outcomes in early childhood classrooms using a performance assessment, WSS were compared to child outcomes in classrooms that did not use WSS. The WSS, developed for children ages 3 to grade 3 uses work samples and teacher observations that are tied to developmental guidelines. The developmental guidelines cover seven major curricular areas. Those children who were in classrooms using the WSS had significantly better reading scores and made greater gains in math than children in non-WSS classrooms (Meisels, Atkins-Burnett, Xue, Nicholson, Bickel, & Son, 2003).

Self-assessment, Peer-assessment, and Assessment by Families

The instructional assessment methods that we have been discussing have focused on the teacher as the assessor. However, self-assessment, peer-assessment, and assessment by families are also valuable instructional assessment methods. We will be examining these in this section.

Self-assessment

Self-assessment can be used to assess children's attitudes, preferences, behaviors, and their work. It is appropriate for any academic area. It is an effective technique for children as young as three (Liebovich, 2000) and for children with and without disabilities. In a study by Sainato, Strain, Lefebvre, and Rapp (1990) children who had autism were able to reduce the need for teacher prompts during independent work through self-assessment. Through self-assessment young children can gather and reflect on evidence and develop goals based on this evidence, plan steps in meeting their goals, and track their progress toward meeting the goal (Warash, & Workman, 2016). This can include assessing knowledge, skills, and behaviors such as the ability to stay on task or interact appropriately with others.

Self-assessment by young children increases child ownership and motivation (Warash, Smith, & Root, 2011) and raises achievement (Smith, 2010). Hattie (2012) found that self-assessment or as he labeled it, self-evaluation had an effect size of 0.62 on student achievement (remember the average effect size is 0.40). Self-assessment is also an important lifelong skill. Through self-assessment, we come to understand our strengths, determine when we need help, become independent learners, and internalize the characteristics of quality work. Through self-assessment, teachers and children can become co-participants in the learning process.

Tips for self-assessment

- Self-assessment works best when it is conducted in the classroom as children are engaged in their normal activities and routines, such as when making play plans, engaging in project work, creating learning logs, and developing learning goals and contracts (Brown, 2008; Liebovich, 2000).
- To effectively self-assess, we need criteria to judge our work against such as a rubric. For example, young children might assess whether their work is clear, detailed, accurate, and complete. They might assess themselves based upon individual or group goals (skip all the way across the playground; tell a story with a beginning, middle, and end; or use words to tell someone when you don't like something rather than hitting).
- Learning to self-assess is a skill that must be taught. You might begin by involving children in the process such as developing criteria together and then critiquing together. You might also model self-assessment through thinking aloud.
- Begin with a simple format and limited criteria. As children become more proficient at self-assessment, the criteria and format can become more complex (Brown, 2008).
- Children can create individual goals based upon their self-assessment. The teacher can assist children to develop steps in meeting the goals, and in assessing and recording their progress.
- Keep children's assessments over time to share with the child and to celebrate the progress that they are making.
- Children are often motivated when they get the opportunity to share their products and goal completion with the other children.

Peer-assessment

Peer-assessment allows children to engage in discussions about their work; describing, defending, challenging, and supporting each other to greater learning (Dunn, 2011). It can also help children develop metacognitive skills and to be active agents in their own learning. Even preschool children can participate in peer-assessment (Learning and Teaching Scotland, 2006). However, to effectively engage in peer-assessment, children must have a clear understanding of the outcomes and the indicators of success.

Peer-assessment is most effective in a non-competitive classroom environment that encourages risk-taking and collaboration. It is critical that teachers help children learn the difference between put-downs and supportive feedback. Put-downs will destroy the process and must not be allowed.

Like self-assessment, peer-assessment is a skill that needs to be taught. This can be accomplished using many of the same techniques used for teaching children to self-assess.

Additionally, children will need training in how to collaborate and how to give effective feedback. It is most effective to explicitly model the process beginning with an anonymous work sample. Skills such as being specific and focusing on the work, not the person can be explicitly taught. Providing prompts that can be used to give feedback is also helpful such as, "I notice that..." "I see that... "I wonder if..." "What if..." These statements can even be posted on the wall as a reminder for children. It is also helpful to teach children the peer-assessment skills needed by reviewing an anonymous work sample as a class.

Providing protocols such as Three Stars and a Wish, the Feedback Sandwich, or Warm and Cool Feedback can be helpful in providing peer-assessment. In the Three Stars and a Wish, the peer-assessor points out three positive things they note about the artifact, idea, or plan and then gives one suggestion as a wish. In the Feedback Sandwich, children provide a positive statement about the work, a suggestion, and then another positive statement (Dunn, 2011). In Warm and Cool Feedback, the peer-assessor points out positive aspects, then areas that need improvement, then provide suggestions on, "how to raise the temperature" by giving suggestions of how to improve.

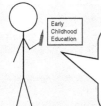

Early Childhood Education

I have used many of these assessment methods with adults as well such as observations, rating scales, oral responses, work samples, and performance tasks. I often use self-assessment. However, I've not had good luck with peer-assessments. It seems that people only tend to tell each other what is good and don't provide constructive feedback. Have you got any suggestions on how to make this better?

Adults, like children, need to learn how to give effective, constructive critiques and be given permission to do so. They don't want classmates to think they are being overbearing. Like with children, it is helpful to give clear expectations, provide helpful prompts, model feedback, and to teach protocols. When modeling feedback, you might use similar work from a previous class (with permission) or a piece of work that you have created. You will want to model how to give feedback that is specific as well as helpful to the student's growth. In addition to the protocols used with children, you might consider using a protocol called Ladder of Feedback. In this protocol, the reviewer first asks clarification questions; then expresses the value they see in the artifact, idea, or plan; next concerns are raised; and finally, suggestions are made (Krechevsky, Mardell, Rivard, & Wilson, 2013). When you provide a protocol, a written form is often used. The form guides the critique and ensures that each area is addressed. Finally, you might use a collaborative rubric that includes descriptors that describe giving both specific, clear positive feedback and also specific feedback that strengthens the work.

Information from Families

Families are critical partners and key informants regarding their children's learning preferences, strengths, routines, and out-of-school activities as well as their goals and dreams for their children. To obtain assessment information from families you might engage in conversation, conduct oral or written interviews, or ask them to complete questionnaires or developmental checklists. You might also find other creative ways to seek information from families. For example, a program serving infants and toddlers begins each year by supplying each family with a plastic baggie and asking the family to place something in the baggie that the child loves. Through this process, they discovered that many of the toddlers loved rocks. This became a foundation for one of their first projects.

In addition to seeking information from families, it is important to share information you have learned through your assessments. There are many ways to do this, both formally during family-teacher conferences or less formally such as sharing an anecdotal record when families pick up children or through an online daily or weekly note to a family.

Rubrics

Because work samples and performance tasks are typically open-ended with a wide range of responses, they are best analyzed using a rubric. Self-assessments and peer-assessments are also often analyzed using a rubric. "A rubric is a coherent set of criteria for students' work that includes descriptions of levels of performance quality on the criteria" (Brookhart, 2013, p. 4). It operates as a bridge between what you see the learner doing and their level of performance. A rubric identifies attributes of quality and is descriptive rather than evaluative (Brookhart, 2013).

Advantages of Rubrics

There are many advantages to using rubrics. As you develop rubrics, you contemplate and clarify criteria and deepen and refine your thinking about what indicates success. This process causes you to focus on what children will learn, determine what is important, to think about and clarify the developmental progression for each of the criteria, and to consider evidence of proficiency. This helps to provide coherence for your unit.

Rubrics also make your expectations explicit. By doing so, they assist the learner in knowing the expectations. The purpose of the rubric is not only to measure learning but also to support learning by showing the learner their strengths, areas needing additional work, and the next steps in the learning progression. Because rubrics assess learners along a developmental continuum, they can be used to show progress. They are also helpful for learners to self-assess their learning.

Rubrics can also make assessment and grading less biased by providing more consistency and accuracy. They prevent teachers from making an immediate judgment and instead encourage a focus on the outcomes and performance levels (Brookhart, 2013). For example, if a teacher is assessing a paper written by a child, the most obvious first impression is often based upon the neatness of the paper. Without a rubric, neatness might become an undue proportion of the grade. The analysis of the data from a rubric can also assist teachers in knowing what areas of teaching to emphasize for each individual as well as common trends and errors for the group.

Are rubrics effective? A study of first- and second-grade children using a 6+1 Trait Writing rubric found that writing improved by a large effect size (Cohen's $d = 0.92$), when the rubric was added (Bradford, Newland, Rule, & Montgomery, 2016). However, rubrics are only as effective as the criteria and performance levels are good.

Types of Rubrics

There are different types of rubrics. For example, holistic, where a single score is assigned to the product and analytic where the score is separated for each criterion. The analytic provides more feedback to children and therefore can be used to enhance learning. It is the recommended method for teaching using backward design since one of the goals of using rubrics is to aid the learner in making improvements.

Rubrics can also be either general or task-specific-based assessments. The advantages of a general rubric are that they can be used over time with multiple assignments, can help students see progress over time, and can be used by multiple teachers. The 6+1 Trait Writing rubric designed by the Northwest Regional Educational Laboratory is an example of a general rubric that is used throughout the United States. It assesses ideas, organization, voice, word choice, sentence fluency, convention, and presentation (Brookhart, 2013). Task-specific rubrics relate to a specific assignment.

Developing Rubrics

A rubric is typically designed as a grid or table which includes performance criteria, performance levels, and descriptors. The performance criteria are the headings for the rows, the performance levels are the headings for the columns, and the descriptors are in the cells of the table. See the example of a rubric for hopping in Table 4.1. The criteria for the rubric on hopping are the use of arms, the use of legs, balance, body position, and the use of the foot. There are three performance levels in this rubric; beginning, nearing proficiency, and proficient. There are 15 descriptors such "as arms swing forward but without intention" placed in the cells. The descriptors allow you to assess the child along a developmental continuum.

Performance Criteria

When designing performance criteria ask yourself, "What criteria will give evidence of the outcome?" Wiggins and McTighe (2012) emphasize four different types of criteria in performance assessment. These are criteria related to:

- impact (achieved the desired purpose).
- content (accuracy and sophistication of knowledge, skills, and understanding).
- quality (overall quality and rigor such as attention to detail and creativity).
- process (quality and appropriateness of the approach and procedures used) (p. 25).

You will want to ensure that children who meet the criteria have developed the desired results you've listed from Step 1. You will match the type of criteria you use with your desired outcomes to determine which are most relevant, focusing on the outcome rather than the product. It is generally not possible to assess all criteria. Therefore, choose the criteria that are most important for the children's developmental level and the criteria that most closely align with the outcomes. When designing performance criteria ensure they are:

- appropriate (directly related to the outcome).
- clearly defined (both the learner and the teacher understand the terminology in the same way).
- observable (the observer can see the criteria in the student's performance).

- distinct from one another (each criterion is unique).
- complete (the criterion when taken together allow you to know the level of mastery the learner has achieved).
- described over a developmental continuum with fairly even distribution between levels (Brookhart, 2013, p. 25).

Performance Levels

Performance levels are listed from left to right as low to high or high to low. I prefer moving from left to right with the highest level of quality on the right. This seems like a more natural progression to highlight quality and growth as a process.

The number of performance levels is based upon how many meaningful differences there are between levels of performance. Typically, there are between three and six. In many educational rubrics, there are four levels. The target level or the level that meets the outcomes is the third level with the fourth level being above standards.

When designing your performance levels, it is important to choose respectful titles. Consider the difference between telling a child her work is in the beginning stages versus her work is poor or insufficient. Our goal is always to motivate learners to work to achieve at the next level not to create discouragement. Some possible titles are listed below.

- Novice, nearing proficiency, proficient, advanced
- Beginning, developing, accomplished, exemplary
- Exploring, developing, mastery
- Learning, working toward, satisfactory
- Emerging, progressing, well-developed

Descriptors

Descriptors allow learners to know how well they have performed based upon the criteria. When designing descriptors:

- whenever possible, focus on descriptive statements rather than subjective statements (some, several, numerous) or quantitative measures (three sources). If you do use quantitative measures also include quality attributes. For example, a paper calls for three sources. Are these reputable, credible sources? Are they primary sources? Are they the most relevant sources for providing information about this specific topic or the first sources that turned up in a search engine? Instead of only stating three sources, you might include three primary sources or three credible sources or three relevant sources.
- cover the entire range of performances with equal distance between levels.
- distinguish among levels of performance.
- provide clear and logical progressions that help scaffold learner's skills, knowledge, and approaches to learning.
- anchor the target performance by placing the level expected at the highest or next to the highest level.
- provide information on what is present rather than only focusing on what is missing.
- provide parallel descriptions from level to level (Brookhart, 2013; Learner Center Initiatives, 2015).

How to Write Rubrics

Begin with the desired results that you want children to achieve. If you have previously taught this unit and still have samples of the children's work, you might analyze the work to determine the different levels for your descriptors. You might also find a rubric that you can modify. Kathy Schrock's Guide to Everything-Assessment and Rubrics provides a variety of examples. RubiStar allows you to create your own rubrics and also to gain access to rubrics created by others. Teach-nology provides a variety of rubric generators that allow you to customize rubrics with the school name, teacher's name, and title of the rubric.

In determining criteria, it is helpful to first brainstorm criteria. After brainstorming, group similar criteria. Then determine which criteria are most critical in meeting the desired results. When writing the descriptors many teachers find it is helpful to begin with the most advanced level or with the level that meets the standard and then move backwards from there. Let's look at two rubrics that examine children's ability to hop.

While the first rubric in Table 4.1 clarifies the task, it doesn't provide the needed information to determine how one would learn to hop better. To effectively hop forward producing distance and height, a child needs to coordinate the use of his arms and legs, use his foot in an effective jump and landing, have an effective body position, and maintain balance. The second rubric clarifies each of these steps along a developmental progression.

Table 4.1 Rubric on the Skill of Hopping: Two Examples

Rubric on the Skill of Hopping: Example 1

Criteria	Beginning	Nearing proficiency	Proficient	Advanced
Hops on one foot	Hops one or two times	Hops ten times in place	Hops ten times while moving forward	Hops ten times while moving forward using either foot

Rubric on the Skill of Hopping: Example 2

Criteria	Beginning	Nearing proficiency	Proficient
Use of arms	Arms kept at sides	Arms swing forward but without intention	Arms move in rhythm with the hop, adding momentum
Use of legs	Non-support leg is inactive and may be held in front of the body	Non-support leg is swung back and forth but without needed projection	Non-support leg is swung back and forth like a pendulum to produce force
Balance	Can hop one or two times before losing balance	Maintains balance for at least ten hops while hopping on preferred foot	Maintains balance for at least ten hops while hopping on either foot
Body position	Upright position	Slight forward lean	Leans toward hopping foot with head up and looking forward
Use of foot	Takes off and lands flat-footed	Takes off from the ball of the foot but lands flat-footed	Lands and takes off from the ball of the foot

Developing Rubrics with Children

Even children in the early childhood years can learn to develop rubrics. As one example, Nancy Harris and Laura Kuehn examined how children in their first-grade classroom would develop criteria concerning what was "a good project." Immediately the children at this age were able to define criteria related to process such as working well with others, planning ahead of time, and taking enough time. As children gained increased experience in viewing projects and brainstorming important criteria, they were able to provide more substantive criteria and were able to provide criteria for the product such as the appearance of the product and the information that was presented. When the children used the rubric they had created to score their work and their classmate's work and compared this with the teachers scoring, they either agreed or were lower than the teacher's rating (Higgins, Harris, & Kuehn, 1994).

For your unit, you will most likely be using performance assessments or work samples and assessing these with a rubric. If you are unable to co-construct the rubric with the learners, it is still important to share the rubric with the learners at the start of the unit, so they can understand the learning targets. When working with young children, this might involve simplifying the rubric and using more child-friendly language for their version. To help the children understand the rubric, you might have them score a sample of work using the rubric.

Cautions in Developing Rubrics

As you design rubrics, it is important that the rubric aligns with the learning outcomes rather than the parts of the assignment or the task. Remember, the assessment task is to determine whether the child has achieved the desired results. Let's look at an example. Beth, a second-grade teacher had just been given a pregnant guinea pig for her classroom. She felt that this would be a good opportunity to develop activities that would meet some of the science standards. She decided to focus on the following enduring understandings.

- Organisms pass on traits to their offspring.
- Many organisms depend on their parents to survive.

For essential questions, she focused on the following

- How do mammals, including humans, help their offspring survive?
- What traits get passed on from organisms to their offspring?

For a final assessment, Beth decided to have the children write a report on the guinea pig. She also designed a rubric for the report, see Table 4.2.

However, as you can see the assessment and the rubric did not align with the essential questions and enduring understandings. Instead, the rubric was aligned with the task and not with the learning outcomes. This is a common error made by teachers.

If Beth wanted to make the assignment more aligned, she might have students investigate the ways that animals care for their young and then write a report. She might also have the children closely observe the guinea pigs and describe the traits that are similar and dissimilar between the mother and the babies. Beth could begin with a Venn diagram.

Table 4.2 Rubric: Guinea Pig Report

	Exploring	*Developing*	*Mastery*
Writing skills	The report does not have a distinct beginning, supporting, or concluding paragraphs	The report contains at least two of the following elements: a beginning paragraph, three supporting paragraphs, and a concluding paragraph	The report has a beginning paragraph, three supporting paragraphs, and a concluding paragraph
Grammar and punctuation	Contains several errors	Contains 3–5 errors	Contains less than three errors
Guinea pig facts	Contains only one or two facts about guinea pigs OR The information is inaccurate	Contains three or four accurate facts about guinea pigs	Contains five accurate facts about guinea pigs

Instead, the rubric Beth designed places an emphasis on extraneous criteria such as grammar and punctuation and writing skills. As stated by Brookhart this creates two issues; first, learners believe that they really have mastered the concept and secondly, the learner may be deprived of learning that will transfer to other learning situations (2013).

Another error that teachers sometimes make in writing rubrics is to focus on form rather than content. For example, a writing rubric included the following criteria:

- turned in on time
- the correct number of pages
- the right size of margins
- includes a title page
- includes five references

None of these criteria address writing skills. They primarily address the child's ability to follow directions and attend to details. Compare this to the 6+1 trait writing rubric which includes ideas, organization, voice, word choice, sentence fluency, conventions, and presentation.

The rubric also needs to match not only the content but the degree of difficulty underlying the desired result. For example, if you are an early childhood adult educator and your goal is that the early childhood teachers in your course are able to demonstrate that they establish positive relationships with families you would want a rubric that could determine if the teacher could, in fact, do this. It would be insufficient to have the teacher write a paper about how they would establish relationships. It is much easier to write a paper about how this would be done than to actually do it.

In summary, as you consider using a rubric make sure that what you are assessing is appropriate for a rubric, that you emphasize content and understanding, and that the rubric is aligned with your desired outcomes rather than the task. The rubric needs to be specific, detailed, and designed to let you and others know the learner's abilities in relation to the desired results. Writing rubrics is challenging work. It is helpful to have others review and provide input on new rubrics. Additionally, as you use a rubric it is common to make changes for subsequent uses.

We use portfolio assessment. How does this fit into this system?

The various forms of assessment that we have discussed can be housed in a physical or online portfolio. A portfolio is a systematic selected collection of children's work that includes an interpretation or reflection regarding what is included. Without analysis of the work, the portfolio is simply a scrapbook. The portfolio is an effective way to organize work samples and other assessments so that they can act as a scaffold in communicating with others.

In developing portfolios, you will want to first determine the primary purpose. Will it be a showcase portfolio that highlights a child's best work in a variety of areas? Will it be a developmental portfolio that documents the child's developmental milestones? Will the focus be on demonstrating growth and progress? For example, showing writing or drawing samples over a period of time. Or, will it be a keepsake portfolio? Some infant and toddler programs develop a keepsake portfolio for families that include documentation of developmental milestones, photos of classmates, and lists of children's favorites such as foods, toys, and books. They might even include such things as lengths of string in an envelope that show the child's size when they started the program and another length of string that shows their size when they left the program.

As you think about the type of portfolio, you will also be considering who the audience will be. Is the portfolio being developed for children and families or is it to pass onto the next teacher or next program? You will want to determine how involved the children will be in collecting, choosing, and reflecting on the portfolio entries. Self-reflection is considered a hallmark of the portfolio process (Martin-Kniep, 2005). Finally, you will want to consider the criteria you will use to assess the portfolio.

Developing portfolios can be overwhelming with children and teachers collecting many entries without the time or structure to sort, choose, organize, and analyze the entries. When you begin using portfolios it is recommended that you begin with a few focused entries (Martin-Kniep, 2005). Instead of focusing on quantity, focus on the quality of entries, ensuring that each entry is representative of the child and that it includes the supporting information needed to make sense of the entry. Once you have determined what you are collecting, you will also need to develop a storage system to contain the ongoing work. For example, some teachers use boxes or oversize folders that are large enough to contain large pieces of paper and sturdy enough to hold 3D work.

How Do I Use Assessment Information?

Gathering assessment information is only one step in the assessment cycle. After gathering the information, we need to:

- document and reflect on the evidence.
- analyze and evaluate the data in relation to the outcomes we have established.
- determine the implications for instruction.
- facilitate learning for the group and individuals (Riley-Ayers, 2014, p. 7).

Developing Summaries and Data Tables

While it is helpful for children, families, and teachers to see rubrics on individual children to determine their proficiency in relation to what is being assessed and to make plans for individualized learning, it is also important for teachers to be able to easily determine the proficiency of the entire class. This allows teachers to determine the effectiveness of their instruction and to determine future instructional needs.

To do this you need to aggregate the information from individual assessments. The way you aggregate the information varies based upon the type of assessment. For example, if you are keeping anecdotal records, you might keep notes of strengths and areas that need attention and create individual and group summaries. If you are keeping electronic anecdotal records, you can tag your records with keywords such as a developmental skill. When you are ready to summarize your information, you can complete a search on the keywords.

If you are completing checklists, you can quickly tally the number of children who are able to perform each of the tasks and those who are not. You can further analyze the data to determine if there are any commonalities among the items that the children are struggling with.

If you are using rubrics for performance assessments and work samples, you will want to create data tables. If you are developing a data table from your rubric, the easiest way to begin is to make an exact copy of your rubric with the descriptors removed. The titles on the rows and columns will remain. Where the descriptors were listed, insert the number of children who scored at each level. You might also add the percentage of children. When you aggregate your data, make sure that you include the relevant information such as the date, the number of children in the setting, and a descriptive title.

Examining and Learning From Your Data

After you have aggregated your data, you are ready to examine, analyze, and reflect upon your data. You might begin by asking yourself the following questions.

- What does the data tell you?
- Do you have enough information to make a decision?
- What additional data do you wish you had?
- What child progress is evident?
- Do you have concerns about specific children or about the overall group?
- What hypothesis do you have regarding the data?

After reflecting upon the data, you are ready to make plans based upon the data. This could include developing activities to meet the needs of individual children, making curricular changes for the group, and sharing the information with others. You might also find that you need to collect more data to confirm or refute your hypothesis (Stevenson-Garcia, Riley-Ayers, & Frede, 2011).

How Do I Choose the Right Assessment Method?

It is critical that we choose the right assessment method and tool based upon the purpose of the assessment. A recent study conducted with 60 teachers using purchased assessments found that while all the teachers used the assessment tool for at least one of the publishers intended purposes, 98% also used the tool for at least one unintended purpose. As pointed out by the authors of the study, this can lead to unreliable data, misinformed conclusions, ineffective teaching techniques and strategies, inaccurate assessment of the progress children are making or not making, and inaccurately referring or not referring children for additional assessment (Khoo, Alarcon, Irwin, Strambler, & Meyer, 2017, p. 7).

Typically, assessment instruments are designed for a single purpose, so it is important to understand the instrument and its purpose. For example, screening instruments are designed to be administered rapidly and so contain few assessment items examining major indicators of health, learning, and development. The assessment is too general to be helpful in instructional planning. It is not designed to inform or to monitor instruction, to diagnose a child with a disability, or to qualify a child for special education services (Slentz et al., 2008, p. 16). However, it is important as we discussed earlier that we screen children as the first step in determining whether a child might need additional assessment.

Assessments are powerful, often driving decision-making and instructional planning. Poorly designed and misaligned assessments provide non-helpful information and waste the children's and your time. As you design or choose an assessment method or instrument ask yourself the following questions.

- Why are you conducting the assessment? What is the purpose?
- Who are you sharing the assessment with (children, families, administrators, co-workers, funders)?
- How does this assessment fit within your overall assessment system?
- What types of assessment will provide you with the information needed?
- Is the assessment developmentally appropriate?
- Is the assessment aligned with your program and instructional philosophy?
- Is the assessment culturally relevant to your group of children?
- Is the assessment feasible in terms of staff time and expertise?
- If you collect this information how will you store it, analyze it, and share it?.

In Summary

In early childhood, we assess children for several reasons; to screen for disabilities, for diagnosis of disabilities, to provide program information, and for instruction. There are a variety of tools that can be used for instructional assessment including observations, checklists and rating scales, oral responses, work samples, and performance tasks. Effective teachers engage in pre-assessments, formative assessments, and summative assessments using tools best matched to the outcomes.

In backward design, designing the summative assessment is Step 2 in the process. In Step 1, we determined our desired results. In this step, we determine the evidence we need to determine if the child has achieved the outcomes. As teachers design the summative assessment, they will typically further refine their outcomes. As you develop your summative assessments avoid these common errors:

- Using group assessments as summative assessments
- Confusing activities and assessments
- Developing assessments that align with the assessment task rather than the outcomes
- Adding unrelated items to the assessments

Clearly defining the summative assessment and providing clear criteria for success allows for self-assessment, peer-assessment, and families to be involved in the assessment. It allows all to know the expectations and what the next steps are in the learning process.

Apply Your Knowledge

1.   Practice using one of the observation methods described in the chapter. What did you learn about the child using this method?
2.   In the section on cautions in developing rubrics, there is a story about Beth, who is fo-cusing on essential questions and enduring understandings related to science. Develop an assessment and rubric that would allow Beth to know if children had achieved these desired results.
3.   Try one of the feedback protocols listed in the chapter such as Three Stars and a Wish or Warm and Cool Feedback. You can learn more about these protocols through an online search.
4.   Build upon your knowledge by reviewing the modules in the Assessment Design Toolkit created by the Reform Support Network (RSN). The 13 modules provide information on how to choose, select, and create assessments and include activities, PowerPoints, and videos. Create an assessment using the information provided.
5.   Apply what you have learned to the challenge in the module, *Classroom Assessment (Part 1) An Introduction to Monitoring Academic Achievement in the Classroom*, by the IRIS Center. Complete the module to learn more.

References

Baio, J., Wiggins, L., Christensen, D. L., Maenner, M. J., Daniels, J., Warren, Z., ... & Durkin, M. S. (2018). Prevalence of autism spectrum disorder among children aged 8 years–Autism and Developmental Dis-abilities Monitoring Network, 11 Sites, United States, 2014. *MMWR Surveillance Summaries, 67*(6), 1-23. doi:10.15585/mmwr.ss6706a1

Bates, C. (2013). How do Wii know: Anecdotal records go digital. *Reading Teacher, 67*(1), 25-29. doi:10.1002/TRTR.1178

Birbili, M. (2006). Mapping knowledge: Concept maps in early childhood education. *Early Childhood Research & Practice, 8*(2), 2. Retrieved from http://ecrp.uiuc.edu/v8n2/birbili.html

Black, P., & Wiliam, D. (1998). Inside the black box: Raising standards through classroom assessment. *Phi Delta Kappan, 80*(2), 139-148.

Blaiklock, K. (2013). What are children learning in early childhood education in New Zealand? *Australasian Journal of Early Childhood, 38*(2), 51-56. doi:10.1177/183693911303800207

Boyle, C. A., Boulet, S., Schieve, L. A., Cohen, R. A., Blumberg, S. J., Yeargin-Allsopp, M., ... & Kogan, M. D. (2011). Trends in the prevalence of developmental disabilities in US children, 1997-2008. *Pediatrics, 2011*(127), 1034-1042. doi:10.1542/peds.2010-2989

Bradford, K. L., Newland, A. C., Rule, A. C., & Montgomery, S. E. (2016). Rubrics as a tool in writing instruction: Effects on the opinion essays of first and second graders. *Early Childhood Education Journal, 44*(5), 463-472. doi:10.1007/s10643-015-0727-0

Brookhart, S. M. (2013). *How to create and use rubrics for formative assessment and grading.* Alexandria, VA: Association for Supervision and Curriculum Development (ASCD).

Brown, W. (2008). Young children assess their learning: The power of the quick check strategy. *Young Children, 63*(6), 14-20.

Carr, M., & Lee, W. (2012). *Learning stories: Constructing learner identities in early education.* London: Sage.

Charlesworth, R. (2016). *Math and science for young children* (8th ed.). Boston, MA: Cengage Learning.

Cheuk, T. (2012). Relationships and convergences found in the Common Core State Standards in Mathe-matics (practices), Common Core State Standards in ELA/Literacy (student portraits), and a Framework for K-12 Science Education (science & engineering practices). Unpublished manuscript. Stanford, CA: Stanford University, Understanding Language Initiative. Retrieved from http://nstahosted.org/pdfs/ngss/ExplanationOfVennDiagram.pdf

Cidav, Z., Munson, J., Estes, A., Dawson, G., Rogers, S., & Mandell. D. (2017). Cost offset associated with early start Denver model for children with autism. *Journal of the American Academy of Child & Adolescent Psychiatry, 56*(9), 777–783. doi:10.1016/j.jaac.2017.06.007

Clarke, D. M., Mitchell, A., & Roche, A. (2005). Student one-to one assessment interviews: A powerful tool for teachers. In J. Mousley, L. Bragg, & C. Campbell (Eds.), *Mathematics: Celebrating achievement* (pp.66–80). Melbourne: Mathematical Association of Victoria.

Dawson, G., Rogers, S., Munson, J., Smith, M., Winter, J., Greenson, J., ... Varley, J. (2010). Randomized, controlled trial of an intervention for toddlers with autism: The early start Denver model. *Pediatrics, 125*(1), e17–e23. doi:10.1542/peds.2009-0958

Dunn, D. (2011). Using peer assessment in the primary classroom. Retrieved from https://www.teachprimary.com/learning_resources/view/using-peer-assessment-in-the-primary-classroom.

Forman, G., & Hall, E. (2013). Wondering with children: The importance of observation in early education. *LEARNing Landscapes, 7*(1), 187–202.

Gallenstein, N. (2013). Concept mapping for learners of all ages. *Journal for Educators, Teachers and Trainers, 4*(1), 59–72.

Ganz, M. L. (2007). The lifetime distribution of the incremental societal costs of autism. *Archives of Pediatric and Adolescent Medicine, 161*(4), 343–349. doi:10.1001/archpedi.161.4.343

Goode, S., Diefendorf, M., & Colgan, S. (2011). *The importance of early intervention for infants and toddlers with disabilities and their families.* The National Early Childhood Technical Assistance Center. Retrieved from http://www.nectac.org/~pdfs/pubs/importanceofearlyintervention.pdf

Graham, S., Hebert, M., & Harris, K. R. (2015). Formative assessment and writing: A meta-analysis. *The Elementary School Journal, 115*(4), 523–547. doi:10.1086/681947

Halle, T., Zaslow, M., Wessel, J., Moodie, S., & Darling-Churchill, K. (2011). *Understanding and choosing assessments and developmental screeners for young children: Profiles of selected measures.* Washington, DC: Office of Planning, Research, and Evaluation, Administration for Children and Families, U.S. Department of Health and Human Service.

Hattie, J. (2012). *Visible learning for teachers: Maximizing impact on learning.* London, United Kingdom: Routledge.

Helm, J. H., & Katz, L. G. (2016). *Young investigators: The project approach in the early years.* New York: Teachers College Press.

Higgins, K., Harris, N., & Kuehn, L. (1994). Placing assessment into the hands of young children: A study of student-generated criteria and self-assessment. *Educational Assessment, 2*(4), 309–324. doi:10.1207/s15326977ea0204_3

Johnson, H. M. (1933). *The art of block building.* New York: The John Day Company.

Johnson, M. (2014). *Analyzing observations.* Retrieved from http://toddlers.ccdmd.qc.ca/observing/analysis

Katz, L., & Chard, S. C. (1996). *The contribution of documentation to the quality of early childhood education.* Urbana: ERIC Clearinghouse on Elementary and Early Childhood Education, University of Illinois.

Kellough, R. D., Carin, A. A., Seefeldt, C., Barbour, N., & Souviney, R. J. (1996). *Integrating mathematics and science for kindergarten and primary children.* Englewood Cliffs, NJ: Prentice-Hall.

Khoo, L., Alarcon, S., Irwin, C. W., Strambler, M. J., & Meyer, J. L. (2017). *Assessment use in early childhood classrooms in southwestern Connecticut: Alignment between reported uses and intended uses.* Retrieved from https://medicine.yale.edu/psychiatry/peer/Publications/PEER%20Brief_Alignment%20in%20ECE%20Assessment%20Use_316685_284_31376_v3.pdf

Kingston, N., & Nash, B. (2011). Formative assessment: A meta-analysis and a call for research. *Educational Measurement: Issues and Practice, 30*(4), 28–37. doi:10.1111/j.1745-3992.2011.00220.x

Knauf, H. (2018). Learning stories: An empirical analysis of their use in Germany. *Early Childhood Education Journal, 46*(4), 427–434. doi:10.1007/s10643-017-0863-9

Krechevsky, M., Mardell, B., Rivard, M., & Wilson, D. (2013). *Visible learners: Promoting Reggio-inspired approaches in all schools.* San Francisco, CA: Jossey-Bass.

Learner Center Initiatives. (2015). *Quality rubrics.* Retrieved from http://qualityrubrics.pbworks.com/w/page/992395/Home

Learning and Teaching Scotland. (2006). *AifL early years: Self-assessment toolkit.* Glasgow: Learning and Teaching Scotland.

Lee, W., & Carr, M. (2002). Documentation of learning stories: A powerful assessment tool for early childhood. Retrieved from http://newzealand.anniewhite.cikeys.com/wp-content/uploads/2016/04/Documentation-of-Learning-Stories-Wendy-Lee-Margaret-Carr.pdf

Liebovich, B. (2000). Children's self assessment. *Proceedings of the Lilian Katz Symposium (Champaign, IL, November 5-7, 2000).* Champaign, IL: Early Childhood and Parenting (ECAP) Collaborative.

Martin-Kniep, G. O. (2005). *Becoming a better teacher: Eight innovations that work.* Upper Saddle River, NJ: Pearson/Merrill Prentice Hall.

McAleese, R. (1998). The knowledge arena as an extension to the concept map: Reflection in action. *Interactive Learning Environments, 6*(3), 251-272. doi:10.1076/ilee.6.3.251.3602

McTighe, J. (2015). Why should we use performance tasks (Part 2) [Blog post]. Retrieved from https://blog.performancetask.com/why-should-we-use-performance-tasks-part-2-76431024e160

Meisels, S. J. (1996). Using work sampling in authentic assessments. *Educational Leadership, 54*(4), 60-65.

Meisels, S. J., Atkins-Burnett, S., Xue, Y., Nicholson, J., Bickel, D. D., & Son, S-H. (2003). Creating a system of accountability: The impact of instructional assessment on elementary children's achievement test scores. *Education Policy Analysis Archives, 11*(9). Retrieved from http://epaa.asu.edu/epaa/v11n9/

Meisels, S. J., Dombro, A. L., Marsden, D. B., Weston, D., & Jewkes, A. (2003). *The Ounce scale: An observational assessment for infants, toddlers, and families.* New York: Pearson Early Learning.

Meisels, S. J., Marsden, D. B., Jablon, J. R., & Dichtelmiller, M. (2013). *Work Sampling System* (5th ed.). New York: Pearson Early Learning.

Müller, G., & Zipperle, M. (2012). Educational and learning stories in practice. An interim assessment from an empirical point of view. In K. Fröhlich-Gildhoff, H. R. Leu, & I. Nentwig-Gesemann (Eds.), *Research in early childhood education IV. Focus: Observing, understanding, interpreting, diagnosing* (pp. 121-150). Freiburg, Germany: FEL Publishing House.

National Association for the Education of Young Children (NAEYC). (2005). *Screening and assessment of young English-language learners: Supplement to the NAEYC position statement on early childhood curriculum, assessment, and program evaluation.* Retrieved from https://www.naeyc.org/sites/default/files/globally-shared/downloads/PDFs/resources/position-statements/ELL_Supplement_Shorter_Version.pdf

National Association for the Education of Young Children (NAEYC) & National Association of Early Childhood Specialists in State Departments of Education (NAECS/SDE). (2003). *Early childhood curriculum, assessment, and program evaluation: Building an effective, accountable system in programs for children birth through age 8, joint position statement.* Retrieved from www.naeyc.org/files/naeyc/file/positions/pscape.pdf

National Research Council. (2000). *Eager to learn: Educating our preschoolers.* Washington, DC: The National Academies Press. doi:10.17226/9745

Newton, N. (2016). *Math running records in action: A framework for assessing basic fact fluency in grades K-5.* New York: Routledge. doi:10.4324/9781315682389

Riley-Ayers, S. (2014). *Formative assessment: Guidance for early childhood policymakers* (CEELO Policy Report). New Brunswick, NJ: Center on Enhancing Early Learning Outcomes.

Ross, J. A. (2004). Effects of running records assessment on early literacy achievement. *The Journal of Educational Research, 97*(4), 186-195. doi:10.3200/JOER.97.4.186-195

Sainato, D. M., Strain, P. S., Lefebvre, D., & Rapp, N. (1990). Effects of self-evaluation on the independent work skills of preschool children with disabilities. *Exceptional Children, 56*(6), 540-549. doi:10.1177/001440299005600605

Schwendimann, B. A. (2015). Concept maps as versatile tools to integrate complex ideas: From kindergarten to higher and professional education. *Knowledge Management & E-Learning, 7*(1), 73-99. doi:10.34105/j.kmel.2015.07.006

Shepard, L. A., Kagan, S. L., & Wurtz, E. (Eds.). (1998). *Principles and recommendations for early childhood assessments.* Washington, DC: National Education Goals Panel.

Slentz, K. L., Early, D. L., & McKenna, M. (2008). *Washington State a guide to assessment in early childhood: Infancy to age eight.* Washington State Office of Superintendent of Public Instruction. Retrieved from http://www.k12.wa.us/EarlyLearning/pubdocs/assessment_print.pdf

Smith, K. (2010). *The effects of preschoolers' goal setting, decision making, and self-recording on academic achievement.* Morgantown, WV: West Virginia University Libraries.

Stevenson-Garcia, J., Riley-Ayers, S., & Frede, E. (2011). *Looking at student work: Using peer-to-peer teacher workgroups to establish accuracy and usefulness of child observations.* Retrieved from http://nieer.org/wp-content/uploads/2016/08/Teacher_Workgroups_for_Child_Observations_NAEYC_2011.pdf

Sundararajan, N., Adesope, O., & Cavagnetto, A. (2018). The process of collaborative concept mapping in Kindergarten and the effect on critical thinking skills. *Journal of STEM Education, 19*(1). Retrieved from https://www.learntechlib.org/p/182981/

U.S. Department of Education, Institute of Education Sciences, National Center for Education Statistics. (2016). *Digest of education statistics.* Retrieved from https://nces.ed.gov/programs/digest/index.asp

Venn, J. (1881). *Symbolic logic.* London: Macmillan.

Warash, B., Smith, K., & Root, A. (2011). "I want to learn my phone number": Encourage young children to set their own learning goals. *Dimensions of Early Childhood, 39*, 12-19.

Warash, B. G., & Workman, M. (2016). Teaching preschoolers to self-assess their choices in Pre-K. *Journal of Educational Research and Practice, 6*(1), 97-104.

Wiggins, G., & McTighe, J. (2012). *The understanding by design guide to advanced concepts in creating and reviewing units.* Alexandria, VA: Association for Supervision and Curriculum Development (ASCD).

Zhang, Q. (2017). Do learning stories tell the whole story of children's learning? A phenomenographic enquiry. *Early Years, 37*(3), 255-267. doi:10.1080/09575146.2016.1151403

5 What We Know about Learning in the Early Years

As there has been more emphasis on learning in the early years, there has been a desire to capitalize on this period by using evidence-based practice. In this chapter, we will explore research on how children learn. We will also examine how we choose practices that are evidence-based.

How Do Children Learn?

Before we can determine how children learn we must consider what is the goal of learning? Most would say that it is transfer. Transfer, defined as the ability to transfer what one has learned to a different task or context, is at the heart of learning (Bransford, Brown, Cocking, & National Research Council, 2000). Amy, a kindergarten teacher has been teaching a social curriculum that emphasizes using conflict resolution strategies. Her goal is that children will use these strategies when they have conflict situations not only in her classroom, but also on the playground, and in their home life. She wants them to be able to use conflict resolution not only this year but also use it as a lifetime skill. Like Amy, as teachers we want learners to be able to transfer what they are learning. However, so often what we learn and teach is not transferred. Learners forget it or are unable to apply the information. How can we increase the likelihood that what we learn and teach is transferable? The National Research Council synthesized decades of research on how people learn, producing a report entitled *How People Learn: Brain, Mind, Experience, and School* (Bransford, Brown, Cocking, & National Research Council, 2000) that addressed this question. We will examine the criteria they found were necessary for teaching and learning leading to transfer. To transfer information, we have learned we must:

- Learn with understanding. This typically involves conceptual understanding. For example, the children in Amy's class are unlikely to be able to use conflict resolution skills if they only memorize the steps. They must understand the values that underlie conflict resolution and why conflict resolution is important.
- Adequately learn the information in the first place. For example, the children will not learn the process of conflict resolution through one circle time activity. To learn they will need multiple opportunities to learn about the steps and to practice these in their lives. Amy will need to coach the children as they have opportunities to apply their knowledge. Adequately learning involves not only learning the steps but understanding the nuances involved in carrying out the steps and knowing under what conditions one would use conflict resolution.
- Take the time needed to learn. Learning concepts and information that can be transferred is time-consuming. As we discussed in earlier chapters, recognizing the need for time to learn, national standards are calling for curriculum that is more narrowly focused but deep rather than curriculum that is "a mile wide and an inch deep."

- Use appropriate learning methods. Some methods that have been found to aid transfer are practice, self-monitoring, feedback focused on the degree of understanding, aiding the learner in seeing potential transfer possibilities, and using contrasting cases. For example, when teaching young children about triangles, their learning is enhanced by providing them with a variety of non-triangles (Clements & Sarama, 2014).
- Enhance motivation to learn. The proper level of difficulty is important in motivation, learners need to be developmentally capable of learning the skills, knowledge, or concepts. If the material is too easy the learner gets bored. If too difficult they get frustrated. Both of these feelings decrease motivation. As emphasized by Vygotsky, we need to focus on children's zone of proximal development (ZPD). That is the difference between what a learner can accomplish independently and what they can accomplish or learn with assistance. By supporting their learning, we can act as a scaffold to new learning. We also motivate learners by helping them to understand the usefulness of the information. One way this occurs is when children can apply the information to a real-world situation. For example, children may be more motivated to write if they are writing a letter requesting the opportunity to visit a pet store than if they are simply conducting a writing exercise. The report also emphasized that children are more motivated when the skill can be used to help others and when learning involves a social opportunity.

Some other factors that influence transfer are the context of the original learning and the overlap between the learning and the transfer condition. Teaching the same concept in different contexts increases the likelihood of transfer as does increased overlap.

As we ponder children's learning, we realize that much of their learning occurs outside an educational setting. So, what is the difference between what children learn in and out of formal educational settings? According to the National Research Council, "More than any other species, people are designed to be flexible learners and, from infancy are active agents in acquiring knowledge and skills" (2005, p. 1). However, while children can learn much informally, "mastery of the accumulated knowledge of generations requires intentional learning, often accomplished in a formal education setting" (2005, p. 1). There are specific ways that we need to teach in formal educational settings to enhance learning. So, what are these? In addition to the report, *How People Learn: Brain, Mind, Experience, and School* the National Research Council of the National Academy of Sciences developed two additional reports including *How People Learn: Bridging Research and Practice* (National Research Council, 1999) and *How students learn: History, mathematics, and science in the classroom* (National Research Council, 2005). These reports list three principles of learning that are critical for teachers to understand.

1. Students come to the classroom with preconceptions about how the world works. If their initial understanding is not engaged, they may fail to grasp the new concepts and information, or they may learn them for purposes of a test but revert to their preconceptions outside the classroom.
2. To develop competence in an area of inquiry, students must (a) have a deep foundation of factual knowledge, (b) understand facts and ideas in the context of a conceptual framework, and (c) organize knowledge in ways that facilitate retrieval and application.
3. A "metacognitive" approach to instruction can help students learn to take control of their own learning by defining learning goals and monitoring their progress in achieving them (National Research Council, 2005, pp. 1-2).

The book (National Research Council, 2005) relates this to a familiar children's book by Leo Lionni, *Fish is Fish*. In this story, the frog leaves the pond and returns to tell the fish all he has seen in the world. As he talks about people, the fish imagines a fish walking upright, wearing clothes. The bird is shaped like a fish but has wings. Eventually, the fish decides he must see this wonderful world for himself. As you might guess, the fish immediately gets into trouble since he cannot breathe out of the water. The preconceptions and the background knowledge of the fish influence his thinking about what people and birds look like and why they might be different than the fish. What concept would help the fish to understand this more? If the fish understood adaptation, he would realize that people on land would have different breathing mechanisms, different ways to control temperature, and different ways of moving than water animals. So, what are the implications for teaching and learning? Let's examine each of these concepts in more depth.

Preconceptions

From birth, children are figuring out how the world works through implicit learning. Implicit learning is the "rapid, effortless, and untutored detection of patterns of covariation among events in the world in the absence of conscious, reflective strategies to learn" (Bransford et al., 2006, p. 210). These include the transmission of culture through imitation of parents, peers, and media and from personal experiences. The child develops theories based upon these experiences. Referred to as preconceptions, sometimes called naïve understandings or misconceptions, they are very resistant to change. Even when children appear to have learned a concept in school, they will often hold onto their preconceptions in other environments or combine their preconceptions with their new knowledge creating a new misconception (Smolleck & Hershberger, 2011). This, by the way, is also true for adults. Since learners have often acquired their understandings based on experience, the preconception might not be at the conscious level. Additionally, the preconception often works okay in day-to-day life. The preconceptions may be logical, particularly to the learner, but not make scientific sense.

Preconceptions may be knowledge related to a specific subject such as the shape of the earth. However, preconceptions can also relate to an overall belief about a subject. Fuson, Kalchman, and Bransford (2005) list three common misconceptions about math related not to math facts or concepts themselves but to overall beliefs about math, "mathematics is about learning to compute, mathematics is about 'following the rules' to guarantee correct answers, and some people have the ability to 'do math' and some don't" (pp. 220-221). As with knowledge-based preconceptions, these preconceptions are based upon experiences and can negatively affect learning.

As teachers, we need to determine children's current understandings so that we can build upon these, creating a bridge to new knowledge or to challenge misconceptions. First, it is helpful to be aware of common preconceptions for the age of the child you are teaching. Especially in the area of science, there has been extensive research on children's thinking. For example, Saçkes (2015) reviewed a wide variety of research and summarized children's typical conceptions and misconceptions regarding earth and space science. She found among other things that:

- Most young children believe that clouds are solid and that clouds are created by humans or by God.
- Young children understand that rain is water, but they don't relate the rain to clouds.
- Early elementary children believe that thunder is the result of two clouds colliding.

It is beyond the scope of this book to list all the common misconceptions that exist in young children. However, you can learn more about science misconceptions in the book, *Research in Early Childhood Science Education* (Trundle & Sackes, 2015).

Second, there are many techniques that teachers can use to determine young children's preconceptions and on-going conceptions. Additionally, these techniques can help bring beliefs into the consciousness of the learner. We discussed several of these in the chapter on assessment including KWHL charts, concept maps, webs, Venn diagrams, observations, and probing questions. Another technique is to have children create drawings of their conceptions. There are many rich examples of discovering children's thinking through drawing. For example, in a project called the Amusement Park for Birds at Reggio, Emilia children decided that the birds needed a fountain. Children took photos of pictures of fountains in the town. The teachers made these photos into overheads, placed them on an overhead projector, shown these on a wall, and put paper on the wall so that children could draw. They then asked children how the water got into the fountains and children drew their theories (Malaguzzi, Rinaldi, Forman, & Gandini, 2006). This allowed the teachers to study the children's current understandings and to be able to ask probing questions and provide additional experiences to enhance these understandings. While this was a yearlong, very in-depth project, you can also use this technique for shorter-term projects and activities. Brooks (2009) describes asking a preschool child to draw a picture of stages of a potato plant growing as a pre-assessment before planting. The four-year-old child drew a progression of pictures with the plant growing bigger, finally moving above ground, and then creating potatoes on the top of the plant similar to tomatoes. Her previous experience with growing flowers, beans, and peas caused her to believe that potatoes would grow above the ground.

To fully understand children's meanings in their drawings, we must typically conduct interviews. Let's look at an example. Young children often form the intuitive conclusion that the world is flat. They conclude that if it wasn't flat, they would fall off. Generally, it isn't until they are older that they are exposed to the idea that the world is round. Karin Ehrlen (2009) had children ages six to nine draw a picture of the earth. Many of the children drew the earth as a round ball which might indicate that they understood that the earth was a sphere. However, when interviewed they had many misconceptions. For example, several children believed that people lived inside the round ball of the earth. Others believed that each country had its own earth. Ehrlen reminds us to be cautious about assumptions we make based upon the drawings unless we interview the child to determine their thinking. As this example illustrates, we might believe based upon the child's drawing that they have mastered a concept, when in fact they haven't. The opposite can also be true. When one of my children, Danny, was young, he participated in a draw a house and a draw a person assessment in his kindergarten class. A few days later, the teacher asked me to come in so that we could discuss the assessment. She was concerned because Danny had drawn so few parts on the person. In the middle of the picture, he had drawn a box. Inside the box was a head with eyes, mouth, nose, ears, and hair. Missing were the many body parts that would be in a typical kindergartner's drawing of a person such as arms, legs, body, hands, and feet. I was not concerned since I had seen many of Danny's previous drawings that had contained these details, but I was curious. When I showed Danny the picture of the person he had drawn and asked him to explain it he said that it was him looking out the window of the house. He had drawn our house in the previous picture. He said he didn't draw the other body parts because you couldn't see them when you looked at someone through a window.

Drawings can also reveal the reactions and emotions that someone feels toward a specific subject or object. Our reactions and emotions can also affect our learning. When I was teaching fifth- to eighth-grade children in a rural school, we had a guest who talked about alcohol awareness. She began by asking the children to draw a picture of alcohol. Most of the children drew a picture of bottles of alcohol. However, one child drew a picture of someone hiding under a bed. Further individual questioning revealed it was her hiding under the bed, while parents had loud fights after drinking. The guest, who specialized in alcohol awareness activities for children, said that it was not uncommon that children would draw a picture revealing their personal experiences with alcohol.

Factual and Conceptual Knowledge

As we discussed when learning about the steps of backward design, learners need the opportunity to learn concepts as they are learning facts. Researchers found that learning facts is not enough, stating "deep understanding of subject matter transforms facts into usable knowledge" (National Research Council, 1999, p. 12). When researchers examined novices and experts to see what accounted for the difference in their skill level, they found that experts use concepts that help them make sense of new information. This allows them to see patterns and relationships, remember relevant information, and to quickly identify what is relevant rather than being overwhelmed with information (National Research Council, 2005). It also aids in transfer of information. Using backward design can assist teachers in planning for not only factual teaching but also conceptual teaching.

Metacognition

The term metacognition, introduced by Flavell in the 1970s, is defined as "the individual's own awareness and consideration of his or her cognitive processes and strategies" (Flavell, 1979). This entails being able to accurately self-assess our knowledge and skills, to think about our own thinking, to plan and monitor cognitive processes, and to develop skills in learning to learn. Many studies have shown that teaching children metacognitive skills can result in increases in achievement. A recent review of research found effect sizes as high as 0.69 (Perry, Lundie, & Golder, 2018). There are a variety of strategies that can enhance metacognition. These include:

- Having learners engage in self-assessment
- Utilizing group work with peer-assessment
- Using a thinking curriculum such as Visible Thinking
- Providing tools such as KWHL charts that help learners reflect
- Modeling your own metacognition through talking aloud
- Asking probing questions about thinking such as "What was the hardest information to understand?" or "What was the muddiest point?"
- Embedding metacognitive skills throughout the curriculum, teaching these skills in the learning context

As researchers continue to study how children learn, other researchers are examining evidence-based practice, trying to determine if there are some strategies and curriculum that are more effective than others. We will examine evidence-based practice next. In the next sections of the book, as we review teaching strategies, we will examine them through the lens of how people learn as well as through evidence-based practice.

Evidence-based Practice

As teachers, we often use practices and techniques that we have seen modeled in our own education. Or, we might adopt a practice we've seen other teachers use and never question the effectiveness. We might adopt a curriculum or practice that claims to be research-based, feeling confident in our decision. However, in many cases, this has become a buzz word with little actual meaning. As a result, some of the practices we are using might actually be ineffective or even harmful. For example, the most widely implemented discipline policy in the United States is a zero-tolerance policy. "A zero tolerance policy assigns explicit, predetermined punishments to specific violations of school rules, regardless of the situation or context of the behavior" (Boccanfuso, & Kuhfeld, 2011, p. 1). Punishments are often swift and harsh. These policies are typically designed with the idea that they will keep schools safer, act as a deterrent for misbehavior, and increase academic achievement. However, do they? The existing research shows that zero-tolerance policies do not make schools safer or decrease disruptive behavior and there is actually a decrease in academic achievement. Furthermore, the penalties are disproportionately applied to children of color and those with disabilities, where they receive harsher treatment for the same offenses than other children (American Psychological Association Zero Tolerance Task Force, 2008). Schools that have reviewed the research and found that zero-tolerance policies are ineffective, discriminatory, and lead to lower achievement, would most likely choose other evidence-based disciplinary practices and policies that would meet their objectives. Unfortunately, most schools are not examining the evidence.

We want to provide children with the best opportunity to learn and the greatest chance for success. Our goal is to improve overall outcomes, not only academic but also social and emotional outcomes. We don't want to waste time or money on ineffective policies or practices. So how can we know that the practices we are using are effective? Rather than being a blind consumer of marketing or tradition, we need to constantly be asking the question, "What is the evidence that this works?" The higher the stakes the more crucial it is that we investigate the practice. For example, if we are implementing a strategy such as dialogic reading that we will use daily for an extended period of time, it is important to know if there is evidence that the practice works. There are several solutions to determining if a practice works. These include using evidence-based practices identified by clearinghouses and professional organizations, conducting our own research reviews, and closely examining and developing data on our own practices. We will examine these solutions in this section.

What Is Evidence-based Practice?

Evidence-based practice is a buzz word found in education, medicine, psychiatry, and social policy, based on the "What Works" agenda (Kvernbekk, 2011, 2017). Politicians and federal legislation call for it. The federal legislation, the Every Child Succeeds Act (ECSA) governing public Pre-K through high schools requires it. In the 449-page law, evidence-based is mentioned 64 times in reference to such things as instruction, literacy methods, assessment tools, trauma-informed practice, family involvement, and professional development. The law states that priorities in awarding grants need to be based on the use of evidence-based strategies (ESSA, 2015). As a result, early childhood curriculums are quick to call themselves evidence-based or research-based. You will also find that many textbooks now include evidence-based in their titles.

What is the definition of evidence-based practice (EBP)? What knowledge is considered evidence? It depends whom you ask. We will be looking at where the term originated and how the term is defined by professional organizations, researchers, and the Department of Education in the reauthorization of the Elementary and Secondary Education Act (ESEA).

The term evidence-based practice has its origins in the medical profession, where doctors and other health professionals, use rigorous research-based evidence to determine treatments. The best research evidence in medicine is seen as randomized controlled experiments. However, health professionals also use clinical evidence such as patient history, diagnostic tests, and information on how the treatment is working for the individual patient to make an informed decision about treatment (Masters, 2018). Evidence-based practice in medicine is therefore defined "as the integration of best research evidence with clinical expertise and patient values" (Sackett, Straus, Richardson, Rosenberg, & Haynes, 2000, p. 1).

Professional organizations such as NAEYC have also used a definition that includes professional judgment and research-based information when determining what constitutes evidence. In the *Early Childhood Curriculum, Assessment, and Program Evaluation: Building an Effective, Accountable System in Programs for Children Birth Through Age 8. Position Statement* evidence is defined as "empirical research and well-documented professional deliberation and consensus, with differing weights given to differing types of evidence" (NAEYC, 2003, p. 5).

The American Speech-Hearing-Language Association has a similar view. They state, "The term *evidence-based practice* refers to an approach in which current, high-quality research evidence is integrated with practitioner expertise and client preferences and values into the process of making clinical decisions" (American Speech-Language-Hearing Association, 2005, p. 1).

The IRIS Center, a national center to improve educational outcomes for children, especially those with disabilities, has developed modules on *Evidence-Based Practice* (2014). In their modules, they use this definition by Buysse, Wesley, Snyder, and Winton, researchers from the Frank Porter Graham Child Development Institute and Vanderbilt University. Evidence-based practice for the early childhood field is a "decision-making process that integrates the best available research evidence with family and professional wisdom and values" (2006, p. 3). The definition like those of the medical profession, NAEYC, the American Speech-Language-Hearing Association stresses the use of both clinical- and research-based information.

This view of evidence-based practice is also found in other parts of the world. For example, *Educational Research* authors from Canada, England, and the Netherlands in a special journal issue focused on evidence-based practice argued that we use the term evidence-informed practice and that this include, "the *integration* of professional judgement, system-level data, classroom data and research evidence" (Nelson & Campbell, 2017, p. 129).

How does the federal government define evidence-based? Evidence-based plays a prominent role in the ECSA, the latest revision of the ESEA. This act, first signed over 50 years ago, was a civil rights law designed to provide quality and equality for the nation's schoolchildren. Through this act, congress sets policies and provides federal funding for education. Since its inception, the act has gone through multiple revisions. However, the law has continued to emphasize the need to provide quality and equity. To understand the current regulation, it is helpful to explore the history of the law. You can see the history of the ESEA in Box 5.1.

Box 5.1 A Brief History of the Elementary and Secondary Education Act

- 1965–1980: Promoting Equity in Access to Educational Opportunities' primary purpose was to fund Title 1, a program for low-income children.
- 1981–1988: The Push for Educational Excellence ushered in the Hawkins-Stafford Elementary and Secondary School Improvement Act requiring states to develop levels of academic achievement for Title 1 schools.
- 1989–1992: The Rise of Standards-Based Reform resulted in discussion and promotion of voluntary national standards, national tests, and school choice.
- 1993–2000: Federal Focus on Standards-Based-Reform reauthorization of ESEA, titled Improving America's Schools Act (IASA) was enacted. This act required that children eligible for Title 1 be taught inclusively. Additionally, the state needed to provide evidence that the learning goals and curriculum opportunities were the same for all students in the state. Title 1 schools were required to make adequate yearly progress or actions needed to be taken to improve them.
- 2001–2008: Test-Based Accountability—The reform authorization of ESEA called The No Child Left Behind Act (NCLBA) was enacted. States were required to develop and implement academic standards, test children from grades 3–8 annually, have highly qualified teachers and apply sanctions to schools that did not meet adequate yearly progress.
- 2009–2016: Competitive Grants and Federal Prescriptions—The federal government used Race to the Top and School Improvement grants with prescriptive requirements. The combination of the grant and waivers to NCLBA were used to exert influence over educational policy.

Information from The Hunt Institute (2016, pp. 1–4).

The ECSA was signed into law by President Obama in 2015 and went into effect in the 2017–2018 academic year. Among other things, the bill emphasizes increased access to high-quality preschool and the use of evidence-based practice. The law also gives more flexibility and responsibility to states. For example, while annual standardized testing is still required, the state is now in charge of developing an accountability plan, which needs to be signed off on by the federal government. Another change that occurred in the ECSA is that now public preschools are also included in the act.

So how is evidence-based defined? An evidence-based intervention is one that, "demonstrates a statistically significant effect on improving student outcomes or other relevant outcomes" based on strong evidence, moderate evidence, or promising evidence, or that

> demonstrates a rationale based on high-quality research findings or positive evaluation that such activity, strategy, or intervention is likely to improve student outcomes or other relevant outcomes; and (II) includes ongoing efforts to examine the effects of such activity, strategy, or intervention.

(ESSA, 2015, pp. 393–394)

We will further examine what is meant by strong, moderate, and promising evidence and demonstrates a rationale.

- Strong evidence is provided by at least one randomized controlled experimental study that shows statistically significant, positive results and that includes a large (350 or more children or 50 or more groups each containing ten children), multi-site sample. This result cannot be overridden by statistically significant negative results in other studies of the intervention (US Department of Education, 2016).
- To show moderate evidence, the one required study can be a quasi-experimental study that uses a comparison group that is similar to the treatment group. The research must show statistically significant, positive results and must include a large, multi-site sample. This result cannot be overridden by statistically significant negative results in other studies of the intervention (US Department of Education, 2016).
- Promising evidence is supported by at least one, "well-designed and well-implemented correlational study with statistical controls" such as sampling and/or analytic methods to reduce bias on the intervention (US Department of Education, 2016, p. 9). As with the strong and moderate evidence categories, the promising evidence must show a statistically significant, positive result on child outcomes and these results cannot be overridden by statistically significant negative results in other studies of the intervention.
- The final category of research that the US Department of Education considers evidence-based is a practice that demonstrates a rationale. The rationale uses, "a well-specified logic model that is informed by research or an evaluation that suggests how the intervention is likely to improve relevant outcomes" (2016, p. 9). Additionally, the outcomes need to be studied either as part of the intervention or there needs to be a study being conducted elsewhere.

But, what is a logic model? I've never even heard of one.

A logic model, also sometimes referred to as a theory of action, is defined as a

well-specified conceptual framework that identifies key components of the proposed process, product, strategy, or practice (i.e., the active "ingredients" that are hypothesized to be critical to achieving the relevant outcomes) and describes the relationships among the key components and outcomes, theoretically and operationally.

(US Department of Education, 2016, p. 11)

Logic models include a problem statement, short- and long-term outcomes, strategies and activities, resources, Vand assumptions (Shakman & Rodriguez, 2015).

For example, the Learning by Making is a STEM curriculum for high school that has developed a logic model. They include a visual diagram that includes inputs (organizations involved and financial resources), outputs (activities and participation) and outcomes (short-, medium-, long-term). They also include assumptions and external factors. Arrows on the diagram show relationships between each of these. The logic model is being used to drive the process and the evaluation (Li & Tripathy, 2017).

The Department of Education guidance document on evidence-based practice (2016) emphasizes that when schools choose an intervention program, they need to determine local needs, find evidence-based interventions related to these needs, determine that the research on the interventions are with a similar population, and examine the capacity of the program to implement the intervention. After implementing, the program needs to examine data on the targeted outcomes to determine if the intervention is successful with their population of children and whether it should be continued.

As you can see, the definition of evidence-based practice by the US Department of Education is more focused on research and less on clinical expertise than the other definitions we examined. However, the addition of the practice that demonstrates a rationale does appear to allow for more flexibility. Furthermore, all of these definitions agree that we should not adopt a teaching practice or strategy simply because it is an EBP. Instead, a teacher or program needs to consider other forms of evidence including knowledge of individual learners, their families, and the local culture; how relevant the practice is to the children and current setting, and how children are progressing when the EBP is used.

Selecting an Evidence-based Practice

When selecting an EBP, you will want to answer several questions:

- What are the specific skills you want to address such as reading comprehension?
- How well do the characteristics of children in your program match those in the research studies?
- What resources are required to implement the EBP (cost, time, specialized training)?
- What research supports the practice? Take a deep dive into the research by reading each research report or article that the review is based on. This is especially important if you are choosing a higher stakes practice, for example, a program-wide strategy, a strategy that is designed to be implemented for a long period of time, a practice that requires specialized training, a practice that takes extensive time for teachers to learn and for children to participate in, or a practice with a high cost.

Sources of Evidence

There are many sources of evidence. However, not all sources are equally credible. In this section, we will look at ways to find credible information.

Clearinghouses and Organizations that Provide "What Works" or Similar Briefs

There are several trusted governmental and professional organizations that examine evidence and provide ratings for EBP. Each of these has different criteria about what is viewed as legitimate evidence. Below is a list of some of these trusted sources:

- What Works Clearinghouse (WWC) is sponsored by the Department of Education and reviews both programs and practices. There is a special division for early childhood.
- Best Evidence Encyclopedia (BEE) by the Center for Data-Driven Reform at John Hopkins University review programs.
- The Promising Practices Network provides information on early childhood programs and practices. Although it is still available it has not been updated since 2014.
- The IRIS Center provides Evidence-Based Practice Summaries
- Center for Early Literacy Learning (CELL) provides CELL reviews, practice-based research synthesis

- Center on the Social Emotional Foundations for Early Learning (CSEFEL) provides What Works Briefs and Research Synthesis
- Division for Early Childhood (DEC) of the Council for Exceptional Children provides DEC Recommended Practices
- The National Center on Intensive Instruction (NCII) provides information on evidence-based assessments and interventions.
- Center on Instruction (COI) provides Research: Meta-analyses and Summaries and Practitioner Guides relating to instructional practices.
- Collaborative for Academic, Social, and Emotional Learning reviews programs focusing on social and emotional learning. The CASEL Guide: Early Childhood and Elementary Edition is especially helpful.
- The National Professional Development Center on Autism Spectrum Disorder provides Evidence-Based Practices and training modules that teach how to use the practices
- Teaching LD provides Current Practice Alerts and Online Tutorials
- The Education Endowment Foundation Early Years Toolkit provides summaries of international educational evidence in different educational areas such as mathematics, self-regulation strategies, and family engagement. The Toolkit provides information on costs, the strength of evidence, and how many additional months of learning per year would be added by practicing this intervention.
- Promoting the Educational Success of Children and Youth Learning English provides a Promising Practices Toolkit

I was looking at the practice of Direct Instruction (DI) and I found contradictory information from different sources, with What Works saying that DI such as DISTAR and Ladders for Learning is ineffective and the Promising Practices Network listing DI as a promising practice. Why is that?

Part of the reason for this discrepancy is based upon what each clearinghouse views as credible evidence. Additionally, what outcomes are being examined and the year the clearinghouse evaluates the intervention can also make a difference. Let's look.

The WWC Early Childhood Education rates programs and practices as positive, potentially positive, mixed, no discernible effects, potentially negative, or negative. They include both randomized controlled trials and quasi-experimental designs that meet their criteria in their reviews. They found only one study of DI in preschool populations out of the seven they located met their criteria for inclusion in the review. This study was with 164 preschool and kindergarten children with special needs. In the summary, the WWC stated:

> The WWC reviewed six studies on Direct Instruction. One study met WWC evidence standards with reservations. The remaining studies did not meet WWC evidence screens. Based on the study included in the overall rating of effectiveness, the WWC found no discernible effects for oral language, print knowledge, cognition, or math.
>
> (What Works Clearinghouse, 2007, p. 6)

In WWC, K-12 several specific DI programs were reviewed. However, no studies were found for any of the DI programs that met the criteria for inclusion, so they were unable to rate the programs. However, these reviews were all conducted in 2007, so it would be important to review research that has been conducted since then if you are considering using a DI program.

The Promising Practices Network reviewed 20 studies for children of all ages that met their requirements for inclusion. These included both quasi-experimental and experimental designs. The Promising Practices Network gives ratings of proven, promising, or other reviewed programs. DI is listed as a promising practice. In the rationale, the Promising Practices Network states,

> Many of the evaluations of Direct Instruction were experimental in design, and those that were quasi-experimental used reasonably convincing comparison groups. The results varied significantly from study to study, with ten of the studies reporting mixed results, six reporting no significant differences between groups, and four reporting solely positive and significant differences for DI students. This lack of consistency among studies suggests that the overall evidence of DI effectiveness is limited. However, when results are considered across all studies, the majority of the evaluations reported at least some significant benefit accruing to students who participated in the Direct Instruction program.
>
> (Promising Practices Network, 2005, Issues to Consider, para. 1)

One reason for different ratings between the clearinghouses is the age range that was being included. The WWC Early Childhood examines only research related to preschool. However, the Promising Practices Network includes research from kindergarten through high school. Since there is such a wide age range in the Promising Practices Network, it is important that you read the synopsis of each research study in the report to determine how relevant the findings are for your age range and context. For more detail, you can read the reports themselves. You might also find some new information as you read the reports. In several of the studies that showed mixed results in the Promising Practices review, DI was being compared to more than one other approach. For example, Alaskan kindergarten children (Rawl & O'Tuel, 1982) were placed in a DI, Action-Reading, or a control group. The study examined alphabet skills, visual auditory discrimination, language, pre-reading, and math. There was an interesting finding in this study. The control group outperformed both the DI and the Action-Reading groups. In the test of alphabet skills, there was no significant difference between approaches. The control group scored significantly higher than one or both of the other approaches in each of the other subtests. The Action-Reading group scored significantly higher on the visual-auditory discrimination than the DI group. The DI group scored significantly higher than the Action-Reading group on language and pre-reading.

Reviews of Research

Although there are many clearinghouses and professional organizations that are reviewing research, there are still many practices that have not been evaluated by any of these groups. The IRIS center in their module on evidence-based practice (2014), recommends that if you cannot find an EBP that meets your needs through reviewing trusted organizations, you need to conduct a research review yourself.

While searching for articles, you will want to ensure that the article is peer-reviewed and that you examine all the articles about the given practice. This ensures that you are getting a well-rounded view of the practice. For example, a practice may have shown significant results in one out of ten published research articles. If you only examine one article, you may have a different impression about effectiveness versus if you examine all of them. If you are reviewing multiple articles, it is helpful to keep track of the information as you review.

To save the time required in examining and analyzing all the research articles yourself, it is helpful to examine a research synthesis, meta-analysis, or research review. In these analyses, the author has examined the evidence from multiple studies. These can often be found in educational journals. Google Scholar and ERIC are also two search engines that are helpful in locating this information.

Are there guidelines for examining research? How can I be a savvy consumer of research? Whether a consumer or creator of research, it is important to be research literate. This begins with determining how trustworthy the research is. Following are a list of questions to consider.

- Was the research peer-reviewed? Was the research reported in a scholarly journal or by a trusted organization?
- Is the research question clear?
- Is the literature review thorough, with a range of relevant, current sources? Does the review include conflicting research or only include research that supports its case? Is the case built for the need for this research?
- Is the researcher credible? Are there conflicts of interest? For example, is the author of the curriculum the researcher for the effectiveness of the curriculum? Who is paying for the research? Is there a bias toward pleasing the funder?
- Is the research experimental or descriptive? Was the research design clearly explained and justified? Was the research design appropriate?
- If the research is experimental, does it include a control group? A control group is considered the gold standard for experiential research. If so, are the groups comparable? Were the participants randomly assigned to a group? Many research studies on curriculum do not contain a control group. The authors will use various measures to describe the growth that children have experienced in using the curriculum. However, young children are in a period of life where they gain knowledge and skills rapidly. Without a control group, it is difficult to determine if the growth experienced is due to the curriculum.
- If the research is qualitative, are the methods for establishing credibility, transferability, dependability, and confirmability well described and defended. Some ways of doing this include triangulating of data; member checks; in-depth rich descriptions of methodology; and description of the researcher's qualifications, background, beliefs, and assumptions (Shenton, 2004).
- Are the participants clearly described? What are their characteristics (age, gender, socio-economic status, race/ethnic background, ELL, presence of a disability) How were the participants chosen? Are they representative of the population being studied? What size is the sample? Is the size appropriate for the method? Is the context described (type of program, teacher qualifications, location)? This is very important since you will want to know if the population and context are similar to your own (What Works Clearinghouse, 2014).
- Are interventions clearly described? What skills were targeted? What specific approach was used? What was the duration and intensity of treatment? Who was involved in administering the treatment? (What Works Clearinghouse, 2014).

- Are the methods for data collection clearly described and defended? Would you be able to replicate this study?
- How did the author control other variables that might affect the research? For example, researchers might be looking at how effective a literacy curriculum is. To do so, they use an achievement test to compare classes who use the curriculum with those who do not. However, to teach educators how to use the new literacy curriculum, the researchers provide workshops and in-class mentoring. Unless workshops and mentoring are also provided to the control group, it is impossible to know if a change in achievement test scores is due to the curriculum or the mentoring.
- How was the data analyzed? Was the method for analysis well-described and defended? Was it appropriate for the type of study?
- Are the results generalizable? Does the study describe the limitations? Are the conclusions based on the evidence?
- What is the practical significance of the research? Does the research simulate real life? For example, as I was conducting research on ADHD (Bullard, 1996), I found a series of studies that examined children's off-task and non-compliant behavior. As I reviewed the studies, I found they all had a similar design. They were conducted in a lab setting. In most cases, the observations lasted for only 15 minutes for each condition. The child and parent were in a bare room with five toys and minimal furniture. In one part of the assessment, children could freely play with the toys. In the other part of the assessment, parents had specific tasks they had the child perform. Children were less compliant and more off task when asked to perform specific tasks. However, they were generally compliant and on-task during the 15-minute free play period. As a result of these many studies, pediatricians at this point in time felt it was unnecessary to provide medication to children in the evenings or weekends. However, the 15-minute free-play period does not simulate a child's everyday home life where children are expected to interact positively with others for extended periods of time, share toys and parental attention with siblings, not engage in dangerous activities, stay out of others' possessions, and to comply with mealtime, homework, and bedtime routines.
- Consider unintended consequences. What is the time and cost to implement the curriculum? Will other practices, resources, or time for other curricular areas need to be reduced or eliminated to implement this program or practice? Does the practice align with DAP and with the program's philosophy? What is the likelihood that the program will negatively affect children's positive approaches to learning?

This sounds complicated. How can I keep track of all the information I am reviewing?

One way to keep track of the information is to put your information into a table. For example, you could have a column for each of the following:

Research study (title, year, who conducted)

Population (number of participants, age, geographic area, culture)

Methods (study design)

Trustworthiness (peer review, control group, randomized, data triangulated, etc.)

Results (statistical significance, effect size)

Recommended Practices from Trusted Professional Organizations

You might also examine recommended practices from professional organizations. These practices are often a combination of research and experiential knowledge that are put out by trusted organizations such as NAEYC in the book *Developmentally Appropriate Practice in Early Childhood Programs Serving Children Birth to Age 8* (NAEYC, 2009) or Zero to Three, a national organization that promotes the well-being of infants and toddlers.

Your Own Data

In the chapter on assessment, we discussed collecting summative data. In addition to letting you know if children are achieving the desired results, this data lets you know if your teaching practices are effective. It is important to develop your own data even if you are using a practice that has been deemed evidence-based. As stated in the US Department of Education guidance document on evidence-based practice (2016), you need to know if this specific intervention works in your context, with your children.

Teachers also conduct teacher research (sometimes referred to as practitioner research or action research) to more deeply examine their practice. "Teacher research is intentional and systematic inquiry done by teachers with the goals of gaining insights into teaching and learning, becoming more reflective practitioners, effecting changes in the classroom or school, and improving the lives of children" (Henderson, Meier, Perry, & Stremmel, 2012, p. 1). Teacher research is conducted by teachers or groups of teachers who use a systematic process. This involves following specific procedures and carefully documenting each step of the process. The process involves three phases; conceptualization, implementation, and interpretation (McLean, 1995). The conceptualization begins by identifying a significant problem or interest. This is followed by developing a researchable question. As stated by Andrew Stremmel,

> The impetus to pursue a question often arises out of personal curiosity, a nagging issue, a keen interest, or a perspective that begs examination in order to understand something more fully or to see it in different ways. When teachers pose questions worth asking, they do so from an attitude–a stance–of inquiry, and they see their classrooms as laboratories for wonder and discovery.
>
> (2018, p. 3)

At this point, you also develop assumptions or hypothesis. Next, you gather evidence and data in relation to your questions. This could include such things as classroom maps, anecdotal records, checklists, time or event sampled observations, student work samples or performance assessments, interviews, or teacher research journals (Rust & Clark, 2007, p. 8). After that, you organize and analyze your data and use the information to improve your practice. Finally, you might consider publishing your research. There are many journals that publish teacher research including *Voices of Practitioners*, a NAEYC journal.

Teacher research encourages teachers to continually view themselves as learners, develop an inquiry stance toward their teaching, to address real classroom problems, and to understand and improve their practice through local knowledge. As teachers engage in teacher research, they begin to understand teaching in profound ways and to contribute to the teaching and learning knowledge base. As both consumers and creators of research in the teacher research process, they begin to understand their own and other's research more deeply. Using interviews, surveys, and questionnaires to examine the impact of teacher research within a community of practice, Rust and Meyers found that after engaging in this process teachers were "more reflective, more critical and more aware, regardless of how many years they have been teaching" (2006, p. 14). Teachers implemented new teaching strategies, improved student achievement, and brought about policy changes through their action research (Rust & Meyers, 2006).

> Early Childhood Education
>
> Implementing action research and reading the studies of other teachers' research sounds like something that might be interesting to my adult learners. They often complain that research articles are not that relevant to everyday practice. But, is teacher research a respected method of research?

One way to determine this is to examine whether the profession endorses action research. Professional organizations such as American Educational Research Association (AERA), National Association of Early Childhood Teacher Educators (NAECTE), and NAEYC have embraced action research providing forums, special interest groups, and research nets. Additionally, several national and international educational journals publish peer-reviewed action research articles. These would seem to support the legitimacy of action research.

However, there are still those who view teacher research with skepticism stating that it lacks scientific rigor (Mertler, 2016). Like all research, teacher research needs to be based on sound practice. As a type of qualitative research, teacher research uses many of the same measures to ensure rigor and trustworthiness. Stringer (2013) defines quality teacher research as being:

Credible—Was the research plausible? Was there integrity in the process? Is the analysis thoughtful? There are many methods used to enhance credibility including repeating the research cycle to see if the results are the same, prolonged engagement, conducting intentional observations over a period of time, using multiple sources of data and information (triangulation), incorporating multiple perspectives including those of all stakeholders, involving participants in reviewing the data and findings, and conducting participant debriefings to discuss participants' emotions (Mertler, 2016; Stringer, 2013).

Transferable—Could the outcomes be used in other programs? Does the researcher provide detailed information about the context, participants, and the methods used?

Dependable—Are the research methods adequately described? Does it appear that a systematic research process has been used? Was each step carefully documented? Confirmable—Is there evidence that the research actually occurred? What artifacts are included? (p. 94).

The term evidence-based practice is permeating early childhood education. In this section, we examined different definitions of evidence-based practice, learned about different sources of evidence, and learned about how to determine if research is trustworthy. However, when examining research, we must also consider the research on how children learn. For example, the research is clear that uncovering children's preconceptions are a critical aspect for learning. In reviewing or creating curriculum, this will be an important consideration. Another impact that affects curriculum are teacher preconceptions or assumptions.

Children and Teacher's Assumptions

Children come to the classroom with assumptions about "school," their role in the classroom, and the appropriate way to interact with other children and adults. Just like preconceptions, it is helpful to uncover and examine these. Like children, teachers also have assumptions. This includes assumptions about the nature of teaching, the roles of the teacher and children, whether learner's abilities are fixed or malleable, what constitutes effective teaching, and what knowledge should be valued (Fives & Buehl, 2016). These assumptions or beliefs shape our expectations for children, the way we allocate time for learning, and our curriculum planning. They also affect our day-to-day and minute-to-minute curricular decisions and interactions. We often form our beliefs based on years of schooling. To effectively teach, especially if we are called upon to try new teaching practices, we must begin by reflecting upon our current beliefs (Fives & Buehl, 2016). While there are many steps in being able to effectively teach, including our skills, knowledge, and the context we are teaching in; our underlying beliefs can help or hinder our adoption of evidence-based practices and our abilities to use effective practices based on the way children learn. What are your underlying beliefs or assumptions?

In Summary

In this chapter, we laid the groundwork for choosing effective teaching strategies and experiences. We examined research on how children learn, information on evidence-based practice, and discussed how our assumptions affect our teaching. In the next chapters, we will use this background information as a lens, as we discuss teaching strategies.

Apply Your Knowledge

1. Choose a research article and use the guidelines for examining research found in this chapter to review it.
2. Browse one of the clearinghouses described in this chapter. What early childhood programs or practices were reviewed? What were the findings?
3. Choose an early childhood practice that you are interested in learning more about. Review the evidence that either lends support to the practice or refutes the practice.
4. Make a list of the assumptions that you have about learning. Each sentence can begin with I believe that … It is helpful to look at categories of beliefs. You might choose categories based upon the section on teacher assumptions.
5. Conduct an observation in a classroom looking for evidence of practices that align with how children learn.
6. Learn more about this topic by completing the modules on evidence-based practice found at the IRIS Center. Think about ways that you can apply what you have learned to your professional life.
7. Increase your knowledge by reading one of the books written by the National Research Council on how children learn. You can find these free on their website. Determine one way that you can apply what you have learned to your current or future classroom.

References

American Psychological Association Zero Tolerance Task Force. (2008). Are zero tolerance policies effective in the schools? An evidentiary review and recommendations. *The American Psychologist, 63*(9), 852-862. doi:10.1037/0003-066X.63.9.852

American Speech-Language-Hearing Association. (2005). *Evidence-based practice in communication disorders* [Position Statement]. Available from www.asha.org/policy

Boccanfuso, C., & Kuhfeld, M. (2011). Multiple responses, promising results: Evidence-based, nonpunitive alternatives to zero tolerance. Research-to-Results Brief. Publication No. 2011-09. *Child Trends*. doi:10.1037/e551982011-002

Bransford, J., Brown, A. L., Cocking, R. R., & National Research Council. (2000). *How people learn: Brain, mind, experience, and school*: Expanded Edition. Washington, DC: National Academy Press.

Bransford, J., Vye, N., Stevens, R., Kuhl, P., Schwartz, D., Bell, P., . . . Sabelli, N. (The LIFE Center). (2006). Learning theories and education: Toward a decade of synergy. In P. Alexander & P. Winne (Eds.), *Handbook of educational psychology* (pp. 209-244). Mahwah, NJ: Lawrence Erlbaum Associates.

Brooks, M. (2009). Drawing, visualisation and young children's exploration of "big ideas". *International Journal of Science Education, 31*(3), 319-341. doi:10.1080/09500690802595771

Bullard, J. A. (1996). *Parent perceptions of the effect of ADHD child behavior on the family: The impact and coping strategies* (Doctoral Dissertation). Retrieved from https://scholarworks.montana.edu/xmlui/bitstream/handle/1/7448/31762102345749.pdf?sequence=1&isAllowed=y

Buysse, V., Wesley, P. W., Snyder, P., & Winton, P. (2006). Evidence-based practice: What does it really mean for the early childhood field? *Young Exceptional Children, 9*(4), 2-11. doi:10.1177/109625060600900401

Clements, D. H., & Sarama, J. (2014). *Learning and teaching early math: The trajectories approach* (2nd ed.). New York: Routledge. doi:10.4324/9780203520574

Ehrlen, K. (2009). Drawings as representations of children's conceptions. *International Journal of Science Education, 31*(1), 41-57. doi:10.1080/09500690701630455

Elementary and Secondary Education Act (ESEA) of 1965 [As Amended Through P.L. 115-224, Enacted July 31, 2018]. Retrieved from https://www.ed.gov/essa

ESSA. (2015). Every Student Succeeds Act of 2015, Pub. L. No. 114-95 § 114 Stat. 1177 (2015-2016). Retrieved from https://www2.ed.gov/documents/essa-act-of-1965.pdf

Fives, H., & Buehl, M. M. (2016). Teachers' beliefs, in the context of policy reform. *Policy Insights from the Behavioral and Brain Sciences, 3*(1), 114-121. doi:10.1177/2372732215623554

Flavell, J. (1979). Metacognition and cognitive monitoring: A new area of cognitive-developmental inquiry. *American Psychologist, 34*, 906-911. doi:10.1037/0003-066X.34.10.906

Fuson, K. C., Kalchman, M., & Bransford, J. D. (2005). Mathematical understanding: An introduction. In M. S. Donovan & J. Bransford (Eds.), *How students learn mathematics in the classroom* (pp. 217-256). Washington, DC: National Research Council.

Henderson, B., Meier, D. R., Perry, G., & Stremmel, A. J. (2012). The nature of teacher research. *Voices of Practitioners*. Retrieved from https://www.naeyc.org/sites/default/files/globally-shared/downloads/PDFs/resources/pubs/Nature%20of%20Teacher%20Research.pdf

Kvernbekk, T. (2011). The concept of evidence in evidence-based practice. *Educational Theory, 61*(5), 515-532. doi:10.1111/j.1741-5446.2011.00418.x

Kvernbekk, T. (2017). Evidence-based educational practice. *Oxford research encyclopedias*. Retrieved from http://oxfordre.com/education/view/10.1093/acrefore/9780190264093.001.0001/acrefore-9780190264093-e-187. doi:10.1093/acrefore/9780190264093.013.187

Li, L., & Tripathy, R. (2017). *Blog: Logic models for curriculum evaluation*. Retrieved from http://www.evaluate.org/blog/tripathy-li-2017-6/

Malaguzzi, L., Rinaldi, C., Forman, G. E., & Gandini, L. (2006). *An amusement park for birds*. Amherst, MA: Performanetics Press.

Masters, G. N. (2018). The role of evidence in teaching and learning. *2009-2018 ACER Research Conferences*. Retrieved from https://research.acer.edu.au/research_conference/RC2018/13august/

McLean, J. E. (1995). *Improving education through action research: A guide for administrators and teachers*. Thousand Oaks, CA. Corwin Press, Inc.

Mertler, C. A. (2016). *Action research: Improving schools and empowering educators*. Thousand Oaks, CA: Sage Publications.

National Association for the Education of Young Children. (2003). *Early childhood curriculum, assessment, and program evaluation: Building an effective, accountable system in programs for children birth through age 8, position statement*. Washington, DC: Author.

National Association for the Education of Young Children. (2009). *NAEYC position statement on developmentally appropriate practice in early childhood programs serving children from birth to age 8*. Washington, DC: Author.

National Research Council. (1999). *How people learn: Bridging research and practice*. Washington, DC: The National Academies Press.

National Research Council. (2005). *How students learn: History, mathematics, and science in the classroom*. Washington, DC: The National Academies Press.

Nelson, J., & Campbell, C. (2017) Evidence-informed practice in education: Meanings and applications. *Educational Research, 59*(2), 127–135. doi:10.1080/00131881.2017.1314115

No Child Left Behind Act of (2001). P.L. 107–110, 20 U.S.C. § 6319 (2002). Retrieved from https://www2.ed.gov/policy/elsec/leg/esea02/index.html

Perry, J., Lundie, D., & Golder, G. (2018). Metacognition in schools: What does the literature suggest about the effectiveness of teaching metacognition in schools? *Educational Review*, 1–18. doi:10.1080/00131911.2018.1441127

Promising Practices Network. (2005). *Direct instruction*. Retrieved from http://www.promisingpractices.net/program.asp?programid=146

Rawl, R. K., & O'Tuel, F. S. (1982). A comparison of three prereading approaches for kindergarten students. *Reading Improvement, 19*(3) 205–211.

Rust, F., & Clark, C. (2007). How to do action research in your classroom. *Lessons from the teacher network leadership institute*. Retrieved from https://www.naeyc.org/sites/default/files/globally-shared/downloads/PDFs/resources/pubs/How%20to%20do%20Action%20Research.pdf

Rust, F., & Meyers, E. (2006). The bright side: Teacher research in the context of educational reform and policy-making. *Teachers and Teaching: Theory and Practice, 12*(1), 69–86. doi:10.1080/13450600500365452

Saçkes, M. (2015). Young children's ideas about earth and space science concepts. In K. C. Trundle & M. Sackes (Eds.), *Research in early childhood science education* (pp. 35–65). Dordrecht: Springer. doi:10.1007/978-94-017-9505-0_3

Sackett, D. L., Straus, S. E., Scott Richardson, W., Rosenberg, W., & Haynes, R. B. (2000). *Evidence-based medicine: How to practice and teach EBM* (2nd ed.). Edinburgh and London: Churchill Livingstone.

Shakman, K., & Rodriguez, S. M. (2015). *Logic models for program design, implementation, and evaluation: Workshop toolkit*. US Department of Education, Institute of Education Sciences, National Center for Education Evaluation and Regional Assistance.

Shenton, A. K. (2004). Strategies for ensuring trustworthiness in qualitative research projects. *Education for Information, 22*(2), 63–75. doi:10.3233/EFI-2004-22201

Smolleck, L., & Hershberger, V. (2011). Playing with science: An investigation of young children's science conceptions and misconceptions. *Current Issues in Education, 14*(1). Retrieved from http://cie.asu.edu/ojs/index.php/cieatasu/article/view/

Stremmel, A. (2018). Posing a researchable question. *Voices of Practitioners, 13*(1), Retrieved from https://naeyc.org/resources/pubs/vop/dec2018/posing-researchable-question

Stringer, E. T. (2013). *Action research*. Los Angeles, CA: Sage Publications.

The Hunt Institute. (2016). Development of the Elementary and Secondary Education Act. Retrieved from http://www.hunt-institute.org/wp-content/uploads/2016/09/Development-of-the-Elementary-and-Secondary-Education-Act-August-2016.pdf

The IRIS Center. (2014). *Evidence-based practices (part 1): Identifying and selecting a practice or program*. Retrieved from https://iris.peabody.vanderbilt.edu/module/ebp_01/

Trundle, K. C., & Saçkes, M. (Eds.). (2015). *Research in early childhood science education*. Springer. doi:10.1007/978-94-017-9505-0

US Department of Education. (2016). *Non-regulatory guidance: Using evidence to strengthen education investments*. Retrieved from https://www2.ed.gov/policy/elsec/leg/essa/guidanceuseseinvestment.pdf

What Works Clearinghouse. (2007). *What works early childhood intervention report: Direct instruction, DISTAR, and language for learning*. Retrieved from https://ies.ed.gov/ncee/wwc/Docs/InterventionReports/WWC_Direct_Instruction_052107.pdf

What Works Clearinghouse. (2014). *WWC evidence review protocol for early childhood education interventions*. Washington, DC: Author.

6 Choosing Effective Learning Contexts

In this chapter, we will be examining the different formats for learning including whole group, small group, learning centers, and routines. As part of this discussion, we will be looking at child engagement. Child engagement is multi-dimensional involving a child's behavior, emotions, and cognition (Fredricks, Blumenfeld, & Paris, 2004). An engaged child is attentive, interested, and enthusiastic compared to the disaffected child who is passive, mentally or emotionally withdrawn, and lacking in attention. As you might expect, multiple studies have found that engagement predicts children's achievement (Skinner, Kindermann, & Furrer, 2009).

Whole Group Activities

Whole group activities or whole class activities are a popular participation structure in early childhood programs. For example, in a study of 705 preschool programs in 11 states children spent 28% of the time in a whole group and 6% in small groups (Early, et al., 2005). In a large study of 214 kindergartens in three states, children spent 43% of their time in whole group activities and only 10% of the time in small groups (Rimm-Kaufman, La Paro, Downer, & Pianta, 2005). By third grade, a large national study indicated that children were spending 53% of their time in whole groups and 39% in individual seatwork (National Institute of Child Health and Human Development Early Child Care Research Network, 2005).

While whole group activities are an important part of the preschool and early elementary participation structure, research demonstrates that preschool and elementary children are less engaged and exhibit more off-task behavior in large groups than when they are in a small group (Godwin, et al., 2016; McWilliam, Scarborough, & Kim, 2003; Rimm-Kaufman, et al., 2005). This may be due to teachers needing to spend more energy and time managing whole groups and the lack of opportunity in whole groups for children to gain attention, contribute, and interact (Rimm-Kaufman, et al., 2005).

There are also more incidents of challenging behaviors in whole group circle time. A study of circle times in Head Start classrooms found challenging behaviors in 30% of all observational intervals. This varied by activity. Roll call had the highest incidents where 64% of the observational intervals involved challenging behaviors. In discussions unrelated to the curriculum, 49% of the intervals involved challenging behaviors. Calendar activities also showed high rates of behavioral issues, with 42% of the intervals showing challenging behaviors (Zaghlawan & Ostrosky, 2011). To counteract off-task and challenging behaviors, teachers need to be very deliberate as they plan whole group activities.

As you plan activities, begin by thinking about whether the whole group format is appropriate. For example, in the study by Zaghlawan and Ostrosky mentioned earlier, the children were most inattentive during roll call (2011). This often involved one child counting the rest of the children. Instead, if the emphasis is on counting, the teachers could implement a routine where children moved their magnetic name tag from the out column to the in column when they enter each day. The child in charge of counting could then count the name tags at a time other than circle. If families bring children to the program, they might be encouraged to count the number of nametags in the column with their child, especially for children who need this skill. Since children are at different skill levels, this task could be varied based upon the child's skills. For example, a child who had mastered counting to 15 or 20 might engage in simple addition and subtraction determining if there were more children present or absent. Or, they might write numerals to record the number of children present or absent. This allows for more targeted learning that meets each child's needs. Once children have mastered the skill of counting successfully to 15 or 20, it is not necessary to continually practice this same skill. As one plans any learning experience it is important to always consider how we meet each individual's needs.

Some activities that lend themselves to a whole group are storytelling, discussions, class meetings, group games, movement, and music activities. Teachers might also use a whole group to introduce new centers, give directions for an activity, demonstrate a new strategy such as making a concept map or to engage in group brainstorming.

Planning a Developmentally Appropriate Length

If you decide that a whole group activity is the best choice, then it is important to plan a whole group time that is a developmentally appropriate length. Research tells us that attention span varies based upon age, gender (girls have a longer attention span), the type of task, and the match between the child's abilities, the child's interests, and the task (Salkind, 2002). The amount of distraction in the environment also affects attention. A study of kindergarten children found that in a classroom with sparsely decorated walls, the children were distracted by the environment in only 3% of the instructional time. However, when walls were highly decorated the children spent 21% of their instructional time distracted by environmental stimuli. Additionally, children's learning was greater in the more sparsely decorated classroom (Fisher, Godwin, & Seltman, 2014). We know that children's ability to sustain attention increases throughout childhood corresponding with brain development (Levin & Bernier, 2011). In the early childhood years, attention spans are still relatively short. A large study that examined off-task behavior of kindergarten to fourth-grade children in 52 classrooms found that children were able to maintain focused attention when the instruction was for ten-minute blocks of instructional activities, but that attention began to waiver after that amount of time. Despite this, they found that the teacher's median duration of time during instructional activities was nearly 13 minutes with 25% of the instruction longer than 17 minutes. The researchers found that children were most distracted when in a whole group, with less distraction during individual and small group activities. In calculating the instructional time, they examined times where children needed to concentrate on one thing. For example, if there was a circle time activity where the teacher first read a story, then children sang a song, and then they engaged in a movement activity, this would be considered three instructional times (Godwin, et al., 2016).

While it is difficult to accurately measure attention in young children (Godwin & Fisher, 2018), you can tell when children begin to be bored by their behaviors. The signs of inattention are often obvious including restlessness, blank stares, and behavioral issues. Since learning requires attention, it is important to plan instruction that takes children's attention span into account.

Setting the Stage for Success

Setting the stage for successful group times begins with well-planned transitions, a way of engaging children's attention, setting up the environment, and planning ahead of time for unsuccessful whole group activities. We will examine each of these in more depth.

- In planning successful whole group activities start with a well-thought-out transition. Sometimes our whole group times fail before we even begin with children being bored and acting out before the activity begins. For example, a whole group circle time often occurs after children clean up the centers. Since children complete clean up at different times, some children are seated in the circle waiting for others to arrive and for the circle time to begin. During this time, you might provide books children can look at, paper and markers so that they can draw, or interactive songs on an iPod that they can act out.
- Whether children are seated in a circle on the floor or at tables and chairs, it is important to begin group time by gaining the children's attention. Some teachers establish a protocol for the start of group time with a specific song, fingerplay, or physical activity that they use for every whole group time. Other teachers vary the way that whole group time is opened. In either case, you will want an activity that results in children becoming focused.
- Set up the environment for success. Begin by ensuring that all the children can clearly see what is occurring in the whole group activity. Provide enough space so children aren't bumping into their peers. Some teachers provide designated space such as carpet squares for each child. Also, remove distractions. As we read earlier, visual distractions affect attention. For example, if you are meeting in the block area, you might cover the blocks with a cloth during your circle time activity. Environmental supports will be determined by the needs of the children in your group. For example, providing fidget toys such as squeeze balls, Koosh balls, and sensory bracelets can assist children with high activity levels. Marice made sensory sticks for circle time by wrapping popsicle sticks with different sensory materials such as fur, fleece, sandpaper, pom-poms, ribbon, and felt. Children could choose their choice of a sensory stick to rub during whole group time. Special seats such as wobble seats can also be helpful.
- Plan for alternative activities if the activity planned is not successful. For example, Josephine has a basket that is beside the circle time area containing puppets and high-interest books that she can use for these situations. Songs, fingerplays, and movement activities can also be used at these times.

Planning Interactive and Engaging Whole Group Activities

As might be expected, children's attention spans are longer when they receive more stimulation (Levin & Bernier, 2011). One way that we provide more stimulation is to make the whole group activity interactive and engaging. We will examine ways to increase engagement while reading or telling a story, teaching a concept, or leading a discussion.

When reading or telling a story you can make the activity more engaging if you:

- use props such as puppets, a story time apron, or a flannel board. You can also use props related to the story such as a large pot and plastic vegetables for the story *Stone Soup* (Forest & Gaber, 2009).
- are expressive, varying your voice volume, pitch, and accents.

- involve the children by asking prediction questions, having children supply missing words as you read, or asking clarification questions. While this promotes literacy and cognitive skills, a study of Head Start children during story time also found that asking questions helped children to sustain attention (Gianvecchio & French, 2002).

- encourage group responses when asking questions. One effective technique is to use response cards. Response cards can be a write-on card or a pre-printed card. A mega-analysis examining studies of learners of all ages, with and without disabilities, found that response cards increased learning and participation, decreased off-task behavior, and was superior to hand raising (Randolph, 2007). Pre-printed cards can have pictures or words. They can be as simple as yes or no or can be more complex. For example, if emphasizing social-emotional learning you might have faces with different emotions. Children hold up different cards to the question about how the character is feeling. You might also have strategy cards such as those found in the solution kit at the Center on the Social and Emotional Foundations for Early Learning website. Children hold up a strategy that they think would be effective for the character.

- have the children act out the story or parts of the story. You might also have children go beyond what is in the book, to create what is termed as a subtext. Children step inside the story to take on the role of a character in the book answering questions about what the character is thinking. In explaining this method, Jean Ann Clyde (2003) describes a teacher who uses the book *Freedom Summer* (Wiles, 2001) with a group of six-year-old children. This is a story about two close friends, one white (Joe) and one black (John Henry), that takes place during the civil rights movement. Due to legislation, the public pool must now be integrated and the friends are delighted. But when they go to the swimming pool, they find it is being filled in with asphalt. To add to the indignity, one of the men who is doing this is John Henry's brother, Will Rogers. Although the book does not provide information on Will Roger's feelings, the children who are stepping into this character are asked, "Will Rogers, what are you thinking?" The first graders give insightful answers expressing Will Roger's frustration, anger, and sadness with the pool being filled but also recognize that Will Rogers needs the job and must obey his boss. Jean Ann Clyde states that there are many benefits to this method including "clear, personal connections to text; enhanced ability to make inferences; and sophisticated understanding of multiple perspectives." She further states that "interpretation, the most difficult aspect of reading comprehension, occurs almost naturally and is enhanced by students' thoughtful 'reading' of the illustrations and insights into the character" (2003, p. 158).

- be cautious about disciplinary interruptions since research shows that this decreases the children's sustained attention (Gianvecchio & French, 2002). Instead, you might draw children's attention back through questions or comments about the book or if you have an assistant, they might oversee children who are having difficulty during the story time. Giving children choices of whether to attend the circle, especially younger children, is also an option. When children don't attend the circle, they are often engaged in an alternative literacy activity such as looking at books in the book area or writing in their journal. I learned an important lesson as a Head Start teacher when I insisted that all children attend the circle time activity. One of the girls, we'll call her Cindy, would come to the circle, but she would bow her head and arrange her hair so that it totally covered her face. When I understood that being in a large group was traumatic for her, I quit insisting that children attend. Instead, I made circle time very engaging, so children wanted to come. For example, we often started with a rhythm band. All the children chose to participate, except Anne. However, Anne would sit a distance away and would observe and listen. Eventually, Anne chose to join the group, but it took several months. My ultimate goal was that children would love musical activities and reading, two focuses of the group time. I realized by forcing children to participate if they weren't ready or perhaps interested, I might be having a long-term impact on their love of books and musical experiences.

These strategies not only affect children's engagement but also increase learning. A mega-analysis of 16 studies and 466 children examining repeated book reading found that encouraging child participation by using props (0.66), asking open-ended questions (0.60), responding positively to children's comments (0.80), and providing explanations in response to children's comments (0.68) had a medium to large effect on children's learning. The average effect sizes are in parenthesis (Trivette, Simkus, Dunst, & Hamby, 2012).

When teaching concepts:

- provide a model. For example, if you are discussing shapes provide three-dimensional models of the shape as you discuss their attributes.
- provide manipulatives for each of the children. In a study by DiCarlo, Pierce, Baumgartner, Harris, and Ota (2012) this was found to be one of the top ways to engage children. For example, if you are discussing shapes you might provide each child with pipe cleaners or wiki sticks so that they can create their own shape as you are discussing them.
- use hand signals to determine if children are understanding. One finger, I did not get it. Two fingers, I think I got it. Three fingers, I got it. Four fingers, I got it and can explain it to someone else. This can give you feedback that you can immediately use in determining the next instructional steps. Additionally, as children reflect on their understanding, it increases their metacognition (Nagro, Hooks, Fraser, & Cornelius, 2018).

In group discussions, you might try the following techniques to engage the children.

- Use a technique such as Whip Around, where each child gets a chance to talk and also a chance to pass if they choose.
- Use Think, Pair, Share where children think through their response, pair with another child, and share information.
- Take a poll, this can be quickly done with a thumbs up or down or with paddles with yes on one side and no on the other.
- Provide think time before children answer a question.
- Provide a parking lot for questions or concerns that arise during group time that can't be addressed immediately.

Promoting Learning during Whole Group Times

While it is important that whole group times are designed appropriately and are engaging, it is also crucial to examine what children are learning in the whole group activity. What is the purpose of the whole group time? Is it to build community, provide information, to introduce new materials and spark interest in them, to teach routines, to problem solve dilemmas that are occurring in the classroom, or is it to increase specific social-emotional or academic skills?

After we determine the purpose of our whole group time, we must determine the best ways that we accomplish the purpose. For example, teachers often use ritualized practices that they have inherited such as roll call or calendar activities. As described earlier, both of these activities tend to be non-engaging to children and times when children are off-task (Zaghlawan & Ostrosky, 2011). However, if asked, teachers would state that these practices are a way of building math skills. We've already examined roll call. What about calendar activities? Is this the best way to build math skills? Early childhood experts emphasize that calendar concepts are abstract and that children are not developmentally ready for these concepts. They call for an end to this practice for young children (Beneke, Ostrosky, & Katz, 2008; Ethridge & King, 2005; Freeman & Swim, 2009). Often even at the end of the year, you will find children who are guessing at the days of the week and the months. It is also important to think, "Are these the most important concepts for children to learn?" "Is this content worth spending 180 days learning?" Instead, you might engage the children in "math talks." This could include such things as providing a group of objects and having children brainstorm all the ways that they might classify the objects, exploring a new material that will be added to the math center, reviewing and discussing a graph that had been created of bugs seen on a field trip, playing a game "guess the pattern," or teaching a mini-lesson such as modeling how to measure, stressing that when we measure we must align the measuring tool with the object being measured. These rich experiences provide variety and can assist children in gaining competencies called for in math standards. Throughout the book, we will be examining ways to enhance learning based on research. It is important that we use this type of information in planning whole group time.

In summary, attention is essential for learning. We know that during whole group time children are less attentive than when in small groups or when engaged in individual activities. However, teachers can increase the length of time children attend by planning whole group times that are an appropriate length and that are engaging. Effective whole group activities are also aided by well-planned transitions, gaining children's attention at the beginning of whole group, ensuring all children are comfortable and can see, and planning alternative activities for individual children and for unsuccessful group times. Finally, it is important that activities for whole group are chosen wisely to promote learning.

Small Group Activities

As we learned earlier, children are more engaged and less off-task when they are in small groups versus large groups (Godwin, et al., 2016; McWilliam, Scarborough, & Kim, 2003; Rimm-Kaufman et al., 2005). However, small groups are underutilized in early childhood programs. Additionally, they are often implemented ineffectively (Wasik, 2008). In this section, we will examine the value and challenges of small group learning and discuss how to make a small group effective.

Studies of toddlers, preschoolers, and elementary age children demonstrate the advantage of small groups. For example, when toddlers are in small groups versus large groups the amount that children talk is doubled (Phillips & Twardosz, 2003). A study of 63 Pre-K classrooms found that children's early literacy skills were greater when the teacher used more small group formats rather than whole group (Bratsch-Hines, Burchinal, Peisner-Feinberg, & Franco, 2019). Studies with elementary age children find that small groups increase achievement related to high levels of cognitive functioning. However, achievement on low levels of cognitive functioning was not affected by whether children learned in small or large groups (Sharan, Ackerman, & Hertz-Lazarowitz, 1979).

In comparison to whole groups, well-planned small groups allow children to be more engaged with the teacher, expand prospects to learn from their peers, and provide enhanced opportunities to contribute. Small groups allow teachers opportunities to scaffold learning and be more responsive to children than when facilitating whole groups. This includes assessing children's understanding and providing immediate individualized, targeted feedback. However, to experience these benefits teachers must structure the activity to take advantage of these opportunities to interact.

Small groups can be used for a variety of different types of activities. For example, teachers might create an engineering challenge where children are working in groups to try to figure out a way to make a bridge ten inches long that will hold a matchbox car. Children might also be engaged in book clubs, writing circles, cooking activities, math activities, discussions, or project work. Groups might be more teacher-directed such as the teacher reading a story or leading a math activity, or the group might be more child-directed as children create a car from a refrigerator box when engaged in a project.

> You haven't mentioned outdoor time. We use small groups outdoors as well, especially as we work on projects.

Tony makes a good point. Children not only learn during inside time but also as they participate in the outdoor environment. As children engage in learning zones established in the outdoor environment, they often interact in child-initiated individual and small group learning. At times, the teacher might also plan small group activities that pertain to a project. For example, small groups might visit their adopted tree throughout the year examining changes and collecting data. During a bug project, the teacher might help children to find insects, identify them, and chart where they are located. A garden project might entail children working in small groups to take soil samples, determine what nutrients the soil needs, plant, and care for their garden.

Planning Effective Small Group Activities

When planning small group activities, keep the following points in mind.

- Determine the size of the group based on the learning goal. However, research demonstrates that the group should not generally exceed three to four children (Lou, Abrami, Spence, Poulsen, Chambers, & d'Apollonia, 1996).
- Be thoughtful and deliberate about forming groups. For example, the teacher might consider children's strengths, their interests, and their abilities in working with other children in the class. It is generally better to have heterogeneous grouping where children with different ability levels are mixed within groups (Marzano, Pickering, & Pollock, 2001). However, there may be times where you establish a group that all need to learn a specific skill.
- Have clear goals for the group work. What is the purpose? What will the group accomplish? How will you and the children know if the group work is successful? Some teachers create simple rubrics that children complete not only on their product but also on how well the group worked and how well they worked within the group.

- Provide an opportunity for children to learn the routines associated with group work. We will be discussing effective thinking routines in Chapter 8.
- Provide the needed structure for the activity. For example, for the engineering challenge, the teacher might set up a process for the group to follow. This could include first listening to each child's ideas, then choosing one idea to test, testing the idea, etc.
- Start slowly with short time periods especially when introducing child-led groups.

> **What are the other children doing while the teacher is working with only some of the children?**
>
> While in some Pre-K classrooms there may be enough teachers and assistants to have a teacher in each group, this is not common in elementary schools. While teachers work with a small group, the other children engage in related activities on an individual or small group basis. For example, Kissel and Miller (2015) describe a writer's workshop process used with Pre-K children. The children begin with a short whole group experience where they gather together to hear a story, see a writing demonstration, engage in a discussion, or participate in a related experience. They then spent 15 minutes writing and conferring. The teacher confers with a small group offering encouragement, making suggestions, and honoring the children's work. Children that aren't involved in the conference engage in writing, choosing what to write, where to write, and whom to write with. At the end of the workshop, two or three children share their writing with the large group.
>
> In other classrooms, all the children are working in small groups and the teacher is rotating between groups. For example, in a second-grade class, children meet twice a week for 30 minutes to discuss a book. The teacher begins the book clubs by introducing three or four different books to the children. During this time, she gives a brief description and generates excitement about the different books. The children then choose a book they would like to read. The teacher then arranges children into groups based upon their preferences. The children read the book independently during silent sustained reading time. The teacher provides prompts for the children to use as they are reading their books, which become the focus of the book club discussion. For example, one prompt might be, "What in the book reminds you of something in your life?" Depending upon the prompt, children might prepare for their book club by taking notes, writing in their journal, or using sticky notes to mark pages. The teacher has taught the children a book share protocol. Jointly established ground rules, facilitation tasks, and protocols for the book club help to ensure that the book club runs smoothly. For example, for each small group, children choose a facilitator to facilitate the protocol and a taskmaster to ensure the group stays focused. As the children participate in the book clubs, the teacher rotates, joining in on one or more group's discussions (Candler, n.d.).

Small group learning has many advantages but is an underutilized learning context in early childhood. To take advantage of the benefits of small groups, the teacher needs to allow for increased interaction possibilities. Small groups can be teacher-led or child-led. If child-led, the teacher needs to provide a structure that will help the group to be successful. This can include providing a protocol, ground rules, and facilitation tasks.

Learning Centers

A learning center is a "self-contained area with a variety of hands-on materials organized around a curriculum area or topic" (Bullard, 2017, p. 97). Teachers might also refer to these as learning stations, studios, interest centers, workstations, or activity areas. Learning centers will vary based upon the age of the child but will typically include an art studio (art, music, dance), science lab, dramatic play, literacy center (reading, writing, listening), math and manipulative, building and construction, and alone/retreat space. See Table 6.1 for an example of how learning centers change from Pre-K through second grade. Note that in this example from the Boston Public Schools, what the centers are called change, from learning centers to studios. Additionally, the type of learning centers that are offered to children change, as does the time allocated for centers.

While interacting in centers children have the choice of where they participate and with whom. Since learning centers provide a range of materials, children can choose materials of interest that are also developmentally challenging. Because children have choices, well-designed centers are highly motivating. Learning centers provide children the opportunity to learn academic skills through hands-on, inquiry-based learning in a real-life context. Further, children practice social and self-regulation skills as they engage in centers.

Although it is beyond the scope of this book to deeply examine the learning that takes place in every center in the early childhood classroom, we will discuss one center as an example, the block and building center. Blocks have a rich tradition in early childhood programs, having been included in programs for over a century (Trawick-Smith Swaminathan, & Liu, 2016). The block center might have different titles and different materials, depending upon the children's age. A toddler program will typically have a block area that contains such things as unit blocks, large foam or cardboard blocks, Duplos, and accessories. Preschool and kindergarten classrooms might call this center a building and construction center. This area will still contain unit blocks but might also contain other building materials such as tree blocks, architectural blocks, KEVA planks, and more advanced and smaller accessories. In elementary schools, the center might be called a maker space, engineering space, or tinker area. Regardless of title or age, this area involves creating two- and three-dimensional objects.

In this area, children create and build. As they do so, they learn and apply their knowledge and skills in math, science, and engineering. Additionally, as they interact with others, they have a real-life opportunity to practice social-emotional, language, and literacy skills. Finally, this area allows children to engage in motor skills and aesthetic awareness (Bullard, 2017).

Table 6.1 Boston Public School's Centers and Studios

	Pre-K Centers	Kindergarten Centers	First-Grade Studios	Second-Grade Studios
Centers and studios	Art Studio Block Area Dramatization Library/Listening Discovery Table Writing/Drawing Math Puzzles/Manipulatives	Art Studio Block Area Dramatization Library/Listening STEM Center Writing/Drawing	Art Dramatization Building Writing/Drawing Library/Listening	Art Building Discovery Research Writing and Storytelling
Time spent in centers	60 minutes daily	60 minutes daily	150 minutes a week	90 minutes a week

Information from the Boston Public School Department of Early Childhood (n.d.).

Several studies have found links between block building and mathematical skills. One of the interesting studies was a longitudinal research study that examined the complexity of children's block building in preschool with later math outcomes. Although the researchers didn't find a relationship in the first years of schooling, they found a significant relationship between this early building success and later math abilities especially in geometry. Children who were more proficient builders took more math classes and these classes were more likely to be honor courses. They received higher standardized math test scores and had better math grades in middle and high school than children who showed less proficiency in building. This correlation held true even when considering gender, social class, and intelligence (Wolfgang, Stannard, & Jones, 2001). Short-term studies also link block building with mathematical learning. For example, Trawick-Smith, Swaminathan, Baton, Danieluk, Marsh, and Szarwacki (2017) found that children who created more complex block structures had higher achievement test scores. In examining what influenced children's posttest math scores, researchers found that 81% was related to the child's demographics and their pretest score. However, 13% was related to block play. Given that these children participated in many other math activities, this is especially surprising. Block play complexity was significantly related to social participation. Why is this? As children work together, they need to create a shared understanding resulting in a high use of spatial language and "math talk" (Trawick-Smith & Savalli, 2013) and the frequency of math talk has been found to be a predictor of early math learning (Trawick-Smith et al., 2016).

There is also a strong relationship between spatial skills and mathematics (Casey & Bobb, 2003).

For example, researchers examined first-grade girls' spatial skills. They found that the spatial skills were a predictor of children's fifth-grade geometry, measurement, number, and algebra skills (Casey, Pezaris, Fineman, Pollock, Demers, & Dearing, 2015). Two important spatial skills that are linked to block building are spatial visualization and mental rotation (Casey, Andrews, Schindler, Kersh, Samper, & Copley, 2008). However, for children to effectively mentally complete these tasks, they need hands-on opportunities for exploration. Research shows that when children have the opportunity to actually manipulate objects, their ability to mentally manipulate the objects improves (Frick & Wang, 2014; Möhring & Frick, 2013). This is true for the infants in these studies and also for older children. A large national study of four to seven-year-old children found that children who played more with spatial toys such as blocks had higher scores on spatial skills assessments (Jirout & Newcombe, 2015). Why do spatial skills matter? We use spatial skills in our everyday functioning such as navigating our environment. Additionally, over 50 years of research has shown that spatial thinking is critical for student's success in STEM subjects and for later careers in STEM fields (Gagnier & Fisher, 2017). Spatial skills are also important in geography and in visual and performing arts.

In addition to gaining mathematical and spatial skills, as children build with blocks and other materials, they gain knowledge and skills in science. This includes experimenting with the properties of materials, stability, balance, force, and motion. They learn about simple machines as they create ramps and use pulleys, wheels, and axles.

Children also learn process skills in the block area. National and state science and math standards not only emphasize content skills but also process skills. These skills such as questioning, problem-solving, analyzing, reasoning, communicating, investigating, and using representation are very apparent in the building center (Chalufour, Hoisington, Moriarty, Winokur, & Worth, 2004). Children also engage with engineering thinking and design as they build. Bagiati and Evangelou who conducted extensive observations of three to five-year-old children during block play found that they approached building in a similar way as engineers. As young children create with blocks, they follow an engineering design process of identifying needs and problems, setting goals, testing solutions, collaborating with each other, and borrowing each other's ideas (2016, p. 83).

Literacy is also increased in the building center. A longitudinal study that followed children from preschool to age eight found that a higher level of representation in block constructions was linked to higher reading skills. This was true for children with and without disabilities (Hanline, Milton, & Phelps, 2010). Why might this be the case? Reading involves using a symbol system where a letter or word represents something else. It also involves visual discrimination such as being able to distinguish between similar looking letters such as b and d. Both symbolism and visual discrimination are also part of block building. Additionally, construction is a very social activity involving complex language (Cohen & Uhry, 2007; Sluss & Stremmel, 2004). In fact, Trawick-Smith and associates found that children engaged in more social interactions in the block area than when using any other play material (2017). Also, literacy is enhanced when teachers add literacy materials to the construction area giving children opportunities to engage in these activities as they build. For example, teachers might add books on construction and architecture, paper and drawing implements for creating plans and documenting buildings, and signs for saving structures.

When planning for children's learning, many teachers immediately think of small and whole group activities that are teacher-led. However, as you've learned through examining the block center, children gain many skills through play in a rich environment. For example, research demonstrates that children who build with blocks have statistically increased mathematics, spatial, and reading scores. As you plan your unit, providing learning opportunities using centers is a highly engaging, research-based way for children to learn.

> How does the teacher ensure that children are learning if they are each making their own choices?

There are several ways that the teacher affects the children's learning in classroom centers. First, the teacher is the environmental designer determining what is placed in the center and how the center is arranged. Both the materials available and the arrangement of space affect learning. The teacher also facilitates learning before, during, and after children use centers. For example, in the Boston Early Childhood programs, center time begins with introducing centers, providing experiences that will provide background. For example, to enhance the learning in the block area teachers might invite a carpenter and architect to visit, read books such as *The three little pigs: An architectural tale* (Guarnaccia, 2010) to the children, and introduce block challenges and provocations. Challenges are most effective when introduced as part of a story. For example, as part of a story about a king and queen who need to get into their castle, children are asked to help by building a bridge with steps or a ramp to get onto the bridge (Casey et al., 2008).

During center time, the teacher acknowledges the work children are creating in the center by taking photos and videos and by having them share their work with the class. Teachers might interact with children as they use the centers, scaffolding their learning by asking open-ended questions and through providing vocabulary and information. For example, the use of spatial language by adults has been found to increase the amount of spatial language used by children. This, in turn, is linked to better performance on spatial problem-solving (Pruden, Levine, & Huttenlocher, 2011). However, it is important that interactions are a "good fit" with what the child needs. It is important to not interrupt children's play or thinking by asking irrelevant questions (Trawick-Smith & Dziurgot, 2011). For example, quizzing the child on the shape of the block or color of the block can be distracting.

At the conclusion of center time, teachers might do like the teachers in the Boston Public Schools and have a specific time for thinking and reflecting. For example, focusing on the block area, one or more children might share their building, describe what they have created, the challenges they faced, and their future plans. The class might also go on a "walkabout" where children examine each other's structures. Children might also reflect on what they have built, create sketches of their building, and write or draw future plans.

Designing Effective Learning Centers

When designing centers:

- create an enclosure around individual centers. Rather than having shelving placed on the walls, you can place the shelving to create small spaces for each learning center. This helps to keep materials in the correct area, allows children to engage in smaller groups, and assists children to stay focused.
- make sure that children can easily access the materials that they need and that they know where to return materials when they have finished using them. For example, labels might be put on shelves and baskets so that materials are returned to the proper place.
- provide an abundance of interesting, interactive materials. You will want these materials to be either open-ended (material that can be used in multiple ways) or if closed-ended (material designed to be used in a certain way such as puzzles) you will want to ensure that you have materials for a range of developmental levels. There should be enough materials that each child has a range of choices. You will want duplicates of popular materials, especially for toddlers since they often have difficulty sharing. You will also want duplicate materials that enhance cooperative play such as telephones and baby buggies.
- have enough materials to allow children to deeply engage in learning. For example, in the block area, it is recommended that you have at least 100 blocks for each preschool child and 200 blocks for each kindergartner or elementary age child that will be using the blocks at any given time (Phelps, 2012). While this may seem excessive, children's complex block structures often use 50-100 blocks. Remember, it is the complexity of block structures that is linked to higher math achievement.
- provide enough time for centers. The book, *Developmentally Appropriate Practices for Children Birth to Age 8* recommends that center time be at least one hour (Copple & Bredekamp, 2009, p. 153). It takes time to engage in deep learning such as building complex block structures or developing and enacting complex dramatic play episodes. When we only give children short periods of time, we limit their ability to engage in deep learning.

You will want your room design to be functional, but also homelike and aesthetic. Natural materials can add to the ambiance of the room and can provide an inexpensive alternative to purchased materials. For example, instead of plastic teddy bear counters, children might sort different types of pinecones. In addition to a richer classification experience, children can also learn about their natural environment. Your room should be a place that is enjoyable and comfortable for both you and the children. This includes using materials from the children's cultures such as lamps, rugs, baskets, toys, musical instruments, music and dramatic play props and materials.

The learning center context allows children to gain academic skills in a highly motivating context, provides for differentiation, and is an ideal format for practicing self-regulation, social-emotional, and language skills. Teachers enhance this learning through the environmental design and their facilitation of learning before, during, and after center time.

Early Childhood Education

Are there advantages to using centers with adults? If so, would you use children's centers or centers especially designed for adult learners?

I have been using adult learning centers in college coursework and in workshops for many years. These are typically designed specifically for adults. When designing centers for adults, I will typically have five or six centers with multiple activities at each center. All the materials needed are also at the center. Centers will also have task cards that will allow adults to know their options. For example, when teaching a multi-day workshop on outdoor environments the goal was that by the end of the workshop participants would leave with a plan for a well-designed outdoor play space that was safe, healthy, and engaging for young children.

In addition to tours of playgrounds, mini-lectures, power points of many different playgrounds to use as examples and to critique, and small and large group discussion, I also included adult learning centers. These included:

- problem-solving issues—This center contained written scenarios of common playground issues. On the back side of the scenarios were some of my solutions to these issues. Participants were also encouraged to write their own issues on large sheets of paper and to post it so that others in the group could add solutions. For example, one participant wrote that they were a director and they often found that staff grouped together and visited during outdoor time rather than engaging with the children. Participants provided many ideas for solving this issue.
- gaining insights and ideas through videos, websites, and a Pinterest site on outdoor environments that I had created. This center contained several computers. Each computer had a page of links that led to a wealth of outdoor environments to look at and to critique. Participants were encouraged to critique centers, create lists of ideas to incorporate into their design, or to create a Pinterest site as a way of saving their ideas.
- gaining insights and ideas through books. This center had 25 books of outdoor environments that participants could review for ideas. Some suggested activities at this center were to find ideas for their plan, make lists of inexpensive ideas that they

could incorporate, make lists of loose parts, or make a wish list of ideas to incorporate at a later time. Several participants took pictures of book covers with the plan to purchase them.

- exploring playground regulations and safety. This center contained short videos on playground safety, the Playground Report Card to review with discussion questions, an investigation activity (Is it safe to use rubber mulch on playgrounds?), a scenario (The climbing rock: What do the regulations say?) with state and national regulations to help determine the answer, and an answer your own safety question using *The Handbook for Public Playground Safety* from the U.S. Consumer Product Safety Commission.

- designing your own outdoor physical play space or developing a playground process or procedure. This center contained many examples of playground processes and procedures, two-dimensional and three-dimensional materials for creating models of play spaces, and a computer and design software.

As participants used the centers, I interacted with individuals and small groups providing information, reviewing their design plans, providing suggestions for resources that would be helpful, and brainstorming issues with them. As is often the case when I use adult learning centers, the participants become excited about all the options and several stayed during lunch hours and after the end of the workshop to continue to explore.

Adults experience the same advantages as children when engaging in learning centers. When using adult learning centers, learners can determine what activities to engage in, for how long, and whether to work independently or with others. If the centers are well designed, learners can work on areas of interest that meet their current level of understanding, learning styles, and current needs. When we use learning centers as adult educators, we are modeling trusting the learner, relinquishing control, and meeting the needs of individual learners. To see more examples of adult learning centers, read the article *Practicing what we teach: Developing appropriate practices for early childhood preservice teachers* (Maloney & Bullard, 1997).

Daily Routines

As teachers, we often bemoan the lack of time we have with the children to complete all the activities and to accomplish all the goals that we have set. What if we could find more time? One place to look for more time is by examining how we are planning for and implementing routines. A large, multi-state study of Pre-K programs found that routines consumed 34% of the day and that during 88% of this time there were no social-emotional or academic learning occurring. Routines in these studies included mealtime, transitions, cleaning up, and personal care (Early, et al., 2010). A multi-state study of kindergarten found similar results, 39% of the time children were non-engaged in any instructional activity. Most of this time was spent in routines such as transitions. Instructional activities were defined very broadly to include such things as visiting about non-school activities. The authors pointed out that activities such as saying a poem while waiting would classify the time as instructional. However, few teachers used this time wisely

(Paro et al., 2009). Reducing the amount of time spent in routines and using routine times as opportunities for learning could significantly increase instructional time. How do we do this? Let's look at one classroom as an example.

Imani, a Pre-K teacher, began by closely observing the daily routines in her classroom. She wondered, "Was there a way to make them more efficient?" "Was there a way to provide more learning during routine times?" She was shocked to discover that she had 15 transitions during the Pre-K day. However, this is not unusual, multi-state research shows that children spend 22% of their time in transitions (Early et al., 2005). As Imani studied her schedule and visited with her assistant and other teachers in the building, she discovered several ideas for reducing transitions. For example, she had a special period of time where children participated in an art activity of their choice. Instead, she could incorporate this time and activity into her center time. This would eliminate two transitions. Each morning, the program served breakfast in their classrooms. However, many of the children had already eaten and were restless as they sat at the breakfast tables. Imani found that some of the teachers had breakfast available during center time. She decided to try this out. Again, this extended the time available for centers, while eliminating two transitions.

However, some transitions were necessary but time-consuming and difficult. The program met in an old elementary school with bathrooms down the hall. This necessitated having the children go as a group to the bathroom and for the child to wait for their turn to use the bathrooms. Since they had to be quiet, they couldn't sing songs or visit. Imani had wanted to incorporate some time each day for journaling. She decided to try having the children journal during this time. They could sit in the hallway next to the lockers as they waited.

Another long transition occurred as children cleaned up the centers and then went to the circle area where they waited until everyone was finished. Children would become restless as they waited and behavioral issues would surface. Imani had just started a new unit on insects and had checked out many books from the library on this subject. She displayed the books in the circle time area with their covers showing and invited children to look at the new books as they waited. This reduced behavioral issues and also contributed to children's interest in insects and to their learning. After Imani made these changes, her classroom ran more smoothly. She had freed up time for learning and children were more engaged.

With school mandates for how time is spent, it is sometimes difficult to incorporate all the unit activities you would like into the school day. As you plan your unit, think creatively about how activities can be incorporated into routine times.

In Summary

In this chapter, we have examined different types of learning contexts that are used in early childhood classrooms. As you plan your unit, the type of activity and the goals for the activity will help dictate whether a small group, whole group, or learning center is the most appropriate context. Further, taking advantage of routine times can increase instructional time. The younger the child, the more individualized their care needs to be. However, by the time children reach preschool age an approach that includes small group, whole group, and centers is important. Farran, who reviewed research on learning contexts for Pre-K programs concluded that a balanced approach is the most effective (2017). Based on the studies discussed in this chapter, it appears that this is true for early elementary school, as well.

Apply Your Knowledge

1. Jenny is an adult educator who is conducting a workshop on infant-toddler development for teachers. Her enduring understanding is that "A young child's development is affected by internal processes and also by opportunities within the environment." Her essential question is, "How can early learning environments support a child's development?" Her assessment focuses on knowledge of research, socio-emotional environments that support development, and physical environments that support development. Brainstorm some adult learning centers that Jenny might set up to enhance participants learning? What materials should be placed in the centers?

2. Stephanie, an early childhood student is required to conduct a backward design unit for a curriculum course. However, the lead teacher in a second-grade classroom is reluctant to have Stephanie use any small group or whole group time. The class is studying habitats and so Stephanie is planning a unit on animal habitats that will supplement the teacher's unit. Her essential questions are "How do habitats affect animals? How do animals affect habitats?" She has designed a summative assessment based upon a scenario of a well-described animal being introduced into a new environment. How might Stephanie prepare children for this assessment using the classroom learning centers, outdoor time, and routine times?

3. Observe the routines in a classroom. Brainstorm ways that learning could be enhanced during these times.

4. Observe a whole group activity. What strategies does the teacher use to keep the children engaged?

References

Bagiati, A., & Evangelou, D. (2016). Practicing engineering while building with blocks: Identifying engineering thinking. *European Early Childhood Education Research Journal, 24*(1), 67-85. doi:10.1080/1350293X.2015.1120521

Beneke, S. J., Ostrosky, M. M., & Katz, L. G. (2008). Good intentions gone awry. *Young Children, 63*(3), 12-16.

Boston Public Schools Department of Early Childhood. (n.d.). *Curricula*. Retrieved May 7, 2019, from https://www.bpsearlylearning.org/our-curricula

Bratsch-Hines, M., Burchinal, M., Peisner-Feinberg, E., & Franco, X. (2019). Frequency of instructional practices in rural prekindergarten classrooms and associations with child language and literacy skills. *Early Childhood Research Quarterly, 47*, 74-88. doi:10.1016/j.ecresq.2018.10.001

Bullard, J. (2017). *Creating environments for learning: Birth to age eight* (3rd ed.). Upper Saddle River, NJ: Pearson.

Candler, L. (n.d.). *Literature circles made easy: Classroom book clubs*. Retrieved April 23, 2018, from https://www.lauracandler.com/book-clubs/

Casey, B. M., Andrews, N., Schindler, H., Kersh, J. E., Samper, A., & Copley, J. (2008). The development of spatial skills through interventions involving block building activities. *Cognition and Instruction, 26*(3), 269-309. doi:10.1080/07370000802177177

Casey, B., & Bobb, B. (2003). The power of block building. *Teaching Children Mathematics, 10*(2), 98-102. Reston, VA: National Council of Teachers of Mathematics.

Casey, B. M., Pezaris, E., Fineman, B., Pollock, A., Demers, L., & Dearing, E. (2015). A longitudinal analysis of early spatial skills compared to arithmetic and verbal skills as predictors of fifth-grade girls' math reasoning. *Learning and Individual Differences, 40*, 90-100. doi:10.1016/j.lindif.2015.03.028

Chalufour, I., Hoisington, C., Moriarty, R., Winokur, J., & Worth, K. (2004). The science and mathematics of building structures. *Science and Children, 41*(4), 30-34.

Clyde, J. A. (2003). Stepping inside the story world: The subtext strategy: A tool for connecting and comprehending. *The Reading Teacher, 57*(2), 150-160.

Cohen, L., & Uhry, J. (2007). Young children's discourse strategies during block play: A Bakhtinian approach. *Journal of Research in Childhood Education, 21*(3), 302-315. doi:10.1080/02568540709594596

Copple, C., & Bredekamp, S. (2009). *Developmentally appropriate practice in early childhood programs serving children from birth to age 8.* Washington, DC: National Association for the Education of Young Children.

DiCarlo, C. F., Pierce, S. H., Baumgartner, J., Harris, M. E., & Ota, C. (2012). Whole-group instruction practices and children's attention: A preliminary report. *Journal of Research in Childhood Education, 26*(2), 154–168. doi:10.1080/02568543.2012.657744

Early, D., Barbarin, O., Bryant, D., Burchinal, M., Chang, F., Clifford, R., ... & Barnett, W. S. (2005). *Pre-kindergarten in eleven states: NCEDL's multi-state study of pre-kindergarten & study of state-wide early education programs (SWEEP).* Retrieved from http://fpg.unc.edu/node/4654

Early, D. M., Iruka, I. U., Ritchie, S., Barbarin, O. A., Winn, D. M. C., Crawford, G. M., ... & Bryant, D. M. (2010). How do pre-kindergarteners spend their time? Gender, ethnicity, and income as predictors of experiences in pre-kindergarten classrooms. *Early Childhood Research Quarterly, 25*(2), 177–193. doi:10.1016/j.ecresq.2009.10.003

Ethridge, E. A., & King, J. R. (2005). Calendar math in preschool and primary classrooms: Questioning the curriculum. *Early Childhood Education Journal, 32*(5), 291–296. doi:10.1007/s10643-005-4398-0

Farran, D. C. (2017). Characteristics of pre-kindergarten programs that drive positive outcomes. In D. A. Phillips, M. W. Lipsey, K. A. Dodge, R. Haskins, D. Bassok, M. R. Burchinal, ... & Weiland, C. (2017). *The current state of scientific knowledge on pre-kindergarten effects* (pp. 45–50). Retrieved from https://www.brookings.edu/wp-content/uploads/2017/04/duke_prekstudy_final_4-4-17_hires.pdf

Fisher, A., Godwin, K., & Seltman, H. (2014). Visual environment, attention allocation, and learning in young children: When too much of a good thing may be bad. *Psychological Science, 25*(7), 1362–1370. doi:10.1177/0956797614533801

Forest, H., & Gaber, S. (2009). *Stone soup.* Paradise, CA: Paw Prints.

Fredricks, J. A., Blumenfeld, P. C., & Paris, A. H. (2004). School engagement: Potential of the concept: State of the evidence. *Review of Educational Research, 74*(1), 59–109. doi:10.3102/00346543074001059

Freeman, R., & Swim, T. J. (2009). Intellectual integrity: Examining common rituals in early childhood curriculum. *Contemporary Issues in Early Childhood, 10*(4), 366–377. doi:10.2304/ciec.2009.10.4.366

Frick, A., & Wang, S. H. (2014). Mental spatial transformations in 14- and 16-month-old infants: Effects of action and observational experience. *Child Development, 85*(1), 278–293. doi:10.1111/cdev.12116

Gagnier, K., & Fisher, K. (2017). Spatial thinking: A missing building block in STEM education. Retrieved from http://scienceoflearning.jhu.edu/assets/documents/spatial_thinking_FINAL.pdf

Gianvecchio, L., & French, L. (2002). Sustained attention, inattention, receptive language, and story interruptions in preschool Head Start story time. *Journal of Applied Developmental Psychology, 23*(4), 393–407. doi:10.1016/S0193-3973(02)00125-9

Godwin, K. E., Almeda, M. V., Seltman, H., Kai, S., Skerbetz, M. D., Baker, R. S., & Fisher, A. V. (2016). Off-task behavior in elementary school children. *Learning and Instruction, 44*, 128–143. doi:10.1016/j.learninstruc.2016.04.003

Godwin, K. E., & Fisher, A. V. (2018). Wiggleometer: Measuring selective sustained attention in children. In *Proceedings of the 40th Annual Meeting of the Cognitive Science Society.* Retrieved from https://mindmodeling.org/cogsci2018/papers/0096/0096.pdf

Guarnaccia, S. (2010). *The three little pigs: An architectural tale.* New York: Abrams Books for Young Readers.

Hanline, M. F., Milton, S., & Phelps, P. C. (2010). The relationship between preschool block play and reading and math abilities in early elementary school: A longitudinal study of children with and without disabilities. *Early Child Development and Care, 180*(8), 1005–1017. doi:10.1080/03004430802671171

Jirout, J., & Newcombe, N. (2015). Building blocks for developing spatial skills: Evidence from a large, representative U.S. sample. *Psychological Science, 26*(3), 302–310. doi:10.1177/0956797614563338

Kissel, B. T., & Miller, E. T. (2015). Reclaiming power in the writers' workshop. *The Reading Teacher, 69*(1), 77–86. doi:10.1002/trtr.1379

Levin, E., & Bernier, J. (2011). Attention span. In S. Goldstein & J. A. Naglieri (Eds.), *Encyclopedia of child behavior and development* (pp. 163–163). Boston, MA: Springer.

Lou, Y., Abrami, P. C., Spence, J. C., Poulsen, C., Chambers, B., & d'Apollonia, S. (1996). Within-class grouping: A meta-analysis. *Review of Educational Research, 66*(4), 423–458. doi:10.3102/00346543066004423

Maloney, J., & Bullard, J. (1997). Practicing what we teach: Developing appropriate practices for early childhood preservice teachers. *Journal of Early Childhood Teacher Education, 18*(1), 46–54. doi:10.1080/10901029708549136

Marzano, R. J., Pickering, D., & Pollock, J. E. (2001). *Classroom instruction that works: Research-based strategies for increasing student achievement.* Alexandria, VA: Association for Supervision and Curriculum Development (ASCD).

McWilliam, R. A., Scarborough, A. A., & Kim, H. (2003). Adult interactions and child engagement. *Early Education and Development, 14*(1), 7–28. doi:10.1207/s15566935eed1401_2

Möhring, W., & Frick, A. (2013). Touching up mental rotation: Effects of manual experience on 6-month-old infants' mental object rotation. *Child Development, 84*(5), 1554-1565. doi:10.1111/cdev.12065

Nagro, S. A., Hooks, S. D., Fraser, D. W., & Cornelius, K. E. (2018). Whole-group response strategies to promote student engagement in inclusive classrooms. *Teaching Exceptional Children, 50*(4), 243-249. doi:10.1177/0040059918757947

National Institute of Child Health and Human Development Early Child Care Research Network. (2005). A day in third grade: A large-scale study of classroom quality and teacher and student behavior. *The Elementary School Journal, 105*(3), 305-323. doi:10.1086/428746

Paro, K. M. L., Hamre, B. K., Locasale-Crouch, J., Pianta, R. C., Bryant, D., Early, D., ... & Burchinal, M. (2009). Quality in kindergarten classrooms: Observational evidence for the need to increase children's learning opportunities in early education classrooms. *Early Education and Development, 20*(4), 657-692. doi:10.1080/10409280802541965

Phelps, P. C. (2013). *Let's build: Strong foundations in language, math, and social skills*. Lewisville, NC: Gryphon House.

Phillips, L. B., & Twardosz, S. (2003). Group size and storybook reading: Two-year-old children's verbal and nonverbal participation with books. *Early Education and Development, 14*, 453-478. doi:10.1207/s15566935eed1404_5

Pruden, S. M., Levine, S. C., & Huttenlocher, J. (2011). Children's spatial thinking: Does talk about the spatial world matter? *Developmental science, 14*(6), 1417-1430. doi:10.1111/j.1467-7687.2011.01088.x

Randolph, J. J. (2007). Meta-analysis of the research on response cards: Effects on test achievement, quiz achievement, participation, and off-task behavior. *Journal of Positive Behavior Interventions, 9*(2), 113-128. doi:10.1177/10983007070090020201

Rimm-Kaufman, S., La Paro, K., Downer, J., & Pianta, R. (2005). The contribution of classroom setting and quality of instruction to children's behavior in kindergarten classrooms. *The Elementary School Journal, 105*(4), 377-394. doi:10.1086/429948

Salkind, N. (2002). *Child development* (Macmillan psychology reference series). New York: Macmillan Reference USA.

Sharan, S., Ackerman, Z., & Hertz-Lazarowitz, R. (1979). Academic achievement of elementary school children in small-group versus whole-class instruction. *The Journal of Experimental Education, 48*(2), 125-129. doi:10.1080/00220973.1979.11011725

Skinner, E. A., Kindermann, T. A., & Furrer, C. J. (2009). A motivational perspective on engagement and disaffection: Conceptualization and assessment of children's behavioral and emotional participation in academic activities in the classroom. *Educational and Psychological Measurement, 69*(3), 493-525. doi:10.1177/0013164408323233

Sluss, D. J., & Stremmel, A. J. (2004). A sociocultural investigation of the effects of peer interaction on play. *Journal of Research in Childhood Education, 18*(4), 293-305. doi:10.1080/02568540409595042

Trawick-Smith, J., & Dziurgot, T. (2011). 'Good-fit' teacher-child play interactions and the subsequent autonomous play of preschool children. *Early Childhood Research Quarterly, 26*(1), 110-123. doi:10.1016/j.ecresq.2010.04.005

Trawick-Smith, J., & Savalli, C. (2013). *A descriptive study of block play: Effects of replica play toys*. Paper presented at the Annual Play Research Roundtables of the Play Policy and Practice Interest Forum, National Association for the Education of Young Children, Washington, DC.

Trawick-Smith, J., Swaminathan, S., Baton, B., Danieluk, C., Marsh, S., & Szarwacki, M. (2017). Block play and mathematics learning in preschool: The effects of building complexity, peer and teacher interactions in the block area, and replica play materials. *Journal of Early Childhood Research, 15*(4), 433-448. doi:10.1177/1476718X16664557

Trawick-Smith, J., Swaminathan, S., & Liu, X. (2016). The relationship of teacher-child play interactions to mathematics learning in preschool. *Early Child Development and Care, 186*(5), 716-733. doi:10.1080/03004430.2015.1054818

Trivette, C. M., Simkus, A., Dunst, C. J., & Hamby, D. W. (2012). Repeated book reading and preschoolers' early literacy development. *Center for Early Literacy Learning, 5*(5), 1-13.

Wasik, B. (2008). When fewer is more: Small groups in early childhood classrooms. *Early Childhood Education Journal, 35*(6), 515-521. doi:10.1007/s10643-008-0245-4

Wiles, D. (2001). *Freedom summer*. New York: Atheneum.

Wolfgang, C. H., Stannard, L. L., & Jones, I. (2001). Block play performance among preschoolers as a predictor of later school achievement in mathematics. *Journal of Research in Childhood Education, 15*(2), 173-180. doi:10.1080/02568540109594958

Zaghlawan, H. Y., & Ostrosky, M. M. (2011). Circle time: An exploratory study of activities and challenging behavior in Head Start classrooms. *Early Childhood Education Journal, 38*(6), 439-448. doi:10.1007/s10643-010-0431-z

7 Facilitating Learning Through Interactions

Over a decade of research in over 6,000 Pre-K through fifth-grade classrooms has consistently shown that the interactions we have with children affect their social, behavioral, and cognitive development and learning (Center for Advanced Study of Teaching and Learning, 2011). Through our interactions, we support relationships, convey information, enhance children's language, and foster learning and thinking skills. As we work with individual children, small groups, or whole groups we can engage in exchanges that support and enhance relationships or that discourage further interaction. We can engage in exchanges that are content and conceptually rich or that are low level and non-significant for learning. Unfortunately, as we will learn in this section, the latter is often the case.

A variety of instruments have been used throughout the years to assess interactions. The Classroom Assessment Scoring System (CLASS) is currently one of the most widely used instruments and is used by QRIS systems, Head Start programs, and Pre-K programs throughout the country. The CLASS instrument, using different versions, assesses teachers working with children from infancy through high school. For infants, the focus is on responsive caregiving (the relational climate, sensitivity of the teacher, ability to facilitate exploration, and support for early language development). The toddler scale examines emotional and behavioral support and engaged support for learning. At the preschool and early elementary level, CLASS examines several dimensions divided into categories of emotional support (classroom climate, teacher sensitivity, and regard for student perspectives), classroom organization (behavior management, productivity, and instructional learning formats), and instructional support (concept development, quality of feedback, and language modeling). Regardless of CLASS age level, the indicators are scored on a seven-point Likert scale with 1-2 indicating low performance, 3-5 moderate performance, and 6-7 high performance (Hamre, Goffin, & Kraft-Sayre, 2009).

While teachers across studies typically score in the higher moderate level for emotional support and classroom organization, instructional support is typically much lower. For example, programs in Head Start are required to use the CLASS assessment. The national Head Start average for emotional support is 6.07, for classroom organization 5.83, and for instructional support 3.00 (Head Start, 2017). Large national studies of Pre-K programs reveal instructional support scores even lower at 2.18 (LaParo et al., 2009) and 2.55 (Hamre, Hatfield, Pianta, & Jamil, 2014).

A multi-state study of 730 kindergartens found that the instructional support scores averaged only 1.98 and that only 1% of the programs scored in the high range on instructional support. Teachers either engaged in little instruction or used inappropriate practices such as an over-reliance on worksheets, simple recall rather than higher order learning, and teaching math and literacy in isolation. The authors point out that this is in "sharp contrast to strong evidence of the importance of developing children's 'usable knowledge,' which is built upon learning how facts are interconnected, organized, and conditioned upon one another" (LaParo et al., 2009, p. 678).

A study of 827 first-grade classrooms in 32 states found higher instructional scores than were evident with younger age groups with instructional conversations rated at 3.13 and evaluative feedback rated at 3.24 (NICHD Early Childhood Research Network, 2002). However, on a seven-point scale, this is still fairly low.

A study of 780 third-grade classrooms in multiple states while not revealing scores did examine how children spent their time. They found that children spent 38% of their time learning basic skills and only 4% of their time engaged in higher learning involving analysis or inference. The authors pointed out that while the social climates are positive, "instruction appears low in quality, focused on rote like activities and lacking in variation within a lesson" (Belsky et al., 2005, p. 318).

Why does this matter? Improving instructional support can significantly affect achievement. Large-scale, national studies demonstrate that instructional support is linked to gains in language, literacy, and math (Hamre et al., 2014; Johnson, Markowitz, Hill, & Phillips, 2016; Mashburn et al., 2008). For example, increasing the instructional support by one standard deviation increases children's achievement by 14% in literacy and 24% in applied problems and math (Johnson et al., 2016). Higher instructional climate scores in Pre-K also translate into higher reading and language skills one year later at the end of the kindergarten year (Burchinal et al., 2008). Further, while it is important to provide opportunities to learn math and literacy skills, the time spent was not as impactful on child outcomes as the quality of the instruction (Johnson et al., 2016; Phillips, Gormley, & Lowenstein, 2009).

> I'm really surprised at this information. I always thought that it was the activities that we plan that makes a difference in children's learning. It does seem that that is what is stressed on lesson plan forms.

I agree, I think that for too long, we've stressed activities over interactions as we plan lessons. Both are important. However, it's harder to pre-plan interactions, because to be effective they are often individualized. However, we can pre-plan some open-ended questions and some academic vocabulary. Additionally, we can choose one of the techniques described in this chapter and practice it as we teach. Eventually, the technique becomes second nature. We can then begin integrating another interactive technique into our teaching.

However, researchers warn us that while the category of instructional support increases achievement, so does responsive teaching which includes all the CLASS categories and dimensions. Increases in these scores are linked to greater gains in children's "cognitive, self-regulatory, and relational functioning" (Hamre et al., 2014).

The instructional support category at the toddler level includes facilitation of learning and development, quality of feedback, and language modeling. The preschool and early elementary level also include quality of feedback and language modeling. Instead of facilitation of learning and development, there is a dimension called concept development. We will examine how we introduce and support concept development; provide effective, targeted feedback, and use language stimulation techniques to enhance children's learning.

Facilitation of Learning and Development

As we've been discussing, teachers influence children's development and learning through their daily interactions. Through these minute-to-minute interactions, teachers can provide emotional support and instructional support to learners (Hamre, 2014). Research reveals that when teachers provide consistent emotional support by being warm, caring, and sensitive to children's needs, children gain social skills, become more compliant, increase their ability to self-regulate their behavior, gain academic skills, and show reduced stress levels (Curby, Brock, & Hamre, 2013; Hatfield, Hestenes, Kintner-Duffy, & O'Brien, 2013; Johnson, Seidenfeld, Izard, & Kobak, 2013; Williford, Vick Whittaker, Vitiello, & Downer, 2013). As mentioned earlier, large national research studies find the average for early childhood classrooms is between five and six on a seven-point scale indicating that teachers are providing a moderate to a high level of emotional support.

Instructional Support

Instructional support includes using interactions to support higher order thinking, to provide effective feedback, and to scaffold language (Hamre, 2014). This type of support is linked to children's academic learning. Since national studies show that this is an area that teacher's struggle with, we will spend time examining how we provide instructional support. Dombro, Jablon, and Stetson describe this type of interaction as a powerful interaction, one where the teacher intentionally interacts with a child to enhance their learning (2011).

Higher Order Thinking and Concept Development

As we discussed how people learn, we found that for learners to transfer information they must learn with understanding. To learn with understanding typically involves conceptual understanding. If using an analogy, we might think of a clothesline with clothespins. The clothesline would be the concepts. The clothespins would be the facts. Without the clothesline, there is nothing to support the clothespins. This is similar for facts. Without concepts, these are unrelated bits of information. In teaching concepts, where do we begin? The first place to begin is to be clear ourselves about what concepts we are attempting to develop. We do this by identifying concepts and then developing enduring understandings and essential questions related to these concepts. Next, we must understand learners' current understanding and background knowledge and use this information in planning instruction. Finally, to help children to develop concepts they must engage in deep rather than superficial learning. As we plan learning experiences, we need to plan activities that will support deep, conceptual learning. However, as the research demonstrates our interactions are crucial for learning as well. It is through our interactions that we are able to act as a scaffold, differentiating for each child and supporting children's learning to a higher level.

Let's look at an example, Josephine is a third-grade teacher who is planning a unit on honey bees. She chose this unit for several reasons. The school where she teaches is near many fruit orchards and the honey bees are very important for pollination. There have been many articles in the newspaper about colony collapse, which has created a crisis in the industry. The school is considering creating a pollinator's garden and Josephine feels this would be a hands-on, real-life opportunity to apply the children's skills and knowledge. For these reasons, she feels the unit will be relevant, interesting, and timely. The concept that Josephine wants to work on is interdependence. This will involve interdependence within the hive and also interdependence between people and honey bees. She has chosen the following essential questions: How do honey bees affect people? How do people affect honey bees? How does cooperative effort affect the honey bee? As a summative assessment, Josephine has developed a scenario where the child needs to help a farmer set up a sustainable hive using the knowledge he has gained. Josephine has developed a rubric that includes the needs of the bees, the needs of the farmer, a conducive environment, hive behavior, and interdependence.

As a provocation for the unit, Josephine shows the children the beehive that has been placed in the science area. One of the parents, who is a beekeeper had brought it in the night before. As part of the pre-assessment Josephine and the children create a KWHL. Josephine also asks children a series of questions about bees that explore children's background knowledge and attitudes. They use their paddles with yes or no to designate their answer. Josephine uses this information in planning her unit.

In addition to the beehive, Josephine has added sketch paper, magnifying glasses, and a digital microscope in the science center for exploring the bees. In the science center are also posters on bees and bulletin boards for bee facts, KWHL charts, photos, and on-going class-work. Josephine also adds QR codes that link to short video clips on bee behavior such as the bee dance. Additionally, a beekeeper suit is available so that children can examine it or try it on. Factual books on bees are added to the literacy center.

There are several planned activities such as watching a video on honey bee roles. Josephine asks the children to think about what would happen to the hive if different roles were removed, for example, if there was no queen. She has children compare the interdependence of the bees to the interdependence of communities and community helpers—a unit they had studied previously. They also brainstorm other examples of interdependence.

The children create a fact board. When they discover a new or interesting fact, they write it on an index card and place it on the board. Each day at group time, they review the new facts and add to the questions they wonder about. For example, why do beekeepers wear white? Why do we need bees and why do bees need us? Josephine planned several activities to assist children in answering this question.

- At mealtime, Josephine asks, "What if there were no bees, how would it affect what we are eating?" Children look in books and on websites that Josephine has added to the tablet computers to find answers. They create a bulletin board with foods and other agricultural products that rely on pollinators.
- Josephine reads newspaper articles on colony collapse to the children. Josephine asks children to brainstorm possible causes. If their responses are unclear, she asks them to explain their thinking. For example, one child thought that the colony collapse was because there were too many red flowers. When Josephine probed for more information, the child told her that bees can see every other color but not red. If the flowers are all red, then the bees wouldn't be able to eat.
- The beekeeper parent comes to visit. In addition to showing children the beekeeping suit, children interview the beekeeper about colony collapse.

- They take a walk with an expert to find pollinator-friendly habitat in the local area and threats to pollinators. Children keep a field journal, take pictures, and create a map of the area showing where friendly and unfriendly habitat is.
- Discussions about making a pollinator garden. Josephine leads a discussion by first having children determine the criteria for the garden. She asks what else do we need to know? How will we find out? The children decide that they need to visit with a nursery to determine the right type of plants to grow.

How did Josephine support children learning about the concept of interdependence? She planned several rich activities that provided hands-on experiences. Josephine asked children why and how questions, she connected concepts, she helped children integrate previous knowledge, and related what they were learning to their lives and their community. As she interacted with children during whole group, small group, and center time she engaged in conversations, asked open-ended questions, provided information, and used new vocabulary words such as interdependence, pollination, larva, nectar, pheromones, and apiarist. She provided feedback on children's garden plans. The garden activity allowed children to generate ideas, make and carry out plans, problem solve, predict, compare, create, ask questions and find information. This is only one example of how to develop higher order and conceptual thinking. However, we can learn from Josephine by applying these techniques to other units.

Specific Interaction Techniques

We can also support children's learning through engaging in powerful interaction techniques. These types of interactions are referred to as language modeling in the CLASS instrument.

Engage in Authentic Dialogue

Strickland and Marinak (2016) refer to authentic dialogue as the teacher-child dance where teachers attend to the child's verbal and non-verbal cues. The teacher uses turn-taking and effective strategies to keep the conversation going. For example, in their study, they found that children's turn-taking was enhanced when teachers were at or below the child's eye level, making eye contact, and smiling and leaning forward. Conversations were enhanced when teachers asked open-ended questions, followed children's lead, gave empathetic responses, reflected the children's words, and made a personal connection to the exchange. The research was conducted as children and teachers examined a photo that children had brought from home. When the teacher asked close-ended questions, corrected children, directed their response, informed the child of what the teacher saw in the photo, or asked multiple questions without waiting for the child to respond, the dance ended. As a teacher, it is important to find opportunities to engage in personalized, authentic interactions. To engage in authentic dialogue, you need to be present, physically and emotionally. You are "in the moment and self-aware" (Dombro, Jablon, & Stetson, 2011, p. 6). Your interactions are purposeful and intentional. You connect with the child, acknowledging her, and letting her know that you want to spend time together. This allows you to extend the child's learning. Authentic responsive dialogue is the foundation for powerful interactions. In this section, we will examine several ways we support children through our interactions. These interactions often occur during center times where there is the opportunity to interact with an individual child. However routine times and group times can also provide opportunities.

I agree that authentic dialogue is good, but who has the time? During center time, I'm busy setting up the next lessons.

It is time-consuming to engage in deep conversations. To carve out this time in a busy day a teacher must place authentic dialogue as a high priority. As a starting point, some teachers make a goal of having an authentic dialogue with a certain number of children each day. They track who they have had deep dialogues with, making sure that be the end of the week they have had at least one deep, personal engagement with each child.

One way that teachers save time in setting up activities is to engage in longer-term units and projects rather than having a theme a week. Often this means that children will engage in activities over a period of days rather than having a different, new activity each day.

Use Sophisticated Vocabulary

As we engage in the dance with children, we are using contingent responding, meaning that we are basing our responses on what the child has said. Vocabulary develops as we engage with children around their interest, their on-going activities, or a shared experienced event (Snow, 2017). As pointed out by Snow (2017), it is not the vocabulary itself that is a strong indicator of children's future success but rather the knowledge of the concepts that the vocabulary represents. The concepts that are developed through rich experiences provide the knowledge base needed to understand vocabulary. For example, in many early childhood classrooms, teachers and children hatch butterflies. As children witness this metamorphosis and the teacher supplies the word for this process, they gain a new vocabulary word linked to a concept. As they later experience this word in their science class, they will have a knowledge base to draw from. This type of language is often referred to as sophisticated or academic language.

As Josephine used new vocabulary words such as interdependence, pollination, larva, nectar, pheromones, and apiarist as children studied honey bees they learned this vocabulary. For many teachers, it does not come naturally to use such rich language. Many teachers have found it helpful to plan ahead and think of the vocabulary they want to stress during a unit, activity, or in different centers. To remind themselves and other adults in the room to use this vocabulary, they might post these on the wall. This has the added benefit of allowing children to see the words in writing.

Use Inferential or Abstract Language

In addition to using sophisticated vocabulary, another way we enhance vocabulary is to use inferential or abstract language. Sometimes this type of talk is referred to as decontextualized, higher level talk, or cognitively challenging talk and includes such things as predicting future events, making hypotheses, summarizing, generalizing, and justifying ideas (Tompkins, Zucker, Justice, & Binici, 2013). The use of more inferential language by the teacher is associated with children having greater comprehension, vocabulary, and abstract language (Dickinson & Smith, 1994; Hindman, Connor, Jewkes, & Morrison, 2008; Van Kleeck, Gillam, Hamilton, & McGrath, 1997).

Josephine used abstract language throughout her unit. For example, she asked children to predict what flowers the honey bees would be most attracted to and asked them to explain their thinking. She asked them to think about how bees affect the food supply.

Provide Background Knowledge

There is heightened concern about literacy in the early years due to studies that show that children who have poor literacy skills by the end of third grade are at high risk of school failure, including dropping out of high school (Lloyd, 1978; Snow & Matthews, 2016). Many early childhood teachers focus on constrained skills to teach literacy such as alphabet knowledge and phonemic awareness. However, Snow and Matthews point out that beyond third grade, unconstrained skills are extremely important (2016). Unconstrained skills include vocabulary, grammar, discourse skills, and background knowledge. These skills help children read more accurately and they are extremely important in children's comprehension of what they read. This might be why research demonstrates that the teacher's use of sophisticated language with preschool children's is found to predict their fourth-grade literacy levels, both comprehension and word recognition (Dickinson & Porche, 2011).

However, teachers need to be cautious about just talking more. Rather than the quantity of teacher talk, it is the quality of the interaction that matters. For example, in examining toddlers' interactions with their mothers, it was the quality of the interaction not the number of words that predicted the child's later language skills (Hirsh-Pasek et al., 2015). A higher ratio of child talk to teacher talk in preschool also predicted kindergarten and fourth-grade literacy outcomes (Dickenson & Porche, 2011). Again, we must remember that this is a coordinated dance, not a solo performance.

In addition to engaging in frequent rich dialogues and intentionally using sophisticated and inferential language, there are other interaction techniques that improve language and cognitive skills. One of these is providing targeted feedback.

Provide Targeted Feedback

Feedback is the information that we provide learners regarding their progress toward achieving goals or outcomes. This feedback can be verbal or written and can come from teachers, peers, or from computer-mediated sources. For the purpose of this section, we will be discussing verbal feedback from teachers.

The Education Endowment Foundation, a What Works Centre for Education in England develops evidence summaries and ratings for educational strategies. Based upon a number of reviews and seven meta-analyses, they rank targeted feedback as a high impact strategy that can increase learning by eight additional months in a one-year period (2018). This is one of the highest-ranking interventions that they review. Hattie who reviewed 100 factors affecting achievement also listed feedback as a powerful strategy. Feedback is listed in the top 5%-10% of these factors with an effect size of 0.79 (Hattie, 1999).

How does feedback support learners? Feedback can assist learners to know where they are in relation to outcomes thereby reducing uncertainty. Supportive feedback can reduce the cognitive load, preventing learners from being overwhelmed. For example, teachers might provide information about how to complete a task more effectively or provide alternative strategies. Finally, feedback can be corrective providing information about misconceptions, faulty interpretations, or errors in strategies or processes (Hattie & Timperley, 2007; Shute, 2008).

Feedback can be about how well a task or product is being accomplished, the process of accomplishing a task, the learner's self-regulation such as emphasizing effort and persistence, or about the person (Hattie & Timperley, 2007). Feedback about the person is often praise and is generally not effective. Some examples are, "You are a great listener." "What a wonderful artist you are." "You are really good at math." These types of comments do not provide information that assists the learner to know where they are in relation to specific outcomes or how they might continue to improve their performance. Hattie and Timperley (2007) state that feedback can help to clarify three major questions:

- Where am I going? What are the goals?
- How am I going? What progress is being made toward the goal?
- Where to next? What activities need to be undertaken to make better progress? (p. 86)

Effective feedback is:

- two-fold. It lets the learner know if they are on target to reach the desired outcome or goal and it also provides specific guidance for improvement. In providing guidance, the teacher might elaborate on the topic, the answer the learner gave, discuss errors, provide examples, or give other specific guidance (Shute, 2008).
- clear. It is targeted to the situation and the learner. Responses that are too long or too complex may obscure the feedback.
- meaningful. Constant feedback can cause learners to tune out the information. Effective feedback is given sparingly and is used for complex or challenging tasks.
- supportive of further effort and perseverance. Feedback that is negative, critical, controlling, lacking in specificity, or that interrupts the student's active engagement can be harmful to learning (Education Endowment Foundation, 2018; Shute, 2008).

Engage in Sustained Attention

As we engage in sustained attention, we learn about the child which helps us to build relationships, understand and empathize with the learner, design more relevant curriculum, and provide more meaningful interactions. We listen to not only the words the child says but also to what they aren't saying. We pay attention to their non-verbal cues and underlying feelings of interest, concern, worry, and joy. Through this, we learn about children's hopes, their interests, their lives outside of the classroom, and their cultural beliefs as we take an inquiry stance to our conversation. To listen effectively we focus on the child, giving the child our undivided attention. We are "minds on" not distracted by thinking about other things. We engage in attentive listening behavior, being at the child's level, leaning forward, and making eye contact. As we listen, we suspend judgment so our focus can be on understanding. We show our understanding by nodding and through our facial expressions. We listen with our heart and mind.

Use Reflective Listening

Another way that we demonstrate to the child that we are listening is to paraphrase or restate what they have said. This technique sometimes referred to as reflective listening is often used in counseling. In addition to demonstrating that you are attentively listening, as learners hear what you reflect, they are able to determine if you have understood correctly. This allows them the opportunity to clarify any confusion. Additionally, hearing their ideas and thoughts paraphrased back to them often clarifies and deepens their thinking.

Use Self-talk and Parallel-talk

Self-talk (you describe what you are doing) and parallel-talk (you describe what the child is doing) are especially important for infants, toddlers, and those with low language skills. For example, Angela was sitting at the clay table with a group of young toddlers who were experiencing earth clay for the first time. She uses parallel talk to describe what the children are doing, "I see that Jacob is patting his clay, Teresa is poking holes into her clay, and Jeremiah is smelling the clay." After the children have had many opportunities to interact with the clay, Angela is again sitting with the children at the clay table. She uses self-talk and states, "I am making a ball with my clay. I'm rolling and rolling it on the table to make it round."

Recast or Provide Indirect Correction

When recasting, you repeat the sentence back to the child correcting a mispronounced word or the child's grammar. This assists the child to know the correct word, grammar, and intonation while allowing the conversation to naturally continue. In contrast, if the teacher stops the child and directly corrects the child's speech, the conversation is often derailed. Further, the child might be embarrassed and be less likely to engage in conversation in the future.

Expand and Extend Speech

Expansion and extension are techniques employed based upon the initial child's statements. When you expand on the child's speech, you might make a child's utterance a full sentence. For example, a child points and says "car." You state, "Oh, you see a car." When you extend the speech, you add additional information such as, "Oh, you see a blue car that is going very fast."

Encourage Peer Conversations

There are many ways that we encourage peer conversations dependent upon the age of the child. First, provide many opportunities for peers to interact such as during learning center time, discussions during group times, or outdoor time. Second, set up an environment that is conducive for peer interactions. For example, conversations naturally occur as children develop play episodes in the dramatic play center or build with blocks. Teachers might also deliberately set up situations that encourage conversation such as two telephones near each other, a floor puzzle, a long jump rope, or an easel with two pieces of paper side-by-side. To enhance children working together in small groups, arrange your space to accommodate this. Third, teachers can refer children to each other for help, to get information, and to solve problems. Finally, teachers can plan more structured activities that encourage peer conversation. Later, we will be discussing cooperative learning. Cooperative learning encourages peer interdependence and rich conversations.

I've been impressed with the videos of the deep discussions and debates that children from Reggio Emilia engage in.

I have been too. I think there are several reasons for this. First, when children engage in deep rather than superficial learning there is more to discuss and debate. Additionally, as we encourage children to describe and justify their thinking, it allows this thinking to become visible allowing others to more effectively discuss and debate the ideas and thinking. Finally, when we establish an environment that encourages respectful discussions and disagreements and teach children how to engage in this, we provide permission and skills that encourage deep discussion and debate.

Ask Open-ended Questions

We have saved one of the most important teacher interaction techniques for last, asking questions. In planning a backward design unit, you thoughtfully choose essential questions to explore. Additionally, as you interact with children, you ask questions to encourage children's thinking, to gauge their understanding, and to encourage dialogue. Quality questions can also help a learner to self-assess their knowledge and thinking in relation to the question.

"Questioning as an instructional tool can be traced back to the fourth century BCE, when Socrates used questions and answers to challenge assumptions, expose contradictions, and lead to new knowledge and wisdom" (Corley & Rauscher, 2013, p. 1). Questioning is a common teacher strategy with teachers asking one to three questions every minute during interactions (Appalachia Educational Laboratory, 1994; Gall, 1971). Therefore, it is especially important that these questions are effective. Effective questioning can enhance achievement and provide a model that children can use in questioning their own thinking. However, teachers do not very often ask these types of high-level questions. Only 20% of teacher's questions ask for more than simple recall (Gall, 1970).

What are high-level questions? These are the questions that require learners to think rather than simply recall information. They are authentic questions that do not have a pre-determined correct answer, an open-ended question. Classifications of questions are often based upon Bloom's Taxonomy or the more recent revision by Anderson and Krathwohl (2001). From the lowest level to the highest level, these are:

- Remember
- Comprehend
- Apply
- Analyze
- Evaluate
- Create

Tienken, Goldberg, and DiRocco (2009) divide these into two categories of questions, productive and reproductive. In answering productive questions, learners use higher order skills requiring them to create, analyze, and evaluate. These questions are typically open-ended with divergent answers. Questions that are reproductive require lower order thinking skills asking learners to recall or apply information. The answer is often a pre-specified correct answer with learners reproducing information.

However, it is not just the way that a question is phrased that determines if it promotes higher level thinking, it is the intent of the questioner. For example, if Josephine asks the children what they should consider in making a pollinator garden after they have just read a list of criteria from a book, she is asking them to recall information. If she is asking them to develop their own criteria based upon what they have learned through questioning experts, their field trip visits, their discussions, and through reading books she is asking them to apply what they have learned. Let's analyze questions that Josephine asked children in their investigation of honey bees.

- Do you think the marigolds or petunias would be better for our pollinator garden? Explain why (Apply).
- What do you notice about the honey bee (to children who are looking at the honey bee through a digital microscope)? (Understand)
- How does the honey bee compare to the grasshopper (viewing both through a digital microscope)? (Analyze)
- What do we need to consider in making a pollinator garden? (Apply)
- What plants would work best in the garden? Why? (Evaluate)
- How will you design the pollinator garden? (Create)
- How will we share what we have learned about honey bees with others? (Create)
- What are some examples of interdependence? (Apply)
- What questions will you add to our question wall? (Create)
- What information will you add to the bulletin board on honey bee facts? (Create)
- Why do you think that honey bees might not be returning to their hives? (Analyze)
- What are the strategies we can use to help honey bees? (Analyze or Apply)
- What would happen if we no longer had bees? (Evaluate)

Compare the questions above to these questions

- What are the colors of the flowers? (Remember)
- What is the name for a male bee? (Remember)
- What do worker bees do? (Remember)
- What is another name for a beekeeper? (Remember)

You can see how the first group of questions differs from the second set of questions, requiring the child to think more deeply and demonstrate their understanding. The second set of questions, on the other hand, would assess lower level knowledge. Questioning for lower level knowledge is fairly easy and is readily apparent in classrooms. However, it is challenging to develop higher level questions. So how do we ask questions that help children think more deeply, that allow us to gauge their understanding, and that help them to self-assess their learning? We'll examine some techniques that will assist us to ask better questions.

Enhance Questioning

There are many ways to improve questioning. These include:

- asking authentic questions, these are questions that you really want to know the answer to.
- determining some questions ahead of time. The type of question you design will be based upon your purpose for asking the question. For example, if it is to get learners to think more deeply you will want to focus on questions that are open-ended and require higher order thinking.

- using questions to gauge understanding. As we gauge children's understanding we assist their learning by real-time scaffolding and prompting, by asking further questions to clarify their thinking such as, "What makes you say that?" This type of formative feedback can also provide information about what steps we take next in teaching. Do we need to provide more experiences or re-teach a concept or are we ready to move on? (Walsh & Sattes, 2017).

- building dialogue in the classroom. This involves moving from teacher monologues to encourage child to child, teacher to child, and child to teacher interactions. To do so, we need to establish a culture where dialogue is encouraged. In classrooms that support dialogue,
    - everyone is focused on learning, not just the person answering the question.
    - learning is reciprocal with everyone learning from each other.
    - dialogue is supported by the teacher. In these classrooms, thinking is encouraged and scaffolded. There is an understanding that we are all learners and that incorrect answers are part of the learning experiences.
    - learners build on each other's thinking and responses (Walsh & Sattes, 2017).

- wording questions as invitational rather than interrogational (Walsh & Sattes, 2017). Instead of using evaluative listening, did the learner answer the question right or wrong, use interpretive listening. With interpretive listening, you are asking what the learner is thinking.

- probing answers—if a child answers incompletely or inaccurately rather than using a typical response of answering the question yourself or moving to another child, probe the child's thinking. Ask the learner to explain his thinking, to give an example, or to provide a rationale.

- allowing think time, sometimes referred to as wait time, both after asking a question (think time one) and after hearing a learner provide a response (think time two). Typically, think time should be 3-5 seconds. During think time one all children think about their understanding of the question, their knowledge and understanding in relationship to the question, and they form a response. Think time two gives children the chance to compare their thinking on the initial question to the speakers, decide whether they agree or disagree with the speaker, and to consider a response or a question to ask the teacher or the speaker (Walsh & Sattes, 2017). When teachers increase think time there is more opportunity for learners to ponder questions that require deeper thought. Research demonstrates that with think time, more children get involved in discussions; the length of their response is increased; there is more interaction between children; learners engage in more speculation, more hypothesize building, and provide more evidence for their thinking; they demonstrate more competence; and there are fewer disciplinary issues (Cazden, 2001; Rowe, 1986). Think time has been found to increase achievement on cognitively complex test items. This is true for learners from early elementary through adults, in different subjects, in different countries and cultures, and of differing abilities (Rowe, 1986).

- involving all children in answering questions by teaching and using think time strategies and by using other techniques such as using a round robin technique where you go around the circle having each child answer; having children think, pair, and then share with their partner; or having children write their answers on individual whiteboards.

- avoiding the questioning trivia trap. For example, it is common that teachers ask young children to tell then the shape of an item or the color of the item. However, they are not asking because they are assessing whether the child has learned his colors or shapes, but instead they are under the mistaken impression that this type of questioning will actually teach children their colors or shapes. They view these as "teaching questions." Barraging children with low-level questions to which the child either knows the answer to or does not (closed questions) interrupts children's activities, does not improve their thinking or learning, and wastes their time and your time. Instead of questions, a more effective technique, in this case, is to use color words in your vocabulary as you talk with the child.

Would you recommend using these interactions when teaching adults?

I would. These techniques are important for all learners although they might be used in a slightly different way with adults. For example, let's look at self-talk. In self-talk, we are discussing what we are doing or thinking. With adults, it is more likely we will be discussing our thinking. For instance, we might describe the rationale for choosing a specific class activity. In regard to parallel talk, we might be identifying a technique that a teacher is using. When we extend speech, we will be building upon what the teacher stated.

Scaffold Learning

To understand scaffolding, we must first understand the zone of proximal development (ZPD) described by Lev Vygotsky, a Russian psychologist. The ZPD is the difference between what a learner can accomplish on his own versus what he can accomplish with assistance. Scaffolding is a metaphor that is often used to describe the support offered by the "knowledgeable other" that allows the learner to reach higher levels in their ZPD. However, this should not be construed as a one-way relationship, with the teacher providing direct instruction to a passive learner. Instead, scaffolding must be viewed within the socio-cultural context of Vygotsky's theory. Within this context, learning is a two-way relationship involving the active participation of the learner and the more "knowledgeable other" as they co-construct knowledge. This process is fluid, dynamic, and based upon the needs of the learner (Van de Pol, Volman, & Beishuizen, 2010). The ultimate goal is always for the child to become an independent, self-directed learner (Verenikina, 2008). Scaffolding is effective with all ages of learners from infants through adults and in all developmental domains and curricular areas.

Scaffolding is based on the two premises; the task must be something that the child can accomplish with support and after receiving support the learner must be able to accomplish the task independently. There are three characteristics that are typically associated with scaffolding.

- Contingency—the type of support and the amount of support are tailored to the needs of the learner. This means that the teacher must be keenly aware of the learner's current level of understanding and competence to provide just the right amount and type of support.
- Fading—there is a gradual release of supports over time.
- Transfer of responsibility—the responsibility is ultimately transferred to the learner who then performs the task independently.

A review of research demonstrates that scaffolding is effective in increasing learners' metacognition, cognitive skills such as critical thinking, and engagement (Belland, 2014; Van de Pol et al., 2010). Scaffolding can assist children to learn strategies, use tools, judge whether work is sufficient, and increase transferable skills such as problem-solving and thinking critically. It can also be an effective tool for content specific skills and strategies. However, because of the need for a highly individualized approach that is based upon a deep knowledge of the learner's understanding and competence, it can be a difficult strategy to implement successfully.

There are many ways that teachers provide scaffolding. These include:

- supporting learner motivation by engaging learner's interests and providing encouragement.
- providing feedback on the learner's current level of skill, knowledge, or understanding.
- challenging the learner's perspectives or thinking.
- focusing the learner's attention such as letting the learner know the most important process, content, or concept to focus on at this time.
- providing hints such as clues or suggestions.
- explaining the process or providing the reasons that the process, content, or skills are important.
- modeling or demonstrating the strategies and processes.
- simplifying the task by breaking it into more manageable pieces.
- asking questions that will assist the learner to complete the task or to articulate and clarify their thinking (Belland, 2014; Van de Pol et al., 2010).

While scaffolding can occur during large and small groups, it is often easier and more effective to use scaffolding when working with individual learners. An ideal time for this is during center time. However, there is often debate within early childhood about the amount of teacher scaffolding that should occur during this time period. One way to resolve this is to examine research. A study by Chien et al. (2010) examined 2,751 preschoolers in multiple states. They discovered that children in the group with a high percentage of play with low levels of teacher scaffolding scored lower than children who participated in a high level of play with teacher scaffolding. However, the key is to provide the right amount of scaffolding, at the right time without disrupting children's play.

There are many different scaffolding supports that the teacher can utilize to support learning. The intentional teacher uses supports based upon the individualized needs of the learner, engaging in a reciprocal learning interaction that assist the learner in advancing their knowledge, skills, or understanding.

In Summary

In this chapter, we reviewed how we facilitate learning through our interactions. Using effective interaction techniques can build rapport and enhance learning. It is important that we are continually thinking about and assessing our interactions. Due to the way we often lesson plan, we might think that only our planned activities lead to learning. We might inadvertently use interaction techniques that are counterproductive, or we might focus only on completing the planned learning activity rather than considering the role of powerful interactions. Effective teachers use both interactions and experiences to enhance children's learning. As you plan learning experiences that assist children to answer essential questions, gain knowledge and skills, and hone approaches to learning, consider how you can use your interactions to achieve these desired results.

Apply Your Knowledge

1. Think of a topic. What are some high-level questions you could ask in relationship to the topic?
2. What are vocabulary words that you could stress in relationship to the topic.
3. Either observe in a classroom or watch a video of a teacher. Which of the interaction techniques described in this chapter are they using?
4. Choose one of the techniques described in this chapter and practice it until you feel comfortable with the technique and it becomes a natural part of your interactions. For example, you can practice reflective listening in any interaction whether with a child or adult, whether in a classroom or in your personal life.
5. Engage in a role play where one person is a toddler playing with a toy and the other is the teacher using self-talk and parallel-talk.
6. Add some of the interaction techniques to your unit plan.
7. Visit the powerful interactions website to learn more about powerful interactions with children and adults. Make a list of interactions that you would like to use.

References

Anderson, L. & Krathwohl, D. (Eds.). (2001). *A taxonomy for learning, teaching, and assessing: A revision of Bloom's Taxonomy of Educational Objectives*. New York: Addison Wesley Longman.

Appalachia Educational Laboratory. (1994). *Questioning and Understanding to Improve Learning and Thinking (QUILT): The evaluation results. A proposal to the National Diffusion Network (NDN) documenting the effectiveness of the QUILT professional development program* (ERIC Document Reproduction Service No. ED403230).

Belland, B. R. (2014). Scaffolding: Definition, current debates, and future directions. In D. Jonassen, M. J. Spector, M. Driscoll, M. D. Merrill, J. van Merrienboer, & M. P. Driscoll (Eds.) *Handbook of research on educational communications and technology* (pp. 505–518). New York: Springer. doi:10.1007/978-1-4614-3185-5_39

Belsky, J., Booth-LaForce, C. L., Bradley, R., Brownell, C. A., Burchinal, M., Campbell, S. B., ... & Jaeger, E. (2005). A day in third grade: A large-scale study of classroom quality and teacher and student behavior. *Elementary School Journal, 105*(3), 305–323. doi:10.1086/428746

Burchinal, M., Howes, C., Pianta, R., Bryant, D., Early, D., Clifford, R., & Barbarin, O. (2008). Predicting child outcomes at the end of kindergarten from the quality of pre-kindergarten teacher–child interactions and instruction. *Applied Developmental Science, 12*(3), 140–153. doi:10.1080/10888690802199418

Cazden, C. B. (2001). *Classroom discourse: The language of teaching and learning*. Portsmouth, NH: Heinemann.

Center for Advanced Study of Teaching and Learning. (2011). Measuring and improving teacher-student interactions in PK-12 settings to enhance students' learning. Retrieved from https://curry.virginia.edu/uploads/resourceLibrary/CLASS-MTP_PK-12_brief.pdf

Chien, N. C., Howes, C., Burchinal, M., Pianta, R. C., Ritchie, S., Bryant, D. M., ... & Barbarin, O. A. (2010). Children's classroom engagement and school readiness gains in prekindergarten. *Child Development, 81*(5), 1534–1549. doi:10.1111/j.1467-8624.2010.01490.x

Corley, M. A., & Rauscher, W. C. (2013). *Deeper learning through questioning*. Retrieved from https://lincs.ed.gov/sites/default/files/12_TEAL_Deeper_Learning_Qs_complete_5_1_0.pdf

Curby, T. W., Brock, L. L., & Hamre, B. K. (2013). Teachers' emotional support consistency predicts children's achievement gains and social skills. *Early Education & Development, 24*, 292–309. doi:10.1080/10409289.2012.665760

Dickinson, D. K., & Porche, M. V. (2011). Relation between language experiences in preschool classrooms and children's kindergarten and fourth-grade language and reading abilities. *Child Development, 82* (3), 870–886. doi:10.1111/j.1467-8624.2011.01576.x

Dickinson, D. K., & Smith, M. W. (1994). Long-term effects of preschool teachers' book readings on low-income children's vocabulary and story comprehension. *Reading Research Quarterly, 29*(2), 104–122. doi:10.2307/747807

Dombro, A. L., Jablon, J. R., & Stetson, C. (2011). *Powerful interactions: How to connect with children to extend their learning*. Washington, DC: National Association for the Education of Young Children.

Education Endowment Foundation. (2018). *Feedback*. Retrieved from https://educationendowmentfoundation. org.uk/pdf/generate/?u=https://educationendowmentfoundation.org.uk/pdf/toolkit/?id=131&t= Teaching%20and%20Learning%20Toolkit&e=131&s=

Gall, M. (1971). The use of questions in teaching. *Review of Educational Research, 40*, 707-721. doi:10.3102/ 00346543040005707

Hamre, B. K. (2014). Teachers' daily interactions with children: An essential ingredient in effective early childhood programs. *Child Development Perspectives, 8*(4), 223-230. doi:10.1111/cdep.12090

Hamre, B. K., Goffin, S. G., & Kraft-Sayre, M. (2009). Classroom Assessment Scoring System (CLASS) Implementation Guide. Retrieved from https://www.vbgrowsmart.com/providers/Documents/CLASSImplementationGuide.pdf

Hamre, B., Hatfield, B., Pianta, R., & Jamil, F. (2014). Evidence for general and domain-specific elements of teacher-child interactions: Associations with preschool children's development. *Child Development, 85*(3), 1257-1274. doi:10.1111/cdev.12184

Hatfield, B. E., Hestenes, L. L., Kintner-Duffy, V. L., & O'Brien, M. (2013). Classroom Emotional Support predicts differences in preschool children's cortisol and alpha-amylase levels. *Early Childhood Research Quarterly, 28*(2), 347-356. doi:10.1016/j.ecresq.2012.08.001

Hattie, J. A. (1999). Influences on student learning (Inaugural professorial address, University of Auckland, New Zealand). Retrieved from http://www.arts.auckland.ac.nz/staff/index.cfm?P=8650

Hattie, J., & Timperley, H. (2007). The power of feedback. *Review of Educational Research, 77*(1), 81-112. doi:10.3102/003465430298487

Head Start. (2017). A National Overview of grantee CLASS scores in 2017. Retrieved from https://eclkc.ohs. acf.hhs.gov/sites/default/files/pdf/national-class-2017-data.pdf

Hindman, A. H., Connor, C. M., Jewkes, A. M., & Morrison, F. J. (2008). Untangling the effects of shared book reading: Multiple factors and their associations with preschool literacy outcomes. *Early Childhood Research Quarterly, 23*(3), 330-350. doi:10.1016/j.ecresq.2008.01.005

Hirsh-Pasek, K., Adamson, L. B., Bakeman, R., Owen, M. T., Golinkoff, R. M., Pace, A., ... & Suma, K. (2015). The contribution of early communication quality to low-income children's language success. *Psychological Science, 26*(7), 1071-1083. doi:10.1177/0956797615581493

Johnson, A. D., Markowitz, A. J., Hill, C. J., & Phillips, D. A. (2016). Variation in impacts of Tulsa Pre-K on cognitive development in kindergarten: The role of instructional support. *Developmental Psychology, 52*(12), 2145. doi:10.1037/dev0000226

Johnson, S. R., Seidenfeld, A. M., Izard, C. E., & Kobak, R. (2013). Can classroom emotional support enhance prosocial development among children with depressed caregivers? *Early Childhood Research Quarterly, 28*(2), 282-290. doi:10.1016/j.ecresq.2012.07.003

LaParo, K. M., Hamre, B. K., Locasale-Crouch, J., Pianta, R. C., et al., (2009). Quality in kindergarten classrooms: Observational evidence for the need to increase children's learning opportunities in early education classrooms. *Early Education and Development, 20*, 657-692. doi:10.1080/10409280802541965

Lloyd, D. N. (1978). Prediction of school failure from third-grade data. *Educational and Psychological Measurement, 38*(4), 1193-1200. doi:10.1177/001316447803800442

Mashburn, A. J., Pianta, R. C., Hamre, B. K., Downer, J. T., Barbarin, O. A., Bryant, D., ... & Howes, C. (2008). Measures of classroom quality in prekindergarten and children's development of academic, language, and social skills. *Child Development, 79*(3), 732-749. doi:10.1111/j.1467-8624.2008.01154.x

National Institute of Child Health and Human Development, & Early Child Care Research Network. (2002). The relation of global first-grade classroom environment to structural classroom features and teacher and student behaviors. *The Elementary School Journal, 102*(5), 367-387. doi:10.1086/499709

Phillips, D. A., Gormley, W. T., & Lowenstein, A. E. (2009). Inside the Pre-Kindergarten door: Classroom climate and instructional time allocation in Tulsa's Pre-K programs. *Early Childhood Research Quarterly, 24*(3), 213-228. doi:10.1016/j.ecresq.2009.05.002

Rowe, M. B. (1986). Wait time: Slowing down may be a way of speeding up! *Journal of Teacher Education, 37*, 43-50. doi:10.1177/002248718603700110

Shute, V. J. (2008). Focus on formative feedback. *Review of Educational Research, 78*(1), 153-189. doi:10.3102/0034654307313795

Snow, C. E. (2017). The role of vocabulary versus knowledge on children's language learning: A fifty-year perspective. *Journal for the Study of Education and Development, 40*, 1-18. doi:10.1080/02103702.2016. 1263449

Snow, C. E., & Matthews, T. J. (2016). Reading and language in the early grades. *The Future of Children, 26*(2), 57-74. doi:10.1353/foc.2016.0012

Strickland, M., & Marinak, B. (2016). Not just talk, but a "dance"! How kindergarten teachers opened and closed spaces for teacher-child authentic dialogue. *Early Childhood Education Journal, 44*(6), 613–621. doi:10.1007/s10643-015-0750-1

Tienken, C. H., Goldberg, S., & Dirocco, D. (2009). Questioning the questions. *Kappa Delta Pi Record, 46*(1), 39–43. doi:10.1080/00228958.2009.10516690

Tompkins, V., Zucker, T. A., Justice, L. M., & Binici, S. (2013). Inferential talk during teacher-child interactions in small-group play. *Early Childhood Research Quarterly, 28*(2), 424–436. doi:10.1016/j.ecresq.2012.11.001

Van de Pol, J., Volman, M., & Beishuizen, J. (2010). Scaffolding in teacher–student interaction: A decade of research. *Educational Psychology Review, 22*(3), 271–296. doi:10.1007/s10648-010-9127-6

Van Kleeck, A. V., Gillam, R. B., Hamilton, L., & McGrath, C. (1997). The relationship between middle-class parents' book-sharing discussion and their preschoolers' abstract language development. *Journal of Speech, Language, and Hearing Research, 40*(6), 1261–1271. doi:10.1044/jslhr.4006.1261

Verenikina, I. (2008). Scaffolding and learning: Its role in nurturing new learners. In P. Kell, W. Vialle, D. Konza, & G. Vogl (Eds.), *Learning and the learner: Exploring learning for new times* (pp. 161–180). Wollongong: University of Wollongong, Australia.

Walsh, J. A., & Sattes, B. D. (2016). *Quality questioning: Research-based practice to engage every learner.* Thousand Oaks, CA: Corwin Press.

Williford, A. P., Vick Whittaker, J. E., Vitiello, V. E., & Downer, J. T. (2013). Children's engagement within the preschool classroom and their development of self-regulation. *Early Education & Development, 24*(2), 162–187. doi:10.1080/10409289.2011.628270

8 Using Powerful Strategies to Facilitate Learning

Teachers use many different strategies when teaching. We want these strategies to yield strong results. This chapter will discuss a few of these powerful strategies. The strategies in this chapter were chosen because they are:

- suitable for learners in a wide age range including children in the early childhood years as well as adults who are attending early childhood workshops and courses
- appropriate for a variety of subjects and topics
- learner-centered and aligned with developmentally appropriate practice
- aligned with the research on how people learn
- research-based with research demonstrating that this strategy has a powerful effect on learning

This chapter will be divided into three sections, using a child-centered or learner-centered approach, empowering the learner through teaching techniques focused on how to learn, and teaching techniques that deepen learning. A committee formed by the National Research Council examined deeper learning which they define as "the process through which an individual becomes capable of taking what was learned in one situation and applying it to new situations (i.e., transfer)" (2012, p. 5). When we engage in deeper learning, we not only learn content but also understand how and when to apply this knowledge in answering questions or solving problems. The committee states that this kind of learning occurs over time but that "recent evidence indicates that even preschool and early elementary students can make meaningful progress in conceptual organization, reasoning, problem solving, representation, and communication in well-chosen topic areas in science, mathematics, and language arts" (National Research Council, 2012, p. 9).

Use a Child-centered Approach

Does the type of teaching matter? What are the child outcomes associated with different types of teaching? Since there is a push to have Pre-K children ready for kindergarten is it better to use a more directive and less play-based approach? What about in early elementary school? We will explore these important questions in this section. Why is this important? A teacher's approach to learning affects the way they organize the children's schedule, the value they place on different types of learning, and the relationships they build with children.

The child-centered approach, with a foundation in constructivism, is based on the belief that children actively construct their knowledge. This is in contrast to teacher-directed approaches that are based on learning theories that hold that academic skills are acquired through direct instruction and practice.

A teacher using a child-centered approach acts as a facilitator of children's learning, engages children in active exploration, considers children's ideas and interests, and encourages learner initiative and responsibility. In a classroom using a child-centered approach, you would be more likely to see children making choices, engaging in conversations, and interacting with peers.

A teacher using a teacher-directed approach emphasizes more teacher control, didactic instruction, systematic teaching such as breaking skills into small steps to increase learning, and acquisition of basic academic skills often over social and emotional skills (Lerkkanen et al., 2016). In a classroom emphasizing the teacher-directed approach, you would be more likely to see teacher dominated talk and more rote activities.

Child-centered approaches have been endorsed by many professional organizations and are the focus of many commonly used early childhood assessments. One way that professional organizations have endorsed child-centered teaching is to write position statements promoting this approach. Several organizations have done so. These include the NAEYC in the Developmentally Appropriate Practices Position Statement (2009), the NAEYC and the National Council of Teachers of Mathematics position statement (2010) Early Childhood Mathematics: Promoting Good Beginnings; National Science Teachers Association (NSTA) Position Statement: Early Childhood Science Education (2014); and The Child-Centered Kindergarten: A Position Paper by the Association for Childhood Education International (Moyer, 2001).

Several commonly used early childhood instruments measure at least some aspects of child-centered versus teacher-directed instruction including ECERS and CLASS. These instruments are used extensively as assessment in Quality Rating Improvement Systems (QRIS) and Pre-K initiatives. While CLASS is also used to evaluate interactions in early elementary programs, another instrument, the Child-Centered Teaching Practices is also an instrument used at this age.

Teachers that subscribe to child-initiated or teacher-directed learning typically use both child-initiated activities and direct teaching in their classrooms. The difference is in the degree and the underlying belief in how children learn best. This could be referred to as the teacher's underlying orientation regarding teaching.

What Is the Evidence that Child-centered Approaches Enhance Learning?

Early childhood has a rich history of using child-centered approaches. However, is there research-based evidence to support a child-centered approach? We'll examine this in relationship to preschool and in relationship to elementary education.

Preschool

Evidence for the use of child-centered learning comes from longitudinal studies as well as short-term studies. Research has found links between the type of orientation to learning and academic outcomes, social outcomes, and children's motivation.

One of the longer-term curriculum studies randomly assigned preschool children to a child-centered curriculum approach (High-Scope), a nursery school model, or a teacher-directed approach (DISTAR). For the first decade, there were few differences found in the achievement of children based upon the curricular approach. However, when assessed at age 15 and again at 23, significant differences in social-emotional outcomes emerged. Children who were in the teacher-directed approach engaged in 212 times the number of misconduct deeds as the child-centered group and had three times as many felony arrests. Additionally, 47% of the teacher-directed group had been treated for emotional impairment versus 6% of the children in the child-centered and nursery school models (Schweinhart & Weikart, 1997).

Another longitudinal study by Marcon (2002) followed children from preschool through fourth grade. She found that while children in more academically directed early education were initially retained less often than children in the child-initiated group, long-term outcomes were more positive for those children in the child-initiated approach. While there were no academic differences in the third grade by orientation, by the fourth grade academically directed groups earned significantly lower grades compared to those in child-initiated programs. Not only that, but grades in most subjects declined between third and fourth grade for children who had experienced the academically directed preschool approach, while they improved or stayed the same for children who had experienced the child-initiated approach.

Some additional studies have examined the short-term effects of different orientations. A study of 227 children in preschool and kindergarten found that children in the teacher-directed didactic group had significantly higher scores in reading but not math. However, motivation factors for the didactic group were significantly lower. Children rated their abilities lower, had lower expectations for success, were more dependent on adults, took less pride in accomplishments, and worried more about school (Stipek, Feiler, Daniels, & Milburn, 1995). A later study by some of these same researchers found that preschool children in the teacher-directed didactic group had both lower achievement and lower motivation (Stipek et al., 1998). Research conducted in Pre-K in the District of Columbia public schools and in the state of Georgia found similar results on academic achievement. Children in the child-centered approach had a better mastery of academic skills than those in the teacher-directed approach (Henry et al., 2004; Marcon, 1999). Both studies also examined teaching that they classified as middle of the road. They speculated that these teachers did not have a strong belief preference. Children in the middle of the road approach scored the least well. For example, the study by Henry et al. (2004) found that the children scored more poorly in math, had a less positive attitude about learning, and were more frequently withdrawn. Finally, a more recent study of 444 children in 48 programs, found that when teachers were child-centered, children had a significantly higher level of self-regulation skills. Children with higher self-regulation skills had higher levels of achievement in both math and literacy (Hur, Buettner, & Jeon, 2015). The researchers speculate that child-centered environments give children more opportunity to practice and learn these skills.

Researchers who have conducted these studies all recommend a child-initiated approach. Remember, a child-initiated approach does not mean that the teacher never uses teacher-directed instruction. Instead, it means that the teacher views the child as an active constructor of knowledge. The teacher uses a variety of instructional formats including learning centers and small and large group instruction. Regardless of format, they tap into the child's interests, background knowledge, and experiences to design relevant, engaging environments and curriculum. Unlike the teacher that favors teacher-directed approaches who first consider the content, the child-centered teacher first considers the needs of the child.

K-3

While nearly all studies in preschool have found the results more favorable for children in child-centered classrooms, there have been mixed results in elementary education. Many studies conducted in the 1970s, the 1980s, and the early 1990s found achievement was higher in elementary classrooms that used more teacher-directed instruction versus child-centered instruction (see Perry, Donohue, & Weinstein, 2007 for a review). However, more recent studies have found either mixed results or results that favor child-initiated teaching. For example, a study of kindergarten children found that children's reading and writing were higher with didactic instruction, but child-centered learning was associated with better mathematics achievement test scores (Guarino, Hamilton, Lockwood, & Rathbun, 2006). Contrary to this, Burts et al. (1993) found that first-grade children in child-centered programs had higher grades in reading but lower grades in math. Perry, Donohue, and Weinstein (2007) found that first graders in child-centered classrooms had higher gains on tests in math. Additionally, more children in the child-centered classrooms met end-of-the-year benchmarks for reading and math. Recently, a study in Finland of over one thousand children in 93 classrooms found that child-centered practices resulted in higher skill levels regardless of whether children began with low, average, or high skills. They also found that the more child-centered practices the teacher used, the greater the gain in both reading and math test scores. Teacher-directed practices were especially detrimental to children with average or above-average reading levels (Lekkanen et al., 2016).

Several studies have also examined developmentally appropriate classrooms (DAP) versus those that are less appropriate. Remember, DAP is based upon a child-centered approach. A study by Burt et al. (1993) of children from more developmentally appropriate kindergartens had higher grades in reading in first grade than those who were from more teacher-directed kindergartens. However, there were no differences in other curriculum areas. Another study of 28 kindergarten and first-grade classrooms found that children had significantly higher achievement test scores in classrooms using more DAP than children in classrooms with less DAP (Huffman & Speer, 2000). Most of the children in this study were African American or Hispanic. However, developmentally appropriate practices are not the norm for children who are low income or children of color. Numerous studies have found that children who are low income or children of color are more likely to receive didactic instruction (Stipek, 2004).

But it is not only achievement that is affected by the teacher's orientation to learning. The orientation affects stress levels, peer interactions, and children's interest in subjects. As with younger children, didactic instruction is associated with more stress in children. In studies where children were observed to determine the frequency of stress behaviors, stress behaviors were significantly more frequent in kindergarten classrooms that used didactic teaching (Burts, Hart, Charlesworth, & Kirk, 1990; Burts et al. 1992). Studies in first-grade classrooms have also found that children that are in more didactic classrooms have greater rates of peer rejection (Donohue, Perry, & Weinstein, 2003). Children in classrooms that are more teacher-directed show less interest in reading and math than children in child-centered classrooms (Lekkanen et al., 2012).

Recent research confirms that child-centered orientations are advantageous for children in early elementary programs. Lekkanen et al. (2012) speculate that the different results between earlier studies and current ones might relate to rigor. Earlier studies were less likely to use control groups. Additionally, practices may have changed regarding child-centered classrooms with more emphasis on teachers actively promoting learning versus believing that children will gain all they need through play.

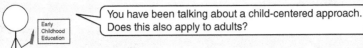

You have been talking about a child-centered approach. Does this also apply to adults?

Yes, andragogy, a model of adult education used throughout the world, also promotes learner-centered approaches. Like constructivism, andragogy promotes the idea that learners actively construct their knowledge based on their engagement, experiences, background knowledge, and beliefs. Their readiness to learn also depends on the learner's "need to know" or how this information will help to solve problems the learner is experiencing.

The teacher is seen as a facilitator of learning rather than strictly an imparter of knowledge. A teacher's role is to design effective learning environments and experiences that are relevant to learners, built upon their interests and prior knowledge and experiences. The teacher may also help to establish the "need to know" by creating a justification for the learning and by creating disequilibrium (Bullard, 2003; Bullard & Hitz, 1997).

Relationship between How People Learn and Child-centered Learning

In Chapter 5, we examined five criteria for transfer (learn with understanding, adequately learn the information having many opportunities to learn and practice, take the time needed to learn, use appropriate learning methods focusing on transfer, enhance motivation through planning "right fit" activities and experiences) and three principles for learning (use children's preconceptions as a starting place for instruction, engage children in deep learning that is based within a conceptual framework and with an organization to enhance retrieval, use a metacognitive approach) (National Research Council, 1999, 2005). How do these relate to child-centered learning?

The most obvious alignment between how people learn and child-centered learning relates to the knowledge of the learner. The National Research Council calls for teachers to enhance learner's motivation through "right fit" activities and experiences and through using children's preconceptions as a starting point. In the child-centered approach, we place the learner at the center of the experience. In comparison, some approaches place the subject as the curricular center. Each of the other criteria and principles can also be accomplished within the child-centered classrooms. However, teachers need to be very intentional. Let's look at two child-centered classrooms, both studying farm animals.

In Gaby's classroom, the unit begins with children visiting a farm. While there, they see several different animals and their babies. The following days, they study an animal a day. During group times they read a story about the animal and sing songs about animals such as, "Old McDonald Had a Farm." During movement activities, they move like the animal of the day. Gaby has added many things to the learning environment, including animal pellets to the sand and water table, books on animals to the reading area, and animal masks and costumes to the dramatic play center. While this classroom is most likely child-centered, it is difficult to see examples of "deep learning" or "conceptual learning."

Let's look at another teacher in this same school. Before going on the field trip, Amelia has her class vote on one animal they would like to study in-depth. They choose to study horses. During small group time, the children complete a KWHL chart on horses. Using their KWHL as a starting point, they determine what they might be able to learn on the field trip through observation, interviewing, and collecting samples. When they go on the field trip they observe, conduct interviews, take photos, draw sketches, and collect samples such as hay, hair the farmer had trimmed from the horse's tail and mane, body horse hair from the horse brush, and horse manure (in a plastic Ziploc bag). Although they visit all the animals, their focus is on the horse. Amelia collects props and information that will help children answer their questions such as books, short videos, curry combs, horseshoes, empty horse shots, a horse blanket, and a saddle. She places these along with the samples they have collected into the various learning centers. Circle times consist of reading books, sharing information they have learned, creating and adding to graphs and webs and their KWHL charts. During center time and small group time children engage in active investigations such as determining if the hair from the tail, mane, and the body are the same. To determine this, they feel the hair, look at the hair through the microscope, and conduct some simple experiments. Since many of the children have had limited exposure to the digital microscope, Amelia had introduced it during a whole group activity. They had examined different items, discussed how the microscope worked, and the type of care it needed. Throughout the unit they also have activities and discussions related to the topical essential question, "What are the needs of horses and how does this compare to the needs of humans and other animals?" Through this unit children are improving their knowledge of not only horses but also all animals, learning about the needs that horses have and how this relates to the needs that other animals have, and learning and practicing skills in observing, questioning, finding answers to questions, compiling data, and using tools. Learning these skills are motivating because they are occurring within an authentic context.

As you can see from these two examples, through providing units that are more in-depth with intentional desired results, we can provide the children with a more enhanced learning experience. In *How Children Learn* (National Research Council, 2005), the researchers discuss the importance of learner-centered, knowledge-centered, assessment-centered, and community-centered learning. Community-centered includes the cultural norms. All are necessary and all can and should be embedded within child-centered learning.

Aren't we getting off track? How does this relate to backward design?

That is a great question. Backward design is a framework for curriculum design. One of the primary purposes is to engage learners in deeper, transferable learning. While the framework is very important in providing a process that can assist with this by focusing our attention on enduring understandings and essential questions, knowledge, and skills and by encouraging alignment between our desired results, assessments, and experiences, the framework alone cannot ensure learning. Indeed, there are many other considerations. We must choose desired results that are developmentally appropriate, related to standards, and that are critical for learning. We must use pre-assessments, formative assessments, and summative assessments that are aligned in-depth and breadth to our desired results and that are appropriate for the learner. Finally, we must choose experiences that will help learners achieve the desired results and perform well on summative assessments. Our best opportunity to enhance learning is to use evidence-based practices and those that are based upon how people learn.

Teach Learners How to Learn

In this section, we will examine three powerful techniques for helping learners to achieve deep learning. These are helping learners ask good questions, teaching learners how to reflect on their learning, and teaching thinking skills. As stated earlier, these are techniques that were chosen because they are appropriate for all ages and subjects, are research-based, and have a powerful effect on learning.

Help Learners Ask Good Questions

Children learn from their first-hand observations, experimentations, and through others. Much of this learning begins by first asking questions. For example, 13-month-old Aidan bangs a metal spoon on a metal bowl. He then bangs the spoon on the floor. He next toddles around the room looking for other shiny objects to bang the spoon on. His question, "Do all shiny objects sound the same when they are hit with a spoon?" was not verbally articulated. However, it was obvious that it was the center of his investigation. Even before speaking, children show evidence of asking themselves questions. They also ask other people questions through their gestures, such as pointing at a picture when they want to know the name of the object. As children become more verbal, they begin to ask more questions of the "knowledgeable others" around them. Asking others questions is a mechanism for cognitive development, allowing learners to obtain targeted information at the exact time that they need it and are therefore most receptive to the information (Chouinard, 2007). Learners often ask questions when they experience disequilibrium or a disparate event (Ostroff, 2016). In the example above, the disparate event was the difference in sound between banging the spoon on the bowl and banging the spoon on the floor.

Being able to ask questions and to seek answers is crucial for lifelong learning. As children engage in questioning and answer seeking, they become independent learners solving everyday problems and developing new understandings of their physical, social, and biological world (Ruggeri & Lombrozo, 2015). They gain knowledge, build concepts, and solve problems. As teachers and families know, preschool children ask many information-seeking questions. Research shows they ask an average of one question per minute with 13% of their utterances being questions (Chouinard, 2007).

Preschool children generally ask informants effective questions. They can distinguish between informants who are more or less knowledgeable and their ability to do so increases with age (Mills, Legare, Grant, & Landrum, 2011). They also adapt their questions based upon others' responses to increase efficiency (Ruggeri & Lombrozo, 2015) and are persistent in obtaining the information that they seek (Chouinard, 2007). Like other skills, children become better at asking good questions through practice, mentoring, and instruction (Vale, 2013).

Information seeking questions can be further divided into questions asking for facts or questions asking for explanations. Explanation questions often begin with why, what about, or how. While research shows that children in western and non-western countries ask questions, the type of questioning varies by culture. For example, in the United States, about one-quarter of preschool-age children's questions are asking for explanations and these types of questions increase during the preschool years. In a study examining four non-western cultures, only 4.5% of questions were explanatory (Gauvain, Munroe, & Beebe, 2013).

What Is the Evidence that Questioning Increases Learning?

Some of the evidence on the effectiveness of children's questions on learning comes from intervention studies that were designed to assist children to ask questions. A review of 26 intervention studies specifically examining comprehension found that when children generated questions about what they had read they increased their comprehension by a median effect size of 0.86 on experimenter-developed tests. Most of these studies were interventions with elementary children, several were with children who were in third grade (Rosenshine, Meister, & Chapman, 1996). In other intervention studies, King (1994) found that children who were able to ask better questions had more complex knowledge construction. King and Rosenshine (1993) found higher posttest knowledge for children who asked better questions.

Further evidence comes from a study by the National Reading Panel. They examined 203 studies to determine the most effective ways to increase reading comprehension. They found an effective technique was for learners to generate questions and then answer these questions as they read. They point out that questioning is both a cognitive and metacognitive activity (2000). Finally, researchers found that when children are completing a task, they remember information better if they ask questions rather than if they are simply given the information (Chouinard & Imberi-Olivares, 2011).

How Can You Assist Learners in Asking Effective Questions?

There are many ways that teachers can assist children in asking effective questions. Several ideas are presented below.

- Provide interesting stimuli and experiences to ask questions about.
- Interpret questions that non-verbal children ask by giving a voice to their questions.
- Promote a climate of curiosity, where questioning and seeking answers is valued (Vale, 2013). We begin by treating children's questions seriously, encouraging children to pursue the answers to their questions, and providing opportunities for them to share what they find out with others.
- When answering questions provide information about the function of objects, not just the name. When children ask, "What is it?" they are often more interested in knowing the function of the object versus just its name. This information helps them to form a concept of the item (Nelson, Egan, & Holt, 2004).
- Model asking questions. For example, as you read stories model asking different types of questions. You can ask questions that encourage children to look for similarities and differences, examine cause and effect, link previous learning with the book, look for evidence, find other examples, speculate on what will occur next, and look at how characters could make different choices. Children who hear a range of questions ask more advanced questions themselves (Birbili & Karagiorgou, 2009).
- Directly teach children how to ask questions. For example, you might create a dice with question stems of why, how, what if (Wrobel, 2018). As children explore an object, you can roll the dice and the children can brainstorm questions based on the question stem.
- Provide some opportunities for formalized question asking such as creating a KWHL chart or creating a topical web of questions.

Asking questions is a lifelong learning skill, allowing us to gain the information we need to increase our knowledge and gain conceptual understanding. We assist children to gain this valuable skill through treating children's questions as serious inquiry, modeling and teaching, and providing opportunities for questioning.

Help Learners Reflect on Their Learning

Reflecting or thinking about our learning has many benefits. First, it is a metacognitive skill. As children reflect, they clarify their thinking, synthesize their learning, and gain new insights and meaning from experiences. This allows them to use what they have learned in new situations, to transfer their knowledge, skills, and understandings. Without reflection, experiences often remain as isolated events.

Additionally, as pointed out by Carr (2011)

> one of the reasons for enabling children to reflect on their learning is to contribute to their developing views about how they learn, and their identities as learners; these views may be established in the early years and are often resistant to change.

(p. 258)

When children believe that their efforts and strategies contribute to their learning, they are more likely to attribute their success to their efforts rather than to conditions outside of their control. As we engage in reflection with children, we also demonstrate to them that we value their learning. Finally, as learners share their reflections with others, they practice articulating their thinking and they learn from others' perspectives.

What Is the Evidence that Reflection Aids Children's Learning?

The National Research Council in a landmark publication, *Eager to Learn: Educating our Preschoolers* (2001) synthesized research from cross-disciplinary sources related to preschool children. Based on this research, they state that preschool children are capable of reflection and that metacognitive skills such as reflection increase engagement and raise achievement scores in science, math, and literacy.

In a large national study that featured a variety of curricular approaches, children who were able to plan and reflect on their learning scored higher on language, literacy, social skills, and overall development (Epstein, 1993, 2012). The research was sponsored by the HighScope Educational Research Foundation but was conducted by independent observers.

How Do We Assist Children to Reflect on Their Learning?

There are many different techniques that aid in reflection including creating and revisiting learning stories, reviewing and revisiting documentation, group discussions, and keeping reflective journals or logs.

As we discussed in Chapter 4, learning stories typically include a learning event that is often documented with text, photos, and sometimes video. The text describes the context and the nature of the learning experience and suggestions for future work. Teachers have conversations with a child about the learning story, allowing the child to revisit the experience and to reflect upon his or her learning. Several strategies were found to enhance these conversations including, teacher authenticity, where the teacher talks with the child in a conversational tone similar to conversations they would have with an adult; co-authoring the story; using artifacts and photos as a basis for the story; helping make personalized connections between the story and the child's interests and past learning; and group discussions (Carr, 2011).

These same strategies can be used to revisit and review other forms of documentation. Having the documentation readily available makes revisiting more likely. Providing graphics such as a series of photos make revisiting easier for children who do not yet read. Finally, establishing a routine for revisiting such as families reviewing children work samples as they come each morning provides a systematic way to ensure that this important aspect of learning is not forgotten (Carr, 2011).

Group discussions are another way to aid reflection. During group discussions, individual children can share their work and their strategies while others ask clarification questions. Reflective discussions can also be a place where each child shares briefly a goal they have for the day or something they have learned that day.

Journals and logs are also a popular reflection strategy. Both adults and children can use journals and logs as a method to reflect on what they learned, how they learned it, and the techniques and strategies that were helpful and unhelpful. Younger children might dictate or draw their responses. Providing a specific prompt to respond to can assist learners. Following are some prompts.

- Use the 3-2-1 technique. In this technique, the child lists three things she has learned, two things she wants to learn, and one question she still has.
- Write a one-minute summary.
- Draw a picture or create a model of something learned.
- Choose a question probe to answer. Question probes include "I learned … I'm confused about…. An aha idea I discovered was….. I disagree with …………… I agree with…………… The muddiest point was….."
- Complete two stars and a wish. Evaluate your work and your process with two things you feel good about and one that you would like to change
- Make a list of dos and don'ts. For example, "When adding numbers do….. don't…." "When writing a story do…. and don't……."
- Describe what you do when you get stuck. This could relate to a specific skill such as writing a story.
- Describe the specific strategies you used and how they helped or hindered the learning process. This is easier to answer if it relates to a specific task or exercise.
- Compare intended and actual outcomes.

In guiding children to become more reflective, there are several techniques that you can use. You can:

- model your own reflective process through talking aloud.
- review and critique examples of reflection. These could be from previous students (with permission) or examples that you have created.
- teach specific techniques such as the 3-2-1 technique.
- discuss metacognitive strategies such as strategies you might use to comprehend a story or solve a problem and have children practice the strategies.

- establish a regular time for reflecting.
- provide props such as videos, photos, artifacts or other forms of documentation to assist children in remembering the event.

Reflection is a critical metacognitive skill that is important for learners of all ages. Without reflection, our learning is hindered and our ability to change behavior is limited.

Teach Learners to Think Critically

From birth, babies engage in thinking and this skill improves with age. However, according to Paul and Elder, who are with the Foundation for Critical Thinking, our thinking is often biased, distorted, and uninformed. They state, "Humans have a natural tendency, all other things being equal, to make decisions and to reason egocentrically or sociocentrically" (2014, p. 24). Without specific training we fall into the following forms of egocentric thinking:

- Innate egocentrism—it's true because I believe it
- Innate sociocentrism—it's true because many people believe it
- Innate wish fulfillment—it's true because it feels good to believe it, it supports my other beliefs, and I don't have to change my beliefs
- Innate self-validation—it's true because it's a long-held belief
- Innate selfishness—it's true because it allows me to maintain power, money, or personal advantage (Paul & Elder, 2014, p. 21).

What causes our thinking to be egocentric? Either we've never examined the underlying basis or justification for these beliefs or there is no evidence or reasoning to support the beliefs.

Sociocentric thinking is our uncritical belief that our culture is superior to others. Without examination, we accept and abide by group norms, identities, restrictions, and traditional prejudices. As a result, we may view other cultures in a negative light and we fail to enhance the breadth and depth of our thinking by studying and gaining insights from other cultures (Paul & Elder, 2014, p. 22).

Other researchers point out that we tend to have my-side bias where we believe information that conforms to our existing beliefs and to dismiss information that does not conform to our current beliefs. Engaging in egocentric thinking, sociocentric thinking, or my-side bias can lead us to make poor judgments and decisions, become trapped by mistaken beliefs, and affect our ability to engage in deep learning.

There are many different types of thinking programs that attempt to improve thinking skills. We will review a popular program, Visible Thinking, that is used throughout the world for children from Pre-K through high school. This is a project originating from Harvard's Project Zero. A focus of the program is on developing a culture of thinking. Teachers who want to develop a culture of thinking focus on learning versus the completion of activities. For example, children in a second-grade classroom are reading the book *The One Day House* by Julia Durango. The story is about a young boy, Wilson and his elderly neighbor, Giga. Wilson is concerned about the decrepit condition of Giga's house and wants to fix it. But Giga reminds him of how much his companionship means to her. Ultimately, Wilson organizes an event to fix Giga's house. A teacher might simply focus on completing the activity of reading or a teacher might focus on how the book can be used to increase learning and thinking. For example, children might think about connections between the book and their neighbors and neighborhoods, about ways that they can help those in need. They might consider the different viewpoints of Giga and Wilson. A culture of thinking is enhanced by teaching learners to use thinking tools or routines. We have discussed some thinking routines previously in this book including KWHL charts and Think, Pair, and Share.

Just like backward design, an important component of Visible Thinking is understanding. According to Ritchhart, Church, and Morrison, the authors of *Making Thinking Visible*, understanding is a primary goal of all thinking (2011). The Visible Thinking team has developed a map of thinking that is useful across curriculum areas and that is especially important for understanding. These are:

1. Observing closely and describing what's there
2. Building explanations and interpretations
3. Reasoning with evidence
4. Making connections
5. Considering different viewpoints and perspectives
6. Capturing the heart and forming conclusions
7. Wondering and asking questions
8. Uncovering complexity and going below the surface of things (Ritchhart, Church, & Morrison, 2011, pp. 11-13).

Additionally, thinking helps us in problem-solving, decision-making, and in forming judgments. Some types of thinking that assist with these goals include (Ritchhart et al., 2011, p. 14):

- identifying patterns and making generalizations.
- generating possibilities and alternatives.
- evaluating evidence, arguments, and actions.
- formulating plans and monitoring actions.
- identifying claims, assumptions, and bias.
- clarifying priorities, conditions, and what is known.

By first creating a culture where thinking is valued, then providing tools to assist with thinking, and finally by making thinking visible to learners and to those who work with them we are able to enhance thinking skills.

What Is the Evidence that Thinking Routines Are Effective?

Project Zero researchers have conducted several studies on thinking routines. The routines were originally developed using a design-research paradigm across three different thinking routine projects in Sweden, Netherlands and Belgium, and the United States. Based upon classroom data such as observations, interviews, journals, logs, and surveys, routines were created, critiqued, modified, and eliminated. Researchers found that children who had previously lacked a voice became more confident and active learners (Ritchhart, Palmer, Church, & Tishman, 2006). In a project where thinking was reviewed using concept maps, researchers found that children of all ages made statistically significant gains in using thinking strategies, exceeding normal developmental projections by over 68% (Ritchhart, Turner, & Hadar, 2009). State and district test scores in reading, writing, and social studies significantly increased in a school district that adopted Visible Thinking ideas (Ritchhart & Perkins, 2008).

Additionally, learning became more collective for both children and teachers and children became more engaged and self-directed in their learning.

In a study of 366 fourth- and fifth-grade children studying art in New York City, the children who received visual thinking had a statistically significant increase in evidential reasoning and awareness of the subjective nature of interpretations in comparison to the control group. These thinking skills transferred to a later science experience. Visual thinking was successful for children of all ability levels. As might be expected, children experienced greater increases when teachers were more skilled (Tishman, MacGillivray, & Palmer, 1999).

How Can You Facilitate Thinking Routines?

There are many techniques that teachers use to facilitate thinking routines.

- Effective teachers teach thinking routines at the beginning of the year and use them frequently. As children learn and internalize routines, they are able to use them on their own. They become thinking dispositions or thinking habits (Ritchhart, 2002).
- Make thinking visible and explicit by noticing, naming, and highlighting children's thinking techniques.
- Model and name your own thinking techniques.
- Create opportunities for thinking through providing challenging projects, and through questioning, listening, and documenting.
- Provide the needed time for deep thinking. Initial thinking is often shallow, as we continue with the thinking process, we build upon these initial ideas and thinking becomes deeper.

Use thinking routines. Thinking routines are like tools, you will want to choose the right one based upon what type of thinking you are promoting. For example, as you develop and implement your unit there are routines that are especially helpful for different phases of your unit. We will examine one routine in each category. However, to learn more routines, visit the Visible Thinking website where you can see a variety of different routines or read the book, *Making Thinking Visible* (Ritchhart et al., 2011).

Routines for Introducing and Exploring New Ideas That You Might Use at the Beginning of a Unit

One of the most popular of all routines is See-Think-Wonder (Ritchhart et al., 2006). The stimulus for this routine can be a piece of art, a photo, or an object. The children first closely examine and look at the stimulus and share what they see. Take time to closely examine and discuss the stimulus since this provides the information for the next step which is an interpretation of what is seen. The next step is to discuss what they think. Depending on the stimulus the teacher might ask questions such as, "What do you think is going on?" "What do you see that makes you say that?" The final step is wondering, this is where children ask questions. If this is at the beginning of a unit, you might record the questions as a foundation for your unit.

For example, a first-grade class was beginning a unit on frogs. Cindy, the teacher began the unit with a provocation. When the children arrived one morning there was a small child's swimming pool in the classroom filled with tadpoles. The children were very excited. Later that day they completed the See-Think-Wonder routine as a way to begin their unit.

*Routines for Synthesizing and Organizing Ideas That You
Might Use during a Unit*

I used to think_____ but now I think_____ is a simple routine where children examine their past and current thinking. For example, Cindy used this routine shortly after the tadpoles had become frogs. One of the children said,

> I used to think that frogs were like babies, they were born looking like the grown-ups but were smaller but now I think they go through metamorphosis, they begin as eggs, then become tadpoles, and then become frogs, kind of like butterflies.

*Routines that Allow You to Dig Deeper into Ideas That You
Might Use at the Culmination of a Unit*

As the unit progressed the children began to explore a community issue which was the loss of habitat for the frogs. They read books and articles, visited with a land developer who wanted to fill in some wetland to make room for a low-income housing complex, and they visited with an environmentalist who wanted to protect the frogs. The children then engaged in a Step Inside routine to more fully explore these ideas. In the Step Inside routine, someone steps inside the role of another person or thing. Cindy used a hula hoop as a visual reminder of stepping inside. Other teachers of young children use props related to the role. When the child was inside the circle, they answered several questions based upon their character such as

- What can this person see, observe, or notice?
- What might the person know, understand, or believe? During this phase, you might also ask children to defend their thinking by asking "What makes you say that?"
- What might the person care deeply about? Again, asking children to provide evidence is helpful.
- What might the person wonder about or question? (Ritchhart et al., 2011).

Children performed this routine through the eyes of the land developer and the environmentalist. This allowed the children to dig deeper into this controversy and to understand the controversy from multiple perspectives. It also allowed them to synthesize their learning.

Visual Thinking routines assist children to learn a process that is at the heart of all learning, thinking. As children learn and repeatedly practice specific routines with the facilitation of a teacher, these ways of thinking become ingrained and children are able to use them independently.

Early Childhood Education

Does Visual Thinking also work for adults?

Many of the Visible Thinking routines are also appropriate for adults. For example, the 4 C's (connections, challenge, concepts, changes) is especially appropriate if reading a complex article. In this protocol, you make connections between the text and your life or learning, you challenge ideas, assumptions, or positions, you determine the concepts you view as important, and you determine changes based upon the text.

Additionally, there is also a movement within teacher professional learning communities to use protocols. These include protocols for reading texts, effective discussions, exploring student work, examining problems of practice, and addressing issues and problems.

One of my favorite protocols is What? So What? Now What? (Thompson-Grove, 2012). During the "What?" part of the protocol the teacher describes a current issue or challenge. During the "So What?" part of the protocol the teacher describes why this issue or challenge is important. During the final part of the protocol, "Now What?" the teacher discusses the next steps that can be taken to solve the issue or face the challenge. In performing this protocol, someone presents the "What" and "So What" and the rest of the group asks clarifying questions. Then the group reflects back what they hear the presenter say. They then give their own thoughts such as "What I wonder ... What this means to me ... What I might suggest......." The presenter listens to the discussion, gains new insights, and then completes the "Now What." I find that the protocol helps to bring clarity to the issue and helps to move the issue to a solution phase. I have found that this protocol also works well for discussing a group issue or even a state or national issue.

Use Powerful Teaching Techniques

Powerful teaching techniques can also assist children with learning. We will examine cooperative learning, authentic learning, identifying likenesses and differences, and using visual representations. These were chosen because they are techniques that can be used with learners of all ages and across curricular areas. They are research-based and show strong potential for increasing learning.

Are there other teaching techniques that are powerful or are these the main ones?

There are many powerful teaching techniques. Some of these are for a specific age group or for a specific curricular area. For example, dialogic reading, an interactive picture book reading technique that improves oral language skills, is listed as being effective in the What Works Clearinghouse. In this technique, the child becomes the storyteller with the adult being a responsive, attentive, and questioning listener. Teachers assist children by using different types of prompts that form the acronym CROWD.

Completion (asking children to complete a fill in the blank sentence).
Recall (asking children to remember key elements of the story).
Open-ended questions related to the story or the pictures.
Wh (asking who, what, where, and why questions).
Distancing (relating the story to children's lives).

The teacher also scaffolds children's learning through a process called PEER.

Prompt (using one of the prompts above).
Evaluation (evaluating the child's response).
Expansion (expanding on the child's response).
Repetition (repeating the prompt).

This technique has an average improvement rating of 19 percentile points for oral language (What Works Clearinghouse, 2007).

Use Cooperative Learning

Cooperative learning is an umbrella term that includes many different cooperative learning approaches such as student team learning, jigsaw, learning together, group investigation, peer tutoring, and response groups. However, in each of these, learners work cooperatively in small structured groups to achieve a mutual goal. Cooperative learning differs from other small group structures in that it includes five key elements (Johnson & Johnson, 2014).

- Positive interdependence where the group must rely on each other to accomplish the group's goal. Each group member is needed to succeed.
- Individual accountability where each person is responsible for a share of the work and also for helping and supporting other group members' learning. In this way, the learning of each team member is strengthened. A learner cannot "hitch-hike" on another member's work.
- Promotive interaction where learners assist, support, and encourage each other. Individuals might explain, model, challenge each other, and make links to past learning.
- Interpersonal and small group skills are needed, supported, and utilized. Learners are taught the skills needed to work cooperatively such as "leadership, decision-making, trust-building, communication, and conflict-management" (Johnson & Johnson, 2014, p. 485).
- Group processing where members systematically reflect on how the group is functioning and on their work progress and process. This includes determining what actions are helpful and unhelpful and based on this what behaviors to continue or change.

Those who promote cooperative learning state that these elements help groups to function effectively and cooperatively. Additionally, these elements are needed for cooperation outside of the classroom; within families, communities, organizations, and among nations (Johnson and Johnson, 2014). Engaging in cooperative learning can provide lifelong learning tools.

What Is the Evidence That Cooperative Learning Is Effective?

Cooperative learning has been widely studied. Over 40 years of systematic reviews and numerous meta-analyses have proven that cooperative learning is effective. The Education Endowment Foundation (2018), an English What Works Centre in Education states that cooperative learning can add an additional five months of learning to an average school year. The United States What Works Clearinghouse has reviewed specific types of cooperative learning and has also found them to be effective. For example, peer tutoring and response groups assisted English language learners to improve their English language development 17 percentile points above the control group. Class-wide peer tutoring raised general reading achievement by 14 percentile points above the control group (U.S. Department of Education, 2007a, 2007b).

Over 685 studies have examined the success of cooperative, individualistic, and competitive learning (Johnson & Johnson, 2014). Research shows that in these comparisons, learners in cooperative learning have higher academic achievement, higher level reasoning, more frequent generation of new ideas and solutions, and greater transfer of learning. Cooperative learning also has social and emotional benefits including higher self-esteem, enhanced perceptions of classmates, more positive interactions, and increased friendships. Additionally, learners enjoy school more when engaged in cooperative learning and there is increased attendance, time on task, and motivation (Johnson & Johnson, 1989, 2014; Kyndt et al., 2013).

Cooperative learning is widely used in schools throughout the world, in all curricular areas with learners from preschool through adulthood (Johnson, Johnson, & Stanne, 2000; Slavin, 1995). It has been found to be equally effective for all ethnic groups and for learners with differing ability levels.

How Do We Implement Cooperative Learning?

Designing effective cooperative group activities involves more than just gathering a group of learners together. To be effective:

- the task needs to be well-designed and structured so that group work is efficient. Goals and criteria for success need to be clear.
- group goals need to be established, but individual accountability must also be built in.
- the teacher needs to support learners in gaining the needed communication and interaction skills.
- the teacher needs to form the groups. Research shows that small group sizes of three to four are most effective (Lou et al., 1996). Typically, it is best to use heterogeneous groups versus homogeneous groups. This provides more opportunities to learn from those with more diverse knowledge and experiences, is more likely to avoid "group think," and more accurately reflects the world of work (Dean, Hubbell, Pitler, & Stone, 2012).
- the teacher needs to monitor groups and provide any needed support. This might include teaching needed skills, providing assistance with understanding the task or process, and helping the group to work effectively with each other.

For example, Tarim (2009) describes the process the teachers used to prepare preschoolers to participate in cooperative learning. In preparing the children to work effectively in groups, the teachers first engaged children in partner activities, then triads, and finally in groups of four. The children completed activities that required the sharing of materials and the development of joint projects such as creating a joint piece of art. They completed several group bonding activities such as corners, where children stood in different corners of the room based upon their preferences of favorite foods and sports. Another bonding activity was an inside-outside circle where children faced a partner and shared information about themselves with their partner. They also completed group cohesion activities such as each group choosing a name, drawing a picture to represent their group, and creating a unique handshake. Finally, they taught children some basic communication skills such as active listening which entailed looking at the person who is talking, listening to the speaker, and keeping hands still. They posted pictures of eyes, ears, and hands as a reminder. They also taught the children to use "happy talk" a method for providing positive feedback to peers. With this support, preschoolers were able to successfully engage in cooperative learning of mathematics problem-solving. As a result, there was a significant difference in problem-solving abilities for the groups experiencing the 20 cooperative learning lessons versus the control group who completed the lessons in a whole class format.

Cooperative learning is perhaps the best studied of educational strategies. Research over many years and in countries throughout the world have proven that it is effective with all age groups, with all ethnic groups, and with learners of multiple abilities. However, to be effective, the teacher must carefully structure the task, provide the needed support, and use the technique on a regular basis. Additionally, choosing tasks that require higher level thinking, problem-solving, or diverse opinions takes the best advantage of the technique.

I have heard about cooperative learning but have not had much success using it. The teachers I work with always complain that some of the members are loafing. What do you suggest?

As a professor for many years, I have also struggled with the most effective ways to form groups and help groups to work cooperatively.

For example, I team-taught an intensive course on Reggio Emilia and the Project Approach each summer that relied on small groups working together to experience the project approach. During this week-long class, we lived and worked together in an isolated mountain setting in Montana. Initially, my colleague and I were unprepared for the intense conflict that occurred within the groups. We had wrongfully assumed that since we were working with adult learners, it was unnecessary to provide a cooperative learning structure. However, as time went on, we experimented with different cooperative learning techniques that made the groups work more effectively. We:

- started the course one-half day earlier and taught group skills such as conflict resolution, active listening, I messages, clear and unclear communication; explored productive and unproductive conflict; and learned about cooperative learning.
- established group and individual accountability by creating rubrics for the final project and also a collaboration rubric that was filled out by each group member on themselves and each other group member. The scores on the group rubric and the aggregated individual collaboration rubric became part of their grade.
- implemented early bonding experiences and getting to know your experiences such as a group hike and bonfire. We had each participant create and post a "Getting to Know Me Poster" that contained such things as the learner's photo, five adjectives

that described them, information about their role in early childhood, and anything else they would like to share with the group. These were posted and we found the class frequently reading them. We also created Venn diagrams where groups of three participants found personal characteristics that were similar and different from other group members.

- debated about whether to let learners choose their own groups or whether we as teachers should form the groups. After experimenting with different methods, we found that it worked best for us to assign groups but base this upon each learner's preferences. Based upon a limited time, the local natural environment, and the need to bring resources we had prechosen topics of water, rocks, or plants to study. We had learners rank which topic they were interested in. They could also list people they would like to work with and list anyone they felt they would be ineffective in working with. Additionally, they could list any types of personality characteristics they found difficult to work with. We used this information and their "Getting to Know Me Posters" to form groups.

- established a peace room for group processing and for groups to use when conflict occurred. The room was a peaceful, quiet setting. It contained a table and chairs, a notebook and pencils, posters reminding the group of strategies, and items that added to a peaceful ambiance such as a beautiful tablecloth, small battery-operated water fountain, flowers, and candles. The groups could use the room independently or ask one of us for assistance. We also met with each group in the peace room to explore how the group process was working and to answer any questions on the task.

- provided more structure. For example, we found that certain types of misunderstandings were likely to create conflict. These typically involved unclear understandings over roles, how the work was to be divided, and how decisions were to be made. When groups first formed, we had them create written ground rules. To do so, they addressed several points. For example, they determined roles, decided how work would be divided (would they complete all aspects of the project work as a group or would they divide the tasks), and determined how decisions would be made (consensus or majority rules, is every group member involved in each decision). They also set up predetermined times the group would meet.

After implementing these strategies, group work was more effective and unproductive conflict was reduced. Since then I have used similar techniques whenever I have a longer-term cooperative group activity.

Provide Authentic Learning

Like cooperative learning, authentic learning is an umbrella term that applies to several different techniques (Great Schools Partnership, 2013). For example, authentic tasks are a focus of project-based learning, problem-based learning (PBL), experiential learning, and situated learning. While there are many different definitions of authentic learning, a common element is that children and adults learn by engaging with real-world activities, problems, and issues. As they do so, they use the skills and knowledge that are used in the fields that they are studying. For example, if learning about history they read and compare original documents. They learn about the scientific process by conducting experiments using the process. A child learns how to measure accurately and the importance of doing so while building a birdhouse for the outdoor playground. If the child doesn't measure accurately, the birdhouse will not be easy to assemble, the seams will not be aligned so the bird will not be protected from the elements, or the hole might not be large enough for the bird to enter. As in real life, as learners engage in authentic learning, they often use inquiry and thinking skills, engage with a community of learners, learn through an interdisciplinary process, and share their learning with others.

Experts view authentic learning as one of the solutions to concerns about inert knowledge, where learners are unable to transfer the knowledge they have gained to another setting. For example, Molly can add fractions at school. However, later at home, when making cookies she needs to add half a cup of sugar. But the measuring cup is missing and she is unable to transfer her knowledge of fractions to this situation. She does not realize that she could use the ⅓ measuring cup and fill it twice. Unfortunately, the inability to transfer knowledge from one setting to another is a common phenomenon (Cho, Caleon, & Kapur, 2015).

As learners engage in authentic learning, they are using the actual skills, knowledge, and understandings present in real life. Additionally, in real-life activities, there are often additional levels of complexity over what occurs in a typical school setting. In schools, we often simplify the experience, provide the exact tools needed, eliminate extraneous information, and practice a specific skill in isolation. However, in the real world, this is often not the case. Providing real-life experiences with the added complexity it entails, aids transfer. Let's look at a relevant early childhood example. Anna has been teaching children letter writing skills. In past years, she has had children write letters to fictional characters as a way to practice. However, she wants to provide the children with a more authentic opportunity. Akio, a child in the classroom, has been in an accident and is expected to have a long recovery. Anna realizes that if children write letters to Akio, they have an authentic reason to write and this also provides support for Akio. When writing a letter to Akio the children consider the audience, an important real-life skill. Since they know Akio, they are able to think about what things he would be interested in knowing and to consider ways that they might cheer him up. They are motivated to write the letters and spend considerable time on the process, wanting to make sure that they write legibly and clearly convey their message. They discuss jokes they are putting in their letters and pictures they are drawing with their classmates. Anna notes that the children's skills and motivation regarding letter writing appear greater than in previous years.

Learning through authentic tasks is not a new concept. For example, John Dewey advocated for authentic tasks in the 1940s (Tan & Nie, 2015). Many fields such as music, drama, and the visual arts routinely use authentic learning. Therefore, most teachers have at least some familiarity with it. However, implementing authentic learning can still be challenging (Newmann, Marks, & Gamoran, 1996).

What Is the Evidence That Authentic Learning Is Effective?

It is difficult to aggregate the research on authentic learning since it occurs under multiple titles. Additionally, many of the studies have not been conducted with learners in the early childhood years. However, following are two studies that report positive successes for this age group.

- A study by Newmann, Marks and Gamoran (1996) of 130 classrooms in 23 public schools examining math and social studies found that authentic learning increased achievement. For example, an average student would increase their test scores from the 30th percentile to the 60th percentile if they were in a classroom with high levels of authentic learning versus low levels of authentic learning. These benefits were equally beneficial for students from different races, ethnic backgrounds, socioeconomic status, and gender.
- John Thomas (2000) in a review of PBL in K-12 schools found that learners engaged in PBL had either equivalent or slightly better general achievement and performance on lower level cognitive skills than their peers. However, those engaged in PBL were superior in several aspects including solving complex problems, using complex processes, and transferring knowledge. There was also some evidence that PBL resulted in improved attitudes, better attendance, and more self-reliant learners (see Thomas, 2000 for a complete review). PBL is one form of authentic learning.

Many studies have been conducted regarding authentic learning for adult learners. We will review one of these.

- A meta-analysis of PBL by Walker and Leary (2009) that reviewed 82 studies across multiple disciplines found that learners in PBL did as well as or better than those participating in lectures. There was a small effect size in favor of PBL.

How Do We Implement Authentic Learning?

Cronin (1993) provided several tips to consider as you begin to implement and expand your use of authentic learning.

- The main point of authentic learning is to let students have real-life experiences. While often this will be exciting and interesting for learners, at times engaging in real-life issues involves some tedious tasks.
- The degree to which an activity is authentic is based on a continuum. Try to find ways that you can make your current activities more authentic, when possible. For example, a simulation or case study might be a way to implement more authentic tasks if you are unable to have a first-hand experience.
- All authentic tasks are not complex, some are fairly simple such as the example of writing a letter to a classmate. However, some project-based learning even for young children can be very complex. For example, in Reggio Emilia, preschool children built a fountain for birds. This involved in-depth study, problem-solving, collaboration with other children as well as experts, and many first-hand experiences with water fountains.
- Take advantage of opportunities for authentic learning whenever possible. For example, I was teaching a college course on learning environments. A new program was being developed for infants and toddlers in the community. With support and appreciation from the new director of the facility, this provided a perfect real-life opportunity for students to practice what they were learning by creating designs for this new environment.

Authentic learning is a well-respected, research-based way to learn skills, gain knowledge, and increase understandings. As students engage in authentic learning, they also have the opportunity to use 21st-century learning skills such as collaboration, critical thinking, creativity, and communication.

Identify Similarities and Differences

Identifying similarities and differences is a fundamental intellectual process that is evident from birth. "Because the operations of identifying similarities and differences help move students from old to new knowledge, and from concrete to more abstract ideas, many scholars consider them to be at the core of all learning" (Apthorp, 2010, p. 14).

Like cooperative learning, identifying similarities and differences is a powerful technique for learners of all ages. Identifying and reasoning about similarities and differences allows learners to clarify thinking, gain new insights, make inferences, generalize, refine schemas, and develop conceptual understanding. As learners engage in identifying similarities and differences, they move beyond examining only superficial commonalities to discover deeper relationships based upon a more connected and abstract understanding. This results in increased learning and achievement (Apthorp, 2010).

Superficial commonalities are often based upon perceptual comparisons such as shape, color, or a distinctive feature (Namy & Gentner, 2002). For example, a perceptual comparison might be that an apple is red and round like a ball. With opportunities to examine likenesses and differences, children can move beyond perceptions to examine the relational commonalities. These are less obvious, conceptual comparisons such as understanding that apples belong to a category called fruit that can be eaten. Relational commonalities go beyond the obvious superficial characteristics to less obvious ones such as the function, the role, the form, and the biological needs.

What Is the Evidence That Identifying Similarities and Differences Enhances Learning?

Researchers at the Mid-continent Research for Education and Learning (McREL) reviewed research on instructional strategies to find the strategies that had the highest probability of enhancing achievement. They found nine strategies that met this criterion. One was identifying similarities and differences. This initial meta-analysis found that identifying similarities and differences was the most powerful of these nine strategies with an effect size of 1.61 (Marzano, Gaddy, & Dean, 2000). A meta-analysis conducted by McREL based upon more recent and more stringent research found an effect size of 0.66. This would be equivalent to a 25-point percentile gain in learner scores (Apthorp, 2010). The meta-analysis included studies conducted with different age levels, in multiple subjects, and in different areas of the world.

How Do We Use the Strategy of Identifying Similarities and Differences in Our Teaching?

Dean, Hubbell, Pitler, and Stone (2013) list four different techniques that we might use when planning activities to identify similarities and differences. These are comparing, classifying, creating metaphors, and creating analogies.

Comparing and classifying are tools for any age group. When comparing, learners look for similarities and differences and use this information to form categories or to classify. Even newborns can form categories based upon sensory inputs such as tastes and smells. Before children can speak, they are able to categorize emotional expressions (Gelman, 1989). At three months, babies can tell the difference between animals and vehicles and between dogs, cats, and birds (Arterberry & Bornstein, 2001; Quinn, Eimas, & Rosenkrantz 1993). Children's early categories might be considered immature since they are often based on superficial characteristics such as the way an object looks. For instance, they might call all round objects a ball.

However, this is often not the case. For example, children who have an extreme interest in a topic and therefore learn a lot about it (dinosaurs, trucks) use categories that are similar to that of older children and adults. Additionally, by the age of four, children are able to develop categories that include non-obvious information such as function and causal properties, information they infer based upon the information that they have (Gelman, 1989; Namy & Gentner, 2002). Let's look at an example, in a study of butterflies children might compare the butterfly to the moth. As they do so, they are likely to more closely examine the different physical features and the behavior of the butterfly and moth such as how they hold their wings, when they rest, or what time of day they gather food. To develop deeper learning, you might extend this to comparing the butterfly (an insect) to a spider (arachnids).

For adults and older children creating metaphors and analogies can be additional ways to explore similarities and differences. Metaphors are "a figure of speech in which a word or phrase literally denoting one kind of object or idea is used in place of another to suggest a likeness or analogy between them (as in *drowning in money*)" (*Merriam Webster Collegiate Dictionary*, 1996, p. 730). When exploring early childhood, one might have students examine some common metaphors that may or may not be true such as, "the child is an empty vessel" or "the child's mind is a sponge." An analogy is a comparison that highlights a relationship between two or more things. For example, a teacher who is teaching a child development course might use the following analogy, "scaffolding is to Vygotsky as _____ is to Piaget" and ask the students to fill in the blank. Analogies are very effective especially when students develop them themselves.

As you incorporate identifying likenesses and differences into your teaching there are some tips to remember.

- Learners must have background knowledge and experience with a topic to identify likenesses and differences.
- Learners need time to move beyond superficial comparisons to develop deeper understandings and comparisons.
- This technique is more effective when paired with cooperative learning, self-reflection, and formative assessment.
- Teachers that are most effective use modeling and cuing, encourage discussions, and provide corrective feedback allowing learners to develop understanding (Apthorp, 2010).
- Learning is enhanced when learners describe and defend their categories.
- When developmentally able, allowing learners to design their own categories, analogies, and metaphors can enhance learning.
- It is important to provide vocabulary to help learners develop categories. Although this seems obvious, research demonstrates that this helps children to form conceptual categories (Gelman & Coley, 1990; Waxman & Kosowski, 1990).
- Graphic organizers such as Venn diagrams can be an effective tool for categorizing (see Chapter 4 for a description of several different graphic organizer descriptions and examples). For example, a meta-analysis by Stone (1983) that examined 112 studies, found that using organizers yielded a mean difference of 0.66 between those using the organizers and those that did not. This was especially powerful for preschoolers with a mean of 1.01. Studies of elementary children revealed a mean of 0.64 and studies of adults yielded a score of 0.49.

Research demonstrates that the following assist young children to focus on relational matches (Namy & Gentner, 2002).

- Compare objects in pairs such as dogs and cats, allowing children to see pictures or actual objects at the same time (Oakes, 2001).
- Compare similar objects or ideas that are a relational match (apple and pear) versus a perceptual match (apple and red balloon).
- Use a unifying label such as fruit for the apple and pear versus labeling each one individually.

Identifying likenesses and differences through comparing, classifying, and developing metaphors and analogies, provide an important tool for enhancing learning for learners of all ages and in all domains and curricular areas. When combined with some of the other strategies discussed in this chapter, this tool can become even more powerful.

Encourage Visual Representations

Visual representations, sometimes referred to as nonlinguistic representations include such things as drawings, models, mapping, diagrams, videos, dramatizations, and graphic organizers (concept maps, webs). Like the other strategies in this chapter, this is a powerful teaching technique that is suitable for all ages.

Imagine you are going to represent an elephant through a painting, creating a model in clay, or dramatizing the elephant's movement. You most likely have a mental picture of an elephant. However, as you ponder how to represent the elephant, you begin to think about new details such as, how large are the ears in relation to the body? How does the elephant hold its head as it moves? To create a visualization, you observe the features more closely and more carefully examine the relationship between these features. While this is a simple representation, imagine now choosing a way to represent your knowledge about how children learn. What are the important ideas and concepts to highlight and how do you show the relationship between these? How will you make your implicit understanding, explicit?

As you think through these questions, you are bringing your ideas "more clearly into consciousness" (Brooks, 2009, p. 319). This focus on and reasoning about your current understanding of ideas and concepts about how children learn leads to a deeper understanding. Imagine now that you share and explain your representation with your classmates and they share theirs with you. This will most likely also further your thinking.

We use a lot of visual representation with our projects. For example, not long ago, we completed a project called "Wildflowers in our meadow." The children sketched the flowers multiple times, used colored pencils and crayons to provide color to their sketches, painted pictures of the flowers using watercolors, and created flowers out of wire. It was amazing to watch them. As time went on their flowers became more detailed and looked more like the flowers they were studying. For example, as they closely examined the flowers they began to notice and add the stamen to their drawings. They noted the color variations on the petals and their artwork reflected this. It really demonstrated what they were learning. When the families came to our culminating event, they were so shocked and surprised that the children had produced such detailed representations.

As we create visualizations, we communicate our understanding of content, but the process also helps us clarify our thinking and to gain new understandings. Visualizations can assist to reveal patterns and to connect information in new ways. For example, Ainsworth, Prain, and Tytler (2011, p. 1096) discussing visualizations in the field of science stress that visualizations are "integral to scientific learning." Visualizations are used to "make discoveries, explain findings, and excite public interest." Through visualizations scientists "imagine new relationships, test ideas, and elaborate knowledge."

Visualizations also help us to develop a mental picture. This can assist in the processing, organizing, and retrieval of information (Clemons, Igel, & Gopalani, 2010). One theory of learning called dual coding states that we have dual pathways (one visual and one verbal) that we use to encode information into memory. According to Cuevas (2016) who examined current evidence on dual coding,

> there is a substantial amount of research evidence that indicates that we encode visual and auditory stimuli differently and that when visual information is paired with and layered upon linguistic information retention is superior to when linguistic information is the sole source of input.

(p. 7)

What Is the Evidence that Visual Representations Are an Effective Learning Technique?

McREL researchers identified nine powerful teaching strategies. They list nonlinguistic representations as one of these strategies. A meta-analysis conducted by McREL of ten studies involving 5,000 learners of all ages in all content areas found that nonlinguistic representations have an effect size of 0.49, allowing a gain of 19 percentile points in one year (Clemons, Igel, & Gopalani, 2010).

How Do We Facilitate the Use of Visual Representations?

There are many different types of visual or nonlinguistic representations. Choose the best form of representation based upon your outcomes, the suitability for the content, and the available time. For example, Andrea's class is hatching caterpillars. If Andrea wants children to explore the physical features such as the hairs of the caterpillar, she might encourage children to create a model using clay and wire. This might occur as part of an enduring understanding of form follows function. If the focus is on the essential question, "What is a cycle?" Andrea might have children create a cycle graphic organizer by drawing pictures of the caterpillar at different stages. They might then use a Venn diagram to compare the cycle organizer of the caterpillar to a cycle organizer of frogs that they had created earlier.

Over time, teach learners multiple ways to represent their knowledge. Used consistently, learners will be able to experience the possibilities of different forms of nonlinguistic representation. As they gain this type of experience, they can choose what nonlinguistic representations they want to use to represent their learning.

To assist learning, ensure that the nonlinguistic representation includes crucial information needed for understanding. For example, Andrea wants children to concentrate on form and function of the caterpillar so she supplies a digital microscope so they can closely examine the caterpillar's mandibles. This gives children the opportunity to examine each of the caterpillar's features in a highly magnified form. This information affects the sketch or model the children create, leading to a greater understanding of how form follows function. Concentrating closely on different features of the caterpillar such as the mandible can assist children to understand that a primary function of the caterpillar is to eat and that the form of the sharp cutting surfaces of the mandible assists with this. Concentrating on the hairs allows the child to see the function of protection and the different forms that this can take in different caterpillars. Compare this type of rich experience and visualization to a commonly used activity of creating a model of a caterpillar using an egg carton and pipe cleaners. The crucial information needed to demonstrate and to gain a deeper understanding is lacking in this visualization.

Have learners describe their representations. As learners explain and justify their representations to others, they often elaborate on their thinking and their thinking is clarified. This results in a deeper understanding of the content (Stone, 2016). This is especially the case if peers or teachers ask questions that assist with this process. For example, teachers might use one of the visual thinking protocols to help learners ask good questions.

Revisit representations. This might be accomplished by revisiting the original format and revising or adding to it. Children might also revisit their ideas using a different representational format. For example, Andrea might have children observe the caterpillars with their naked eye and then draw a sketch. They might revisit the caterpillar sketch after they view the caterpillar with the digital microscope. After this experience, they are likely to add more detail to their sketch. They might also use a different format such as creating a skit to illustrate how form follows function.

Visual representations are a way for learners to demonstrate their knowledge, clarify their thinking, and gain new understandings. Representations, especially through visual art and drama, have been an accepted way of learning especially in the toddler and preschool years. Renewed understandings of the value of this learning occurred with the world learning more about the Reggio Emilia approach and the viewing of their display that traveled the world entitled "The 100 Languages of Children." These displays captured children's representations and the representations of the teachers that worked with them, showing a deep level of understanding by both groups. However, in early childhood, we have not always embraced this type of learning within the elementary years. Additionally, we have not taken full advantage of the many types of representations available for learning.

In Summary

To be an effective teacher you need many different strategies in your tool belt. However, you will want to ensure that any strategy that you use is learner-centered, based on constructivist beliefs and developmentally and culturally appropriate for your group of learners. Using strategies that are research-based and that have a proven record of success is also important. One of the key principles set forth in How People Learn is to teach children metacognitive skills. As we learned in Chapter 5, a recent review of research on teaching children to use metacognitive skills found effect sizes as high as 0.69 (Perry, Lundie, & Golder, 2018). In the section on teaching children how to learn, we discussed several techniques for enhancing metacognitive skills including helping children ask good questions, reflect on their learning, and learn to think. In this chapter, we also discussed powerful teaching strategies that are appropriate for a variety of ages and curricular areas. These include cooperative learning, authentic learning, identifying likenesses and differences, and visual representations. To experience the full benefits of any of the strategies discussed in the chapter, you will want to use them regularly. As you design your unit, using these strategies can assist children's and adult's learning.

Apply Your Knowledge

1. Choose one of the strategies and learn more about it. For example, visit the website on Visible Thinking or watch YouTube videos of teachers implementing a thinking routine.
2. Visit a classroom. Look for evidence to determine the degree to which the classroom is learner-centered.
3. Think of a topic and determine authentic experiences that could be planned for this topic.
4. Experiment with one or more of the strategies listed in the chapter. Be sure to carefully introduce the strategy to the learners. They will need to be taught how to use the strategy.
5. Create a visual representation for what you learned in this chapter.

References

Ainsworth, S., Prain, V., & Tytler, R. (2011). Science education. Drawing to learn in science. *Science, 333*(6046), 1096–1097. doi:10.1126/science.1204153

Apthorp, H. (2010). Identifying similarities and differences. In A. D. Beesley & H. S. Apthorp (Eds.), Classroom instruction that works. *Mid-continent Research for Education and Learning (McREL)* (pp. 14–31). Retrieved from https://www.mcrel.org/wp-content/uploads/2016/03/McREL-research-report_Nov2010_Classroom-Instruction-that-Works_Second-Edition.pdf

Arterberry, M. E., & Bornstein, M. H. (2001). Three-month-old infants' categorization of animals and vehicles based on static and dynamic attributes. *Journal of Experimental Child Psychology, 80*(4), 333–346. doi:10.1006/jecp.2001.2637

Birbili, M., & Karagiorgou, I. (2009). Helping children and their parents ask better questions: An intervention study. *Journal of Research in Childhood Education, 24*(1) 18–31. doi:10.1080/02568540903439359

Brooks, M. (2009). Drawing, visualisation and young children's exploration of "big ideas". *International Journal of Science Education, 31*(3), 319–341. doi:10.1080/09500690802595771

Bullard, J. (2003). Constructivism: Does your practice match your conceptual framework? *Journal of Early Childhood Teacher Education, 24*(3), 157–162. doi:10.1080/1090102030240304

Bullard, J., & Hitz, R. (1997). Early childhood education and adult education: Bridging the cultures. *Journal of Early Childhood Teacher Education, 18*(1), 15–22. doi:10.1080/10901029708549133

Burts, D. C., Hart, C. H., Charlesworth, R., DeWolf, D. M., Ray, J., Manuel, K., & Fleege, P. O. (1993). Developmental appropriateness of kindergarten programs and academic outcomes in first grade. *Journal of Research in Childhood Education, 8*(1), 23–31. doi:10.1080/02568549309594852

Burts, D. C, Hart, C., Charlesworth, R., Fleege, P., Mosley, & Thomasson, R. (1992). Observed activities and stress behaviors of children in developmentally appropriate and inappropriate kindergarten classrooms. *Early Childhood Research Quarterly, 7*, 297–318. doi:10.1016/0885-2006(92)90010-V

Burts, D. C, Hart, C., Charlesworth, R., & Kirk, L. (1990). A comparison of frequencies of stress behaviors observed in kindergarten children in classrooms with developmentally appropriate versus developmentally inappropriate instructional practices. *Early Childhood Research Quarterly, 5*, 407–423. doi: 10.1016/0885-2006(90)90030-5

Carr, M. (2011). Young children reflecting on their learning: Teachers' conversation strategies. *Early Years, 31*(3), 257–270. doi:10.1080/09575146.2011.613805

Cho, Y. H., Caleon, I. S., & Kapur, M. (Eds.) (2015). *Authentic problem solving and learning in the 21st century: Perspectives from Singapore and beyond*. Singapore: Springer Singapore. doi:10.1007/978-981-287-521-1

Chouinard, M. (2007). Children's questions: A mechanism for cognitive development. *Monographs of the Society for Research in Child Development, 72*(1). Boston, MA: Blackwell Publishing.

Chouinard, M., & Imberi-Olivares, K. (2011). Getting information from other people: Who do children turn to? In M. Siegal & L. Surian (Eds.), *Access to language and cognitive development* (pp. 100–115). Oxford University Press. doi:10.1093/acprof:oso/9780199592722.003.0006

Clemons, T., Igel, C., Gopalani, S. (2010). Nonlinguistic representations. In A. D. Beesley & H. S. Apthorp (Eds.), *Classroom instruction that works* (pp. 72–83). Denver, CO: Mid-continent Research for Education and Learning (McREL). Retrieved from https://www.mcrel.org/wp-content/uploads/2016/03/McREL-research-report_Nov2010_Classroom-Instruction-that-Works_Second-Edition.pdf

Cronin, J. (1993). Four misconceptions about authentic learning. *Educational Leadership, 50*(7), 78–80.

Cuevas, J. (2016). An analysis of current evidence supporting two alternate learning models: learning styles and dual coding. *Journal of Educational Sciences & Psychology, 6*(1), 1–13.

Dean, C. B., Hubbell, E. R., Pitler, H., & Stone, B. J. (2012). *Classroom instruction that works: Research-based strategies for increasing student achievement* (2nd ed.). Alexandria, VA: Association for Supervision and Curriculum Development (ASCD).

Donohue, K. M., Perry, K. E., & Weinstein, R. S. (2003). Teachers' classroom practices and children's rejection by their peers. *Journal of Applied Developmental Psychology, 24*(1), 91–118. doi:10.1016/S0193-3973(03)00026-1

Education Endowment Foundation. (2018). *Collaborative learning.* Retrieved from https://educationendowment foundation.org.uk/pdf/generate/?u=https://educationendowmentfoundation.org.uk/pdf/toolkit/?id=152&t=Teaching%20and%20Learning%20Toolkit&e=152&s=

Epstein, A. S. (1993). *Training for quality: Improving early childhood programs through systematic inservice training. Monographs of the High/Scope Educational Research Foundation, 9.* Ypsilanti, MI: High/Scope Press.

Epstein, A. S. (2012). How planning and reflection develop young children's thinking skills. In C. Copple (Ed.), *Growing minds: Building strong cognitive foundations in early childhood* (pp. 111–118). Washington, DC: National Association for the Education of Young Children (NAEYC).

Gauvain, M., Munroe, R. L., & Beebe, H. (2013). Children's questions in cross-cultural perspective: A four-culture study. *Journal of Cross-Cultural Psychology, 44*(7), 1148–1165. doi:10.1177/0022022113485430

Gelman, S. A. (1998). Categories in young children's thinking. Research in review. *Young Children, 53*(1), 20–26. doi:10.1177/109625069800100304

Gelman, S. A., & Coley, J. D. (1990). The importance of knowing a dodo is a bird: Categories and inferences in 2-year-old children. *Developmental Psychology, 26,* 796–804. doi:10.1037/0012-1649.26.5.796

Great Schools Partnership. (2013). *The glossary of education reform: Authentic learning.* Retrieved from https://www.edglossary.org/authentic-learning/

Guarino, C. M., Hamilton, L. S., Lockwood, J. R., & Rathbun, A. H. (2006). *Teacher qualifications, instructional practices, and reading and mathematics gains of kindergartners (NCES 2006-031).* U.S. Department of Education. Washington, DC: National Center for Education Statistics.

Henry, G., Ponder, B., Rickman, D., Mashburn, A., Henderson, L., & Gordon, C. (2004). *An evaluation of the implementation of Georgia's Pre-K program: Report of the findings from the Georgia Early Childhood Study (2002–03).* Atlanta, GA: Georgia State University, Andrew Young School of Policy Studies.

Huffman, L. R., & Speer, P. W. (2000). Academic performance among at-risk children: The role of developmentally appropriate practices. *Early Childhood Research Quarterly, 15*(2), 167–184. doi:10.1016/S0885-2006(00)00048-X

Hur, E., Buettner, C. K., & Jeon, L. (2015). The association between teachers' child-centered beliefs and children's academic achievement: The indirect effect of children's behavioral self-regulation. In *Child & Youth Care Forum* (Vol. 44, No. 2, pp. 309–325). Springer US. doi:10.1007/s10566-014-9283-9

Johnson, D. W., & Johnson, R. T. (1989). *Cooperation and competition: Theory and research.* Edina, MN: Interaction Book Company.

Johnson, D. W., & Johnson, R. T. (2014). Cooperative learning in 21st century. *Anales de psicología, 30*(3), 841–851. doi:10.6018/analesps.30.3.201241

Johnson, D. W., Johnson, R. T., & Stanne, M. B. (2000). *Cooperative learning methods: A meta-analysis.* Retrieved from https://www.researchgate.net/profile/David_Johnson50/publication/220040324_Cooperative_learning_methods_A_meta-analysis/links/00b4952b39d258145c000000.pdf

King, A. (1994). Guiding knowledge construction in the classroom: Effects of teaching children how to question and how to explain. *American Educational Research Journal, 31,* 338–368. doi:10.3102/00028312031002338

King, A., & Rosenshine, B. (1993). Effects of guided cooperative questioning on children's knowledge construction. *Journal of Experimental Education, 61,* 127–148. doi:10.1080/00220973.1993.9943857

Kyndt, E., Raes, E., Lismont, B., Timmers, F., Cascallar, E., & Dochy, F. (2013). A meta-analysis of the effects of face-to-face cooperative learning. Do recent studies falsify or verify earlier findings? *Educational Research Review, 10,* 133–149. doi:10.1016/j.edurev.2013.02.002

Lerkkanen, M. K., Kiuru, N., Pakarinen, E., Poikkeus, A. M., Rasku-Puttonen, H., Siekkinen, M., & Nurmi, J. E. (2016). Child-centered versus teacher-directed teaching practices: Associations with the development of academic skills in the first grade at school. *Early Childhood Research Quarterly, 36,* 145–156. doi:10.1016/j.ecresq.2015.12.023

Lerkkanen, M. K., Kiuru, N., Pakarinen, E., Viljaranta, J., Poikkeus, A. M., Rasku-Puttonen, H., ... & Nurmi, J. E. (2012). The role of teaching practices in the development of children's interest in reading and mathematics in kindergarten. *Contemporary Educational Psychology, 37*(4), 266–279. doi:10.1016/j.cedpsych.2011.03.004

Lou, Y., Abrami, P. C., Spence, J. C., Poulsen, C., Chambers, B., & d'Apollonia, S. (1996). Within-class grouping: A meta-analysis. *Review of Educational Research, 66*(4), 423–458. doi:10.3102/00346543066004423

Marcon, R. A. (1999). Differential impact of preschool models on development and early learning of inner-city children: A three cohort study. *Developmental Psychology, 35*(2), 358–375. doi:10.1037/0012-1649.35.2.358

Marcon, R. A. (2002). Moving up the grades: Relationship between preschool model and later school success. *Early Childhood Research & Practice, 4*(1), n1.

Marzano, R. J., Gaddy, B. B., & Dean, C. (2000). *What works in classroom instruction.* Aurora, CO: Mid-Continent Research for Education and Learning.

Merriam-Webster's Collegiate Dictionary (10th ed.) (1996). Springfield, MA: Merriam-Webster Incorporated.

Mills, C. M., Legare, C. H., Grant, M. G., & Landrum, A. R. (2011). Determining who to question, what to ask, and how much information to ask for: The development of inquiry in young children. *Journal of Experimental Child Psychology, 110*(4), 539–560. doi:10.1016/j.jecp.2011.06.003

Moyer, J. (2001). The child-centered kindergarten: A position paper: Association for Childhood Education International. *Childhood Education, 77*(3), 161–166. doi:10.1080/00094056.2001.10522153

Namy, L. L., & Gentner, D. (2002). Making a silk purse out of two sow's ears: Young children's use of comparison in category learning. *Journal of Experimental Psychology: General, 131*(1), 5. doi:10.1037/0096-3445.131.1.5

National Association for the Education of Young Children (NAEYC). (2009). *Developmentally Appropriate Practice position statement.* Retrieved from https://www.naeyc.org/resources/position-statements/dap

National Association for the Education of Young Children (NAEYC) and the National Council of Teachers of Mathematics (NCTM). (2010). *Early childhood mathematics in the promoting good beginnings position statement.* Retrieved from https://www.naeyc.org/sites/default/files/globally-shared/downloads/PDFs/resources/position-statements/psmath.pdf

National Reading Panel (US). (2000). *National Reading Panel: Teaching children to read: an evidence-based assessment of the scientific research literature on reading and its implications for reading instruction.* Washington, DC: National Institute of Child Health and Human Development, National Institutes of Health.

National Research Council. (1999). *How people learn: Bridging research and practice.* Washington, DC: National Academies Press.

National Research Council. (2001). *Eager to learn: Educating our preschoolers.* Washington, DC: The National Academies Press.

National Research Council. (2005). *How students learn: History, mathematics, and science in the classroom.* Washington, DC: The National Academies Press.

National Research Council. (2012). *Education for life and work: Developing transferable knowledge and skills in the 21st century.* Washington, DC: The National Academies Press.

National Science Teachers Association (NSTA). (2014). Position statement: Early childhood science education. Retrieved from https://www.nsta.org/about/positions/earlychildhood.aspx

Nelson, D., Egan, L. C., & Holt, M. B. (2004). When children ask, "What is it?" what do they want to know about artifacts? *Psychological Science, 15*(6), 384–389. doi:10.1111/j.0956-7976.2004.00689.x

Newmann, F., Marks, H., & Gamoran, A. (1996). Authentic pedagogy and student performance. *American Journal of Education, 104*(4), 280–312. doi:10.1086/444136

Oakes, L. M. (2001). The role of comparison in category formation in infancy. Paper presented at the 68th Anniversary Meeting of the Society for Research in Child Development, Minneapolis, MN.

Ostroff, W. L. (2016). *Cultivating curiosity in K-12 classrooms: How to promote and sustain deep learning.* Alexandria, VA: Association for Supervision and Curriculum Development (ASCD).

Paul, R., & Elder, L. (2014). *The miniature guide to critical thinking concepts and tools* (7th ed.). Tomales, CA: Foundation for Critical Thinking.

Perry, K. E., Donohue, K. M., & Weinstein, R. S. (2007). Teaching practices and the promotion of achievement and adjustment in first grade. *Journal of School Psychology, 45*(3), 269–292. doi:10.1016/j.jsp.2007.02.005

Perry, J., Lundie, D., & Golder, G. (2018). Metacognition in schools: What does the literature suggest about the effectiveness of teaching metacognition in schools? *Educational Review,* 1–18. doi:10.1080/00131911.2018.1441127

Quinn, P. C., Eimas, P. D., & Rosenkrantz, S. L. (1993). Evidence for representations of perceptually similar natural categories by 3-month-old and 4-month-old infants. *Perception, 22,* 463–475. doi:10.1068/p220463

Ritchhart, R. (2002). *Intellectual character: What it is, why it matters, and how to get it.* San Francisco, CA: Jossey-Bass.

Ritchhart, R., Church, M., & Morrison, K. (2011). *Making thinking visible: How to promote engagement, understanding, and independence for all learners.* San Francisco, CA: Jossey Bass.

Ritchhart, R., Palmer, P., Church, M., & Tishman, S. (2006). *Thinking routines: Establishing patterns of thinking in the classroom.* Retrieved from http://citeseerx.ist.psu.edu/viewdoc/download;jsessionid=6D50EBE087E9F6776A6FB0B2451AB2B9?doi=10.1.1.545.213&rep=rep1&type=pdf

Ritchhart, R., & Perkins, D. (2008). Making thinking visible. *Educational Leadership, 65*(5), 57–61.

Ritchhart, R., Turner, T., & Hadar, L. (2009). Uncovering students' thinking about thinking using concept maps. *Metacognition and Learning, 4*(2), 145–159. doi:10.1007/s11409-009-9040-x

Rosenshine, B., Meister, C., & Chapman, S. (1996). Teaching students to generate questions: A review of the intervention studies. *Review of Educational Research, 66*(2), 181-221. doi:10.3102/00346543066002181

Ruggeri, A., & Lombrozo, T. (2015). Children adapt their questions to achieve efficient search. *Cognition, 143,* 203-216. doi:10.1016/j.cognition.2015.07.004

Schweinhart, L. J., & Weikart, D. P. (1997). The High/Scope preschool curriculum comparison study through age 23. *Early Childhood Research Quarterly, 12*(2), 117-143. doi:10.1016/S0885-2006(97)90009-0

Slavin, R. E. (1995). *Cooperative learning theory, research, and practice* (2nd ed.). Boston, MA: Allyn & Bacon.

Stipek, D. (2004). Teaching practices in kindergarten and first grade: Different strokes for different folks. *Early Childhood Research Quarterly, 19*(4), 548-568. doi:10.1016/j.ecresq.2004.10.010

Stipek, D., Feiler, R., Daniels, D., & Milburn, S. (1995). Effects of different instructional approaches on young children's achievement and motivation. *Child Development, 66*(1), 209-223. doi:10.2307/1131201

Stipek, D. J., Feiler, R., Byler, P., Ryan, R., Milburn, S., & Salmon, J. M. (1998). Good beginnings: What difference does the program make in preparing young children for school? *Journal of Applied Developmental Psychology, 19*(1), 41-66. doi:10.1016/S0193-3973(99)80027-6

Stone, B. J. (2016). Four tips for using nonlinguistic representations. Message posted to https://www.mcrel.org/four-tips-for-using-nonlinguistic-representations/

Stone, C. (1983). A meta-analysis of advance organizer studies. *The Journal of Experimental Education, 51*(4), 194-199. doi:10.1080/00220973.1983.11011862

Tan, J. P. L., & Nie, Y. (2015). The role of authentic tasks in promoting twenty-first century learning dispositions. In Y. H. Cho, I. S. Caleon, & M. Kapur, (Eds.), *Authentic problem solving and learning in the 21st century* (pp. 19-39). Singapore: Springer Singapore. doi:10.1007/978-981-287-521-1_2

Tarim, K (2009). The effects of cooperative learning on preschoolers' mathematics problem-solving ability. *Educational Studies in Mathematics, 72*(3): 325-340. doi:10.1007/s10649-009-9197-x

Thomas, J. W. (2000). *A review of research on project-based learning.* Retrieved from https://www.asec.purdue.edu/lct/HBCU/documents/AReviewofResearchofProject-BasedLearning.pdf

Thompson-Grove, G. (2012). What? So what? Now what? Retrieved from http://schoolreforminitiative.org/doc/what_so_what.pdf

Tishman, S., MacGillivray, D., & Palmer, P. (1999). *Investigating the educational impact and potential of the museum of modern art's visual thinking curriculum: Final report, Harvard Project Zero.* Retrieved from http://www.pz.harvard.edu/sites/default/files/PZ-MoMA%20FINAL%20REPORT%2011-99.pdf

U.S. Department of Education, Institute of Education Sciences, National Center for Education Evaluation and Regional Assistance, What Works Clearinghouse. (2007a). *Classwide peer tutoring.* Retrieved from https://ies.ed.gov/ncee/wwc/Docs/InterventionReports/WWC_CWPT_070907.pdf

U.S. Department of Education, Institute of Education Sciences, National Center for Education Evaluation and Regional Assistance, What Works Clearinghouse. (2007b). *Peer tutoring and response groups.* Retrieved from https://ies.ed.gov/ncee/wwc/Docs/InterventionReports/WWC_Peer_Tutoring_070907.pdf

Vale, R. D. (2013). The value of asking questions. *Molecular Biology of the Cell, 24*(6), 680-682. doi:10.1091/mbc.e12-09-0660

Walker, A., & Leary, H. (2009). A problem based learning meta analysis: Differences across problem types, implementation types, disciplines, and assessment levels. *Interdisciplinary Journal of Problem-based Learning, 3*(1), 6-28. doi:10.7771/1541-5015.1061

Waxman, S. R., & Kosowski, T. (1990). Nouns mark category relations: Toddlers' and preschoolers' word-learning biases. *Child Development, 61,* 1461-1473. doi:10.2307/1130756

What Works Clearinghouse. (2007). *Dialogic reading.* Retrieved from https://ies.ed.gov/ncee/wwc/Docs/InterventionReports/WWC_Dialogic_Reading_020807.pdf

Wrobel, S. (2018). *The question game: A playful way to teach critical thinking.* Retrieved from https://www.teachthought.com/critical-thinking/question-game-playful-way-teach-critical-thinking/

9 Designing Integrated Units

At this point, you know how to determine desired outcomes including essential questions, enduring understandings, knowledge, skills, and approaches to learning. You've learned how to assess your desired results and you've learned about powerful strategies and techniques to help learners achieve the desired results. In this chapter, we will examine how you use all of this information to develop effective, interesting, integrated units. Units may also be referred to as investigations, projects, or studies.

There are many different definitions for integrated units and different ways of integrating. For the purpose of this book, integrated units are defined as the use of a topic, concept (family), phenomena or problems, or issue (getting along with others) to form an organizing theme that combines different domains and curricular areas into a coherent study. Integrated units are philosophically aligned with learner-centered teaching where the teacher is a facilitator of learning, learners are actively engaged in experiential learning, and the curriculum is relevant and meaningful to learners.

Integrated units allow learners to experience a curriculum that is less fragmented and more coherent. As proponents point out, the real world is integrated so integrated learning is a more natural way to learn. To solve real-world problems, we use knowledge from multiple disciplines. Units combine knowledge and skills and allow children to apply their knowledge in a real-life context. Because in an integrated curriculum, connections between ideas and subjects are more explicit than when subjects are taught individually, children can more easily connect ideas and form meaningful relationships between curricular areas. This, in turn, aids in conceptual understanding and the ability to transfer learning. Integrated curriculum is also aligned with the way our brain works, as an organism that tries to make sense of the world through seeking patterns.

Since units are often designed by teachers and school districts, the topics are more relevant and meaningful to children than curriculum that is developed elsewhere. Additionally, rather than engaging in isolated exercises, learning material as part of a unit creates, "the need to know." For example, a third-grade class was studying bats and the children had created a list of questions to explore. As children read informational books during literacy centers, they took notes about what they were learning and then shared their notes during whole group time. There was a real purpose to this activity versus taking notes on a book simply to learn note-taking. Children were, therefore, more motivated to learn.

Additionally, as teachers become responsible for an increasing number of standards in an increasing number of areas, it becomes impossible to separately address each one in isolation. Teaching through units can make wise use of limited time by preventing overlap and by combining knowledge and skills from different disciplines. For example, children were completing a unit on bats. As they read texts on bats, they were learning science content while also learning about informational texts.

Integrated learning has gone through periods of increasing and waning popularity. For example, integrated units were promoted by the progressive movement but waned after Sputnik. The successful launch by the Soviet Union of the first space satellite was the start of the space age and the emphasis on competition with Russia. Integrated units were again popular in the 1980s and 1990s but began to experience a decrease during the standards and testing movement (Drake & Burns, 2004). Today while integrated curriculum is common within preschool programs, it is less common in elementary schools. However, integrated curriculum appears to be making a resurgence. Drake and Burns (2004) report on the promotion of integrated learning in Canada, Australia, China, Japan, Korea, Taiwan, and the United States. For example, nearly 700 schools in 70 school districts in Michigan developed an integrated curriculum as part of a five-year grant. Effective school movements and school restructuring projects also often involve curriculum integration (Ellis, 2013). As an example, the A+ school movement features interdisciplinary units that include the arts. A+ schools are found in several states and in South Africa. In Oklahoma alone, 65 schools are part of the movement with 55 of these schools using this method in the early childhood years (Oklahoma A+ Schools, 2018). There are several other examples of public schools designing and using integrated units in Pre-K and early elementary classrooms including Boston Public Schools and Montgomery Public Schools. The 1,652 schools in 109 countries that are part of the International Baccalaureate Primary Years Programme also design curriculum around transdisciplinary themes (International Baccalaureate Organization, 2018).

Integrated curriculum is recommended by NAEYC, the professional organization for early childhood. The NAEYC Developmentally Appropriate Practice in Early Childhood Programs encourages the use of integrated curriculum not only for preschool and kindergarten but also in first to third grade. They state,

> Primary grade teachers may try to fit everything in by tightly scheduling blocks of time for each subject. But this approach grows out of a misguided, adult-imposed scheme, rather than from the way young children learn and construct their understandings.
>
> (Copple & Bredekamp, 2009, p. 259)

Instead, DAP recommends that early elementary teachers provide focused instruction within an integrated curriculum. For example, within a unit on construction, the teacher might teach a focused lesson on measurement.

What Is the Evidence That Integrated Units Are Effective?

For over 70 years, researchers, reformers, and educators have been advocating for integrated curriculum (Martin-Kniep, 2000). But is it effective? Research demonstrates that it increases children's achievement and has many positive effects on children's and teachers' attitudes about school.

Probably the first in-depth study of integrated curriculum was the Eight-Year Study (Aikin, 1942). In this study, 30 progressive high schools were matched with traditional schools that used a college preparatory curriculum. The progressive schools designed integrated curriculum units. The study found that high schoolers attending the progressive schools were as well prepared academically for college as those in traditional schools and that they were more involved in social and extracurricular activities. Not all of the progressive schools in the study were as successful at implementing integrated curriculum. Students who attended those schools that were the most experimental achieved higher achievement than those from more traditional schools and from progressive schools that used fewer experimental techniques.

A more recent meta-analysis examined 30 studies on integrated curriculum, each containing control groups. Hatzler (2000) found that children in classrooms using integrated curriculum consistently outperformed their peers in classrooms who did not use an integrated curriculum. Children had significant gains in test scores ranging from a mean 0.47 effect size in studies that used statewide mandatory assessments to a mean of 0.53 effect size for studies that used other specifically designed assessments. Integrated curriculum was significant for all grade levels and for rural and suburban students. Thirteen of the studies involved children from kindergarten through fifth grade. All of these studies showed positive effect sizes with the mean being 0.56. It was also successful for children coming from different economic backgrounds with the most positive effect on children who were low-income. While the integrated curriculum was most successful for science and language arts, math and social studies assessments were also higher for those that received the integrated curriculum. Achievement was best when content was combined with process skills and when the integration was focused around a theme (Hatzler, 2000).

There are also studies that have emerged from the Oklahoma A+ Schools movement. This is a network of schools that combines interdisciplinary teaching with the arts and that focus on experiential learning. The schools are based upon North Carolina's A+ school programs. The Oklahoma A+ schools have been studied extensively. Researchers have found that children in these schools are at or above state averages in achievement with the most positive effects for children who are low-income or are from ethnic minorities. Schools achieved statistically significantly better results in their API (academic performance index) versus schools who were not using the curriculum, even though the Oklahoma A+ schools tended to have lower income children with more diversity who have traditionally scored lower. Schools that included the A+ method in a more comprehensive way had superior achievement test scores, more community involvement, and better child and teacher attitudes than when A+ was viewed as an add-on. Children reported that they found school more enjoyable, interesting, and challenging while teachers displayed more positive teacher attitudes and reported increased collaboration in the A+ schools that had embraced this method (Barry, 2010).

Another study examined three elementary schools in the A+ programs in North Carolina. All three schools are Title 1 schools indicating that they have a high percentage of low-income children. All these schools have received national recognition for their programs, all have high achievement and/or high growth on the North Carolina end of the year tests in comparison to those who are not implementing integrated curriculum (Whiteman, 2014).

Other research has come from the project-based learning movement. For example, one study integrated second-grade social studies and literacy. Four projects with 80 lessons occurred over a year-long period. The project-based group had statistically significant scores on social studies tests in comparison to the control group with an effect size of 0.48. They also achieved statistically significantly higher scores on informational reading, while the writing scores were similar between the experimental and the control group. Although it was not statistically significant, the experimental group also showed greater motivation than the control group (Duke, Halvorsen, Strachan, Konstantopoulos, & Kim, 2016).

Finally, additional research can be found in the movement started by Marie Kovalek on Integrated Thematic Instruction (ITI), which later became the Highly Effective Teaching (HET) model. Units are designed to integrate science, language arts, social studies, mathematics, and the arts. In this case, science is the conceptual focus that unites the other subjects. In one project, each teacher developed a year-long theme with a different focus each month. For example, Vicki Ogborn, a first-grade teacher, and her students were placed in a temporary building as their new school was being built. With a first-hand view, they studied the different aspects of the building process as it occurred. This included using the design process, creating blueprints, learning about soils and conducting experiments with core sampling, exploring the properties of sound as the new school construction put in sound barriers, and learning about plants as the building was being landscaped. The project that Vicki Ogborn was part of, served 300 teachers and was studied by researchers from Stanford University. They found that the children's achievement showed statistically significant gains, and this was true for learners with various skill levels. They also found increased language acquisition especially for children who were English Language Learners. Additionally, the teachers reported a dramatic increase in the amount of science they taught and indicated that they were teaching more in-depth content. The teachers also indicated that they had increased comfort with science instruction (Greene, 1991).

There are many other studies that examine integrated curriculum. For a review of additional research on integrated learning, see the Integrated Studies Research Review by Vanessa Vega at Edutopia (2015).

What is the difference between units and projects?

In this book, we are using both terms, units and projects. However, while there are similarities, there are also differences. Both are organized around a topic of study, develop integrated curriculum, and embed standards and outcomes into the study. However, the project approach includes specific elements that may not be present in all units. These include (Helm & Katz, 2001):

- designing projects based upon children's interests versus planning based on the curriculum
- creating an emergent curriculum based upon children's questions
- focusing the project on investigation, with children engaged in finding answers to their questions.
- including field site visits as a critical part of the experience.
- permeation of the project across the day and the learning environment.
- children's creation of representation to assist them to integrate concepts and to document learning. These activities are often repeated to show growth. For example, in a tractor project, children drew pictures of tractors at the beginning of the project and again at the end. The pictures provided a powerful view of children's learning.
- ending the project based upon children's interests and the process in investigating questions rather than on a predetermined time frame.

How Do We Organize Units?

There are many different organizational themes for your unit. These could be based on a topic such as the tractor project, the worm unit, or a study of bones. A concept could also be the basis of the organization such as family, community, or supply and demand. The organizational theme could be a persistent problem such as what to do with garbage, how to make sure everyone in the group is included, or how to keep the squirrels out of the bird feeders. Another way of organizing units is through using phenomena. What is happening in the world that we need to figure out or what problems might be solved through engineering design? Since you might be less familiar with this type of organizational theme, we will explore it more deeply.

The STEM teaching tools website houses several practice briefs to assist teachers in implementing science, technology, engineering, and math. One of these briefs is Using Phenomena in NGSS (Next Generation Science Standards)-Designed Lessons and Units. The authors of the briefs state that phenomena are especially effective for learning about science and engineering, that this creates a shift from, "learning about a topic to figuring out why or how something happens" (Achieve, Next Generation Science Storylines & STEM Teaching Tools, 2016, p. 1). This, in turn, provides a hook for learning about science, makes the unit more engaging, leads to deeper and more transferable learning, engages children in exploring big ideas rather than just memorizing facts, and helps children to understand the relevance of science. As children answer their questions regarding the phenomena, they learn science content and process skills. Choosing a phenomenon to study is an art, you want phenomena that children can understand and figure out but not immediately, that allows for deep learning, and that is relevant to children's lives. Rather than using phenomena as an example, the unit begins with the phenomena. Let's look at some examples.

As a child living in the Great Plains of the United States, I witnessed several grasshopper infestations. Grasshoppers would arrive in hoards eating their way through farmers' crops, stripping the plants of their leaves. Their devastation did not end in the fields. Thick clouds of grasshoppers made their way to town where they ate the gardens, plants, and grass. As a child, this immediately raised questions, "Where do the grasshoppers come from?" "Where do they go to?" "How do we stop them?" These types of phenomena are engaging to children, relevant to their lives, and allow active exploration.

As another example, one day, the children at Curious Minds Early Care and Education Center arrived to find their downstairs preschool room had flooded with water. Water was still flowing under the door. Immediately, the children were interested in exploring where the water came from and how it could be stopped. They devised plans and using materials that were available went into action to stop the water from intruding into the center. Through the experimentation, they found some successful and some unsuccessful strategies. Children assumed complementary roles as they worked together. For example, one child assumed the role of a television anchor, describing the flood and the efforts to contain it. Ultimately this phenomenon led to a long-term project where children examined different ways to move water, protection of property during floods, and how landscaping can protect from floods.

After witnessing the solar eclipse of 2017, a group of preschoolers in Nevada became fascinated with light. This study lasted throughout the year as children explored how light measures time, how light moves, visible and invisible light, and the exploration of light in relationship to plants and animals. Throughout the study, the children asked questions and sought answers to their questions through visiting with experts, reviewing books and the Internet for answers, and conducting their own investigations. For example, as children studied visible and invisible light they compared different types of sunglasses and colored filters, used LED and ultraviolet flashlights to examine a variety of different materials, explored which colors were harder and easier to see, and they discussed and studied signs at businesses and restaurants as the application of this to everyday life (Ashbrook, 2018).

Each phenomenon we've reviewed is a relatively rare event. However, we can also study phenomena that occur more commonly. Each spring, dandelions blossom and turn into white seed puffs. Most young children find blowing these seed puffs irresistible. This could become a study on how the wind moves seeds or what makes a plant a weed. When it rains, worms will often emerge covering the sidewalks. This phenomenon could lead to the study of animals and their habitats.

Each of the phenomenon we've discussed provides the opportunity for all the children in the group to have a real-life experience that creates interest, sparks questions, and allows children opportunities to answer these questions through their investigations. Each of these units would be developmentally appropriate for young children and would allow for rich integration with other subject content.

Choosing the Topic

Choosing the right topic is critical to the success of your unit. When determining the topic ensures that it meets the following criteria. According to Helm and Katz (2011), well known for their promotion of the Project Approach, the topic needs to:

- be significant and meaningful, worth the children's time and effort.
- allow experiences that will assist children in meeting the desired outcomes.
- able to address multiple learning outcomes in different curriculum areas.
- contribute to curricular balance and coherence.
- allow for first-hand, deep versus superficial investigations. The child should be able to conduct these investigations with minimal assistance from adults.
- be relevant to the children including being culturally and locally relevant.
- be accessible to children and related to their background experience.
- relate to children's interest or allow for building interest. Interested children learn more and families are more likely to be engaged when children are excited about what they are learning.
- be immediately applicable to children's lives but also prepare children for later learning and life.

As you plan units, you must also consider practical issues such as:

- the amount of time available for the unit. Units and projects are often several weeks, and some may last an entire year.
- the available resources for conducting investigations such as opportunities for field site visits and visiting guests and investigative materials, equipment, and books.
- the time of year, some topics are more relevant at different times of the year. For example, many programs begin the year with a getting-to-know-you unit.
- the teacher's background and knowledge. Sharing your own passions can enrich a unit.
- how broad or narrow the topic should be. For example, it is sometimes easier to learn in-depth information and concepts with a narrow topic (cows versus farm animals).

Let's look at how Delena chooses a topic. She knows that she wants the topic to relate to animals and that she wants to integrate reading, writing, art, math, social studies, and science into the unit. For example, in science, she plans to focus on how energy transfers between organisms in an ecosystem. She also wants to include how living things are dependent upon the environment for air, food, and water. In social studies, she plans to emphasize the economic impact of animals. She realizes that she could conduct a unit on sea animals, farm animals, zoo animals, pets, animals in the wild, or extinct animals such as dinosaurs. As she considers her options, she knows that the children in her class would be interested in any of the options. They are fascinated with large animals such as whales and dinosaurs. Many have beloved pets. However, as she considers which topic will allow first-hand research, deep learning, and relate to the geographic and cultural area they live in, she knows that farm animals are the correct choice. She lives in an area dominated by agriculture and children will have many opportunities with this unit for first-hand investigations. They will be able to explore the economics of farming through discussions with farmers and perhaps through hatching chickens to sell. She also knows that these types of hands-on experiences can be transferred to other types of animals. There are always numerous choices for unit or project topics. We want to choose one that will meet the above criteria and that will provide the most educational value.

With backward design philosophy we begin with desired results, then determine the proof we would need to determine if children had achieved the desired results (our assessments), and finally, we plan our unit topic and experiences. However, at times a serendipitous event occurs, or you notice extreme interest on the part of children that warrants a unit of study. If this happens, you might choose your topic of study first. However, instead of immediately planning activities, you will want to determine your desired results, then determine assessments, and lastly, determine experiences and activities. Using this process, you are more likely to achieve learning that meets standards and that causes children to gain enduring understandings.

I don't understand how you can address children's questions and at the same time address essential questions, enduring understandings, and knowledge and skills developed by the teacher. Is it possible?

That is a good question. Yes, the project can address children's questions and also meet the desired results. Let's look at the flood example above. Because this was a serendipitous event that was of high interest to the children, the teachers immediately looked at the possibility of this as a topic to explore. They determined that the topic was worthwhile and could be infused with desired outcomes suitable for this age group. They, therefore, began to determine desired outcomes. They felt this topic was especially powerful in allowing for the integration of science, social studies, math, and literacy. They arrived at the following essential questions, enduring understandings, knowledge, skills, and approaches to learning.

Essential questions and enduring understandings.

- How do the forces of nature affect humans?
- We are interdependent on our environment. The environment, including weather, affects where people live and how they live. Humans also affect the environment.

- How do humans mitigate the powerful forces of nature?
- Humans can at times mitigate the powerful forces of nature but cannot consistently control it.

Topical questions and understanding.

- How do humans mitigate floods?
- Humans use a variety of methods to try and control floods, but they are not always successful.
- How does flooding affect humans?
- Flooding affects where people live and how they live. There can be advantages and disadvantages to flooding.

Knowledge-Children will know:

- the effects of floods on people, animals, and landscapes.
- the advantages and disadvantages of flooding.
- some examples of what causes floods.
- the steps in the design process.
- tools and procedures for measuring accurately.

Skills-Children will be able to:

- use the design process.
- gain information from informational texts, videos, and visiting experts.
- accurately measure.
- produce data and analyze it.

Approaches to Learning-Children will practice:

- perseverance.

They also examined the children's questions and determined how the desired outcomes fit into these questions.

- How do we stop the water from entering our school?
- What materials work to stop the water?
- How do we move the water to a different place?

Although the teachers were following the children's lead and their questions, because they had determined the desired outcomes, they were able to infuse the project with additional information and experiences. This resulted in ensuring standards were met and led to more in-depth learning.

For example, because the teachers were focused on the design process, they were more intentional about presenting and supporting this content. They conducted mini-lessons on the design process, assisted children to record and discuss the trial and error activities, encouraged children to make plans for the changes they wanted to make and to use the design process, and provided terminology as children went through the steps of the design process. Because they had identified an essential topical understanding as being how do humans mitigate floods, the project was expanded beyond just the immediate flood and the impact on their school to examine the impact of floods in their community and state.

Implementing the Unit or Project

The Provocation

It is important to provide a provocation to capture children's interest and to provide a start to the unit or project. At times a provocation occurs as a result of an event such as a solar eclipse or water flooding a school. Generally, however, the teacher provides the provocation. For example, an infant-toddler teacher hung a bird cut from black construction paper in the window of the classroom. When the sun streamed through the classroom window, the bird made a shadow on the floor that moved throughout the day. The children noticed the shadow and the teacher suggested that they outline the shadow on the floor with chalk. When the shadow moved, the children were surprised (a provocation).

In a study of worms, the teacher placed dirt and worms in the media table. The children discovered the worms and were very excited (a provocation). A teacher placed a pan of goop (cornstarch mixed with water) on a speaker. The goop began to dance, making children wonder what was creating this reaction. This was a provocation that led to a study of sound.

Early Childhood Education

Is it necessary to provide provocations for adults?

Malcolm Knowles is often credited with being the father of andragogy (how adults learn). He stated that we need to create a desire to know (a hook or provocation). He emphasized that without the "desire to know," the adult will not make the effort needed to learn and to incorporate what they are learning into their lives. Often this results in disequilibrium. For example, a program administrator was eager for the teachers to adopt the project approach. However, they were currently using a weekly theme approach and felt that this approach worked very well for the children and for themselves. I was asked to be a consultant to work with the teachers. To have any chance of success, I first needed to create some disequilibrium. Why take the time and tremendous effort to learn and implement a new approach if the current approach is effective? I showed the teachers slides of children's work from Reggio Emilia. I asked the teachers if they saw this type of work from their children. They did not. Then I asked what they felt might have caused these results. After much discussion, we concluded that the most likely reason was the long-term projects that were used. This created disequilibrium and also the desire to learn more.

Can infants and toddlers participate in units or projects?

There are many examples of successful projects with infants and toddlers. These are often referred to as investigations. They are focused on children's interests in investigating materials, objects, and the processes in children's everyday lives. Let's look at an example.

The exploration of light was an investigation that took place at the Ohio University Child Development Center with children who were six months to three-years-old. Jennifer Whited and her colleagues created a light studio. Over time the children explored light from a variety of sources; a light table, overhead projectors, flashlights, rope lights, and battery-operated lanterns. They experimented with a variety of materials such as transparent blocks, cups, and rocks; bottles of tinted water; fabric; fishing line; art media; hair gel; ribbons; and mirrors. They also created art on the light table including clay sculptures, painting, drawing with markers, using glue on plexiglass, and making tissue paper collages. As children used the materials, they explored light sources, color, shadows, and cause and effect. They developed hypotheses and tested their ideas and showed increased attention span.

Determining What Children Know About the Topic

Determining children's current knowledge provides us information on where to start the project, how to spend our time, and what experiences will be most relevant. It allows us to build on children's background knowledge, identify their misconceptions, and allows us to differentiate so that we can increase learning for all children. Many of the assessment techniques we discussed in Chapter 4 are effective for pre-assessing children's knowledge, skills, and approaches to learning including webs, KWHL charts, concept maps, Venn diagrams, checklists, and observations. Some other specific techniques include asking open-ended questions individually or with a group. If you are asking an entire group, children might use hand signals or hold up paddles with answers allowing you to get information from each child, not just a vocal few. Determining common misconceptions regarding the topic will allow you to ask focused questions to look for misconceptions. Older children might complete written self-assessments using a Likert scale. You can also design games that check for current knowledge such as, "Who Wants to Be a Millionaire" or "Jeopardy." As you conduct the pre-assessment, you can also determine what children would like to learn more about.

Planning Learning Experiences

Many teachers begin to plan learning experiences by creating an anticipatory web. This web includes activities that will allow children to meet the desired outcomes and achieve success on the assessments. Other teachers create a list of possible activities. In each case, these are tentative and are based upon formative assessment data. Perhaps in the example of the flood, you had planned a mini-lesson on measurement after which the children would measure the length of PVC pipe they needed to move water from one area of the sandbox to another. However, as you observe the children, you realize that they do not understand how to measure. You would then need to provide additional measurement activities.

As you plan your learning experiences, you need to consider several criteria concurrently. Experiences need to:

- assist children in achieving the desired outcomes and help children succeed on the key assessments. As one begins to plan experiences, it is easy to veer from our desired results. To ensure that our experiences align with our desired results, it is helpful to create webs using the desired outcomes as the organizer. In the example of the flood, one bubble of the web would be the design process, another would be measurement, another would be seeking information, and so on.
- relate to children's interests. All learners are more likely to be motivated and engaged when they are interested. When we capitalize on children's interests, we are more likely to have successful learning outcomes.
- conform to research-based information. For example, we know through research that children learn more when they are engaged in hands-on learning.
- be engaging and allow for genuine exploration. Consider the following two kindergarten classes. It is spring and the classrooms are studying rabbits. In one classroom they do this by reading fiction and nonfiction books about rabbits, labeling the parts of a rabbit on a worksheet, and creating rabbits using stuffed paper bags. In the other classroom, there is a live rabbit. The children have created the rabbit habitat, are studying the rabbit's habits and what it prefers to eat and are learning what the rabbit needs to stay healthy. They have been reading books, interviewing experts, making close observations, and creating drawings and paintings of the rabbit. In which classroom will children likely learn more?
- relate to children's current level of understanding, knowledge, and skill level. Teachers need to be aware of developmental pathways in learning so that they can choose activities that are most likely to lead children along this path.
- meet the needs of all the children in the classroom. Since children will be at a variety of different levels in regard to their understanding, knowledge, and skills, teachers need to plan activities that will allow children to increase their competence regardless of their current levels. This might be done by providing a range of options in learning centers, providing targeted small group instruction, and through tailoring individual interactions based upon children's levels of understanding, knowledge, and skills.
- consider children's cultural backgrounds. We can provide a richer experience for all children when we include information from different cultural backgrounds. For example, a study of bread is enriched when we study different types of cultural bread. It also allows us to honor the cultures that are present in the classroom and introduce children to other cultural practices. When I was teaching Head Start, a family came and made fry bread with the children. They also made pemmican and brought jerky for the children to try. While about a third of my class ate fry bread at home, the rest had never had this opportunity. When children are exposed to only one way, they begin to believe that is the right way. This can pertain to all aspects of our lives, what we eat, what we wear, what we value, what we believe about roles and responsibilities, religion, education, and so on. We can learn about the children's culture from their families and from community members. It is important that we do so. We want to ensure that we honor all the children and families in our program, that we respect different types of cultural beliefs and traditions, and that we take advantage of the richness we gain by being aware of others' cultures.

As you design your learning experiences, you might find that you are unable to meet all the desired outcomes that you have designed and that you might need to revisit them. Don't try to force connections that are not there. For example, when I was a preschool teacher conducting a unit on firefighters, my assistant and I cut out hundreds of different colored fire hats for the children to count and classify as a way of designing math activities that fit with the unit. I soon realized what a waste of time this was. It didn't enhance children's learning and I spent several hours doing this rather than spending my time on planning and implementing an activity that could have led to deeper learning. However, you will also want to be aware of opportunities to embed additional learning. For example, children might help to set up the dramatic play center focused on firefighters and while doing so have an authentic opportunity to classify materials.

As you plan choose strategies that are effective. Revisit chapters seven and eight to review some of these strategies. Remember that your interactions result in powerful learning. To take full advantage of interactions we must develop our own background knowledge. It is our responsibility to be informed, to provide accurate information, to be able to spot misconceptions, to provide needed background information, and to scaffold learning. One way that we can enhance background information is to study the unit topic. Many teachers create an informational sheet on the topic that can be shared with other teaching staff and families. This allows all the adults to be "knowledgeable others."

Visiting Experts

We have probably all experienced a situation where the visiting expert gives a lecture and the children quickly become uninterested and disruptive. How do we prevent this? It begins by preparing both the children and the visiting expert in advance. When setting up the visit with the expert, be clear about the children's developmental level, what children are interested in learning, and interactive techniques that have proven successful in the past such as bringing props and engaging children in discussions and hands-on activities. For example, when firefighters came to visit, they came dressed in their fire clothes. This immediately created interest and children had a lot of questions. They also asked questions they had prepared ahead of time. The firefighters talked about how fires begin and emphasized the danger of playing with matches. They next talked about safety in case of a fire such as not hiding during a fire and showed a short video of what it looks like inside a building on fire. They then had children practice stop, drop, and roll. In small groups, the children then had the opportunity to explore the fire truck. The firefighters left old firefighting clothing and other props for the children to explore. The teachers had taken a video of the firefighter's talk and children had taken photos of the fire truck. The props, video, and photos were placed in the dramatic play area allowing children to revisit what they had experienced. The teacher later conducted a debriefing session with the children where they had a general discussion about the visit and then discussed specifically what they had learned and added this to their web.

This visit was successful for several reasons. The school visit was related to what the children were studying and came at a key time in the project progression. In this case, it was near the beginning of the project. Children were prepared with questions and the firefighters were prepared for the children. The firefighters used a variety of different teaching techniques including discussion, videos, props, and hands-on practice. By using small groups to see the fire engine, children had a richer experience and were able to actually go into the cab of the fire truck and explore the instruments.

While these visiting experts primarily used a large group context, it is also very effective to have visiting experts who work with children individually. For example, children were learning watercolor techniques and had invited an artist. Instead of giving a large group presentation, she sat with children in the art center and provided tips and taught techniques as children engaged in the media. A musician visited a toddler class and sat in a corner of the room playing his guitar, children came and went based upon their interest.

Field Site Visits

When choosing a field site visit, ensure that it relates closely to what the children are learning. Field sites may require transportation to a site. However, they might also be within walking distance of the school. For example, a study of evaporation might entail visiting the mud puddles in the outdoor play space multiple times. A study on babies might entail visiting the infant classroom in the same building.

Whether in the immediate vicinity or further away, an important key to a successful field site visit is planning ahead of time. This allows children to develop a focus for their visit and to prepare questions to explore. As with visiting experts, it is also important to prepare the visiting site with the focus of the visit, the children's developmental level, and what you hope the children will be able to see and do. It is also important to think about the best group size. For example, when visiting the babies, the teachers decided that only two children at a time could visit. Those two children were responsible for gathering the information that the group had requested. For example, one of the questions was whether a newborn baby could hold a rattle. Throughout the project, all of the children were able to make a visit to the baby room. Small groups visited the mud puddles. Since there were several mud puddles, each group had their own puddle to explore.

As you pre-plan your site visit, brainstorm with the children what documentation they want to obtain. For example, a teacher at Curious Minds developed a tractor project. The children visited a farm implement dealer to examine the different types of tractors. Children were interested in the tires and wanted to make casts. Since they were not certain what would work best, they brought both clay and tinfoil. They also wanted to take photos and videos.

Pre-plan questions that the children will ask. The children at Curious Minds had prepared a list of questions before they went to the implement dealer and had decided who would ask what questions. The questions were written on index cards and each child illustrated their card as a way of helping to remember the question. Each child was given their card or cards when they got to the field site. Spontaneous questions will also arise. With both planned and spontaneous questions, it is helpful if the answers are recorded or written down to review later.

Bring the materials that you will need for documentation. This often includes clipboards to create representational drawings, diagrams, and for recording data. Also, provide a way to take photos and videos. This provides documentation and helps children to revisit the experience.

Determine what artifacts might be collected at the site. For example, in the tractor project, the children brought back the tire casts and a collection of brochures about tractors. On a field trip to a pond, children might bring back various samples. When visiting a farm, the children might be able to bring back different products. For example, a group studying chickens visited a farm to receive the eggs that they would incubate and hatch in their classroom. The farm had different types of chickens, an emu, and an ostrich. The farmer gave children several different types of eggs. The teachers blew out the yolks and whites of the emu and ostrich eggs and placed them in the science center so that children could compare these to the chicken eggs that they were hatching.

Establish ground rules with the children. These will vary depending upon the trip but often will include safety rules such as staying with the designated adult and learning rules such as completing the assigned learning tasks.

Typically, when you visit off-site, you will have volunteers to assist you. It is important to use volunteers effectively. For example, assign volunteers to be responsible for certain children or assign volunteers to a specific task such as taking videos. Make sure that volunteers are aware of the goals of the trip, what experiences you hope that the children will have, and what kind of representation and documentation you will be collecting. Also, let the volunteers know the ground rules that you have established with the children (Helm & Katz, 2001).

But, can young children even engage in observational drawing?

According to Helm and Katz (2001), experts on the project approach, even three-year-olds can successfully engage in observational sketching. However, they do better if they are focusing on a small part of an object such as a tractor tire rather than the entire tractor.

If possible, revisit the field site. With an initial visit, children often receive information at a global level, when they go back to the same site, they can attend to more details. They also will have new questions they are seeking answers to. For example, at the Subsidiary Kindergarten of Hangzhou Municipality, the children were studying umbrellas. This began with a visit to an umbrella museum. The children were very interested and wanted to create their own umbrella museum. Each week they went back to the museum and had additional information they wanted to explore. As they began creating their own umbrellas, they wanted to examine the ribs of the umbrellas more closely and to examine how the umbrellas closed and opened. As they developed their display, they wanted to more closely examine how the umbrella museum displayed their umbrellas. They became curious about what type of oil was used to prevent paper umbrellas from getting ruined in the rain and wanted to interview the museum staff.

Debriefing after the field site visit is a way to gather information from various perspectives and to synthesize what has been learned. As with visiting experts, begin with a general discussion about the field site visit and then discuss how what they discovered relates to what they are learning. Children often share answers to their questions and might share their representation with the group.

As the project unfolds, you will also revisit the artifacts you collected from the field site and your documentation. For example, the children at Curious Minds repeatedly watched the video of the tractors and studied the photos as they created their own tractor at the center.

Choosing an Effective Learning Context

When designing unit plans, teachers often think about teacher-directed, small- and whole group activities. As you are planning your unit, also make sure that you include learning centers, routines, and individual interactions in your plans. Also, remember that learning can occur outdoors as well as indoors. For more information on contexts, revisit Chapter 6.

Monitoring for Learning and Understanding

As you engage in the unit or project you will be continually monitoring the children's level of understanding. This is often done through observation, asking questions, listening to children's questions, and through reviewing children's work. Revisit Chapter 4 for formative assessment techniques.

Documenting and Sharing Children's Learning

There are several important reasons to document and share children's learning through a culminating event. One of the most important is that it allows children to revisit what they have learned. As they review documentation and plan culminating activities they articulate and synthesize their learning.

Documenting Learning

Just as with documentation of individual children, teachers need to be purposeful and plan ahead of time what will be collected, determine how to capture both the process and products of learning, decide how the information will be stored, when and how the information will be analyzed, and how the learners will be involved in the collection and interpretation of the documentation. Teachers will also need to think about the purpose of the documentation. Often the purpose changes throughout the project. Initial documentation is often shared within the classroom, assisting children in revisiting ideas and experiences and providing teachers with information to support the learning process. At the conclusion of the project, documentation is often shared with those outside the group of learners such as families, children and teachers from other classrooms, administrators, and policymakers (Krechevsky, Mardell, Rivard, & Wilson, 2013).

As teachers begin to provide rich documentation of projects, they often go through a series of stages, culminating in focusing not only on children's experiences but also on their learning. Let's look at these.

- Special events are documented and displayed. For example, a field trip might be documented with photographs and captions.
- Children's engagements in many different activities and experiences are documented and displayed (often with photographs and captions). A brief description of the project might be included.
- Documentation may include a brief project narrative, photographs of children engaged in activities and experiences, captions explaining the process, and representation of children's work including webs, charts, and other relevant products.
- Children's experiences and learning are documented and displayed. Documentation includes children's questions, description of the process, learning experiences, examples of children's representations, and a detailed analysis of what children learned.

Planning the Culminating Event

Culminating events are a celebration of learning. As children plan and conduct the culminating event, they synthesize their experiences, determine how to share what they have learned with an audience, and collaborate in designing the event. During the event, they typically engage with an audience which allows the development of additional skills. Following are several tips that can make culminating events more successful.

- First, determine the target audience. Will it be another class, families, community, or policy-makers and legislators?
- Involve learners in planning the event.
- Highlight, not just the activities children participated in but also what the children learned.
- Involve the audience.
- Assist children to be prepared for the event. For example, if planning learning centers go through the centers with the children ahead of time and discuss what they might say to families.
- Provide enough space so that the audience can be comfortable. This might entail borrowing a space, meeting outside, or staggering groups.
- Plan for greeters to let your audience know what is expected. For example, are they to get snacks first, sit down, or engage in learning centers?
- Send invitations in advance and also remind your guests shortly before the event. For example, when Kid Kollege concluded a pet project each child created a personalized invitation for their family. The event was also posted in the newsletter and the teacher personally invited each family. Providing multiple opportunities allowed all families to be aware of the event and all children had family members that attended.
- Meet your audience's needs. This begins with choosing a convenient time for the event. For example, you might conduct a survey of families to see when they prefer events. Also, to be more family-friendly it is helpful to provide food. Child care might also be needed if the event is not appropriate for younger siblings.

There are many ways of organizing culminating events. Below are a few examples that I have been personally involved with.

Learning Stations for the Culminating Event

This culminating event occurred at the end of a multi-month human body project by a group of early childhood students. Each student had developed experiences around a different body part. There had been a health fair in the community and children were interested in creating a health fair for their families. For the children's health fair, the program had borrowed a large conference space. As families entered, they were greeted, provided a list of the centers available, and given a passport that was stamped at each center. Each center contained both documentation and also interactive activities. The children had helped develop the centers and they had also gone through the centers and discussed being guides for their families. They were excited about their roles. Let's look at the centers.

- The heart—At this center, families explored a model of the heart and listened to their heartbeats before and after exercising. A list of exercises was posted along with pictures of how to do the exercises. The documentation contained pictures the children had drawn before and after they studied the heart, with children's descriptions of their learning. For example, one child stated, "I used to think that the heart looked like a valentine heart but now I know that it doesn't."
- The digestive system—At this center, participants learned how food goes through your digestive system by walking through the steps. On the floor was a large laminated sketch of

the digestive system. The participant would choose a food, and walk through the system, making sure to churn when they reached the stomach. There was also a piece of yarn that stretched 23 feet, illustrating the length of the small intestine.

- The brain—At the brain center, families could explore a brain model, create their own model with clay, and feel the texture of the brain with a sand and potato flakes mixture. There were graphs of the egg brain experiment the children had conducted, informational books, and a visual of how the brain, if it were unfolded, would be the size of a pillowcase.
- The eyes—At the eye center, there were photos of each of the child's eyes. Families guessed which eyes belonged to which children in the program. They could turn the picture of eyes over to find the name of the child on the back. There was also an activity where participants were blindfolded and tried to guess what sensory items they were feeling. A PowerPoint on the computer showed the different eye experiences the children had participated in.
- Bones—At the bones center there was a life-size puzzle of a person to assemble. There was a display of children's drawings of bodies before and after their study in multiple media such as chalk, markers, and crayons.
- Nutrition—At the nutrition center, there was a guessing game on paper plates created by the children. You turned the plate over to reveal the answer. For example, one child had typed, "I am sweet, green, a fruit, and grow on a tree. What am I?" There were also individual documentation books created by children on nutrition.
- Tooth center—At the tooth center, there was a book that displayed each child's smiling mouth. Families guessed whose mouth it was and could then lift the flap to see the entire face of the child. They also had a display of an experiment the children had conducted where they put screws in different types of soda. Finally, there were skulls of various animals with teeth. Participants tried to guess what animal belonged to each skull.

Also posted were children's webs and KWHL charts and documentation of children's site visits, visiting experts, and children engaged in dramatic play. Each family took home their child's book of "A look at me." This successful event ended with families, children, and teaches sharing a meal.

I have found that when families come to our culminating event and review the documentation, they tend to just look for photos of their children. They don't read the project story or spend much time examining the documentation. After all the work the children and teachers put into it, it is disappointing. What do you suggest?

I have also witnessed this on many occasions and became interested in how we solve this dilemma. What I began to examine was how museums engage visitors. I think we can adopt some of the same techniques for early childhood documentation. When I've seen teachers use the following techniques, visitors do see to spend more time with the documentation.

First, design an attractive display that is easy to read and interact with. For example, while you want to provide information, less is sometimes better. If there is too much information, it can be overwhelming. Print needs to be large enough that visitors can easily read it from a distance away. You need to provide enough space and either staggered times or enough panels that participants feel like they can take the time to read and interact with the documentation. Next, take cues from museums and make your documentation interactive. Following are some ideas:

- Provide hands-on activities with the display.
- Provide treasure hunts where guests look for certain information on a display.
- Build interaction into the documentation panel itself. For example, you might have a guess the answer to a question the children were studying, and you must lift the flap to find the answer.
- Provide passports that get stamped for each type of documentation visited.
- Have child guides that take visitors through the display. For example, when Kid Kollege was culminating the "Pet Project," families came to the center and were greeted by their child guide. There were several centers available and children had practiced different things to point out in the documentation. In case the child guides forgot the directions, there were also labels at each center with instructions. There was a video of what children knew at the start of the unit and what they knew at the end, a pets discovery center with hands-on pet props such as bones, children's work such as webs and graphs, children's stories, drawings by the children of what they had learned, some activities related to the unit such as animal puzzles and matching pets and their paw prints, and a center with the visiting tarantula. The child guides made certain that families participated in each of the centers.

Culminating the Unit with a Community Event

Events might also be held for the community. This is an opportunity for community members and others to learn about the competency of young children. For example, children at a college-based preschool were visiting and studying a gallery that contained a large collection of African animal mounts. The children were very interested in the animals. They studied them, researched them, watched short videos, developed dramatic play scenarios, made elaborate masks of the animals, engaged in shadow puppetry with their masks, and created in-depth artwork with different types of media. The children wanted to create their own art gallery. They did so for the Board of Regents who were visiting the campus. They also gave a short presentation to the Regents. The teachers and early childhood faculty took advantage of the opportunity and created poster displays with information about what children learn during the preschool years. Several Regents and guests who attended the meeting expressed their awe with the children's work.

The children at Kid Kollege had been studying bones and decided to share what they had learned at the community health fair. They set up a documentation display about the project approach, showed some of the activities the children had been engaged in, and had a display of the books they had used in the unit. The highlight of the display was a 20-box sensory walk that the children had created. Each child had taken a box that normally holds four six-packs of pop (the processing plant had donated them). They had decorated their box and filled it with a sensory material, such as sand, packing peanuts, bubble wrap, and sandpaper. Participants could take off their shoes and walk through the sensory walk. Again, those who visited the booth were surprised at the capabilities of young children.

Is it valuable for adult learners to have culminating experiences?

Early Childhood Education

I believe it is. Adults studying early childhood can also use their culminating experiences to inform others of the value of early childhood. For example, a class of students at the University of Montana-Western had been studying the brain and also learning about advocacy. As a final culminating project, the class decided they wanted to share what they were learning with legislators. They developed a large walk-in brain that they placed in the rotunda of the state capital. Inside the brain was a series of posters, showing what children learn in the early years. It was a powerful display.

Creating Project Books or Videos as the Culmination of a Unit

Children might also create project books, either physical books or digital books that they share with families. This can include documentation of children's work and what they have learned, along with photos and if digital, videos. Digital books make it easy for families to share with others and allows all families to easily have and keep a copy of the documentation.

Children are often able to discuss their learning more easily when videotaped rather than when presenting in front of an audience. Even if you are having an event that families attend, it often works best to videotape young children and share the video rather than putting the children on the spot at the event. Instead of asking children, "What did you learn?" it is often easier for children to answer the question, "What did you find out?" (Helm & Katz, 2001, p. 52).

Engaging in a New Experience Together That Also Culminates the Unit

Your culminating activity might also be a new experience that the children and families engage in together. For example, one of my sons was in a third-grade classroom that completed a unit on fish. As a culmination, the teacher had a fish tasting event. As children and families tasted the fish, children told families about what they had learned during the unit.

Be cautious, however, with the type of experience you plan. I have been at events where the teachers show a Disney children's movie. I left wondering what the children had learned during their study. Instead, be purposeful about the experience you plan, linking it back to your desired outcomes.

Culminating events can be an exciting way to end a unit or project. Sharing children's learning can also be a way to develop awareness and appreciation for young children's learning.

Involving Families

We've just examined ways that families were involved in culminating events. However, we don't want to wait until the end of the project to involve families. As we reviewed the research on the effectiveness of integrated learning, we discovered that they encourage more family interaction. This only occurs though, if we are intentional. Long-term projects and units can be very engaging for families. If families are aware of the topic, they can provide more support. For example, I was working with a family child care provider who served 12 children and their families. She was planning her first-ever unit on firefighters and fire trucks. When I asked her about involving the families, she stated that the families had never been involved in curriculum and she was certain that they would not be interested. However, we agreed that she would at least create a flyer about the project and post it on the door to the program. The provider was shocked by the families' interest. They were not only very interested, but they asked if they could bring resources. One of the family members was a volunteer firefighter and he brought his fire suit and hat, another family had some fire truck puzzles and books, and another brought some toy fire trucks. Sometimes as these families demonstrated, families are interested in supporting the curriculum but are unaware of how to do so. Like these families, some families might provide resources, others might be visiting experts, or they might teach children some skills needed to successfully complete the project. Still, others might provide suggestions for activities, field visits, and visiting experts. Families might also attend field site visits, becoming co-learners with their children. Finally, knowing the topic of study and seeing the ongoing documentation provides a focus for talking to their child about what they are learning and also allows families to tie this information to activities and experiences in the home (Helm & Beneke, 2003).

In Summary

Over 70 years of research has demonstrated the effectiveness of integrated units. Units become even more powerful as a learning mechanism when we combine them with essential questions and enduring understandings. This helps to ensure that learners are engaged in deeper learning that will lead to transfer. Choosing a unit topic that will allow for this type of deep, inquiry-based learning is also critical. Additionally, when learners are interested in a topic of study, they are more likely to be engaged and therefore to learn more. Units and projects can be developed around children's interests or we can provide provocations to pique their interest. Field site visits and visiting experts are two ways that children learn more about the topic and are considered essential in the project approach. Therefore, this availability is also an important consideration in choosing a topic. Experiences should be in-depth and hands-on, allowing children to deeply engage in content and increase their skill levels and understanding. As children participate in experiences related to the unit or project you will want to be continually monitoring and documenting their learning. At the end of the unit or project, a culminating event can be a way for children to revisit their learning, synthesize what they have learned, and to share their learning with others.

Apply Your Knowledge

1. Observe a group of children and make a list of their interests. Which of these has the potential for a long-term study?
2. Critique these topics using the criteria in the chapter. To effectively do so, you will want to determine the age of the children that you would develop the topic for and also determine where they live. The topics to critique are starfish, stars, the letter A, bears, triangles, the color blue, Little Blue and Little Yellow (a children's book), fishing, rodeo horses, and our backyard.
3. You are a kindergarten teacher and would like to develop projects rather than use the weekly themes that are now a part of the curriculum. Develop a list of points that you will address with the principal when you meet to present your idea.

References

Achieve. (2016). *Using Phenomena in NGSS-Designed lessons and units* (Practice Brief 42). Retrieved from http://stemteachingtools.org/brief/42

Aikin, W. M. (1942). *The story of the eight-year study: With conclusions and recommendations* (Vol. 1). New York: Harper & Brothers.

Ashbrook, P. (2018). *The power of phenomenon-based learning.* Retrieved from http://nstacommunities.org/blog/2018/06/18/the-power-of-phenomenon-based-learning/

Barry, N. H. (2010). *Oklahoma A+ schools: What the research tells us 2002-2007, Volume 3: Quantitative measures.* Edmond, OK: Oklahoma A+ Schools/University of Central Oklahoma.

Copple, C., & Bredekamp, S. (2009). *Developmentally appropriate practice in early childhood programs serving children from birth through age 8.* Washington, DC: National Association for the Education of Young Children.

Drake, S. M., & Burns, R. C. (2004). *Meeting standards through integrated curriculum.* Alexandria, VA: Association for Supervision and Curriculum Development (ASCD).

Duke, N. K., Halvorsen, A., Strachan, S. L., Konstantopoulos, S., & Kim, J. (2016). *Putting PBL to the test: The impact of project-based learning on 2nd-grade students' social studies and literacy learning and motivation.* Retrieved from https://docs.google.com/viewer?a=v&pid=sites&srcid=dW1pY2guZWR1fG5rZHVrZXxneDoxMDUwYjZlODg4MzE5NWVj

Ellis, A. (2013). *Research on educational innovations* (4th ed.). New York: Routledge.

Greene, Lynda C. (1991). Science-centered curriculum in elementary school. *Educational Leadership, 49*(2), 42-46.

Hartzler, D. S. (2000). *A meta-analysis of studies conducted on integrated curriculum programs and their effects on student achievement.* ProQuest Dissertations and Theses.

Helm, J. H., & Beneke, S. (Eds.). (2003). *The power of projects: Meeting contemporary challenges in early childhood classrooms—strategies and solutions.* New York: Teachers College Press.

Helm, J. H., & Katz, L. G. (2001). *Young investigators: The project approach in the early years.* New York: Teachers College Press.

International Baccalaureate Organization. (2018). Key facts about the PYP. Retrieved from https://www.ibo.org/programmes/primary-years-programme/what-is-the-pyp/key-facts-about-the-pyp/

Krechevsky, M., Mardell, B., Rivard, M., & Wilson, D. (2013). *Visible learners: Promoting Reggio-inspired approaches in all schools.* San Francisco, CA: Jossey-Bass.

Martin-Kniep, G. O. (2000). *Becoming a better teacher: Eight innovations that work.* Alexandria, VA: Association for Supervision and Curriculum Development (ASCD).

Oklahoma A+ Schools. (2018). OKA+ Schools. Retrieved from http://www.okaplus.org/schools

Vega, V. (2015). *Integrated studies research review.* Retrieved from https://www.edutopia.org/integrated-studies-research

Whiteman, B. W. (2014). *Adaptations of the A+ Schools program in three unique contexts.* Retrieved from https://files.nc.gov/ncaplus/pdf/AplusCaseStudiesFinal.pdf

10 Completing the Unit Form

We have now learned how to determine desired results, design assessments based upon our desired results, and how to plan experiences that will allow learners to gain the understandings, knowledge, and skills to achieve the desired results and to pass the assessments. It is now time to put what we have learned into practice. In this chapter, we will explore the unit planning form and tips for completing it. You will be introduced to a backward design rubric that can be used to critique your own and other's units. Additionally, you will see three sample units for different age groups.

Early Childhood Backward Design Unit Planning Form

We will begin by examining the early childhood backward design unit planning form. This form with slight modifications can be used for learners of all ages. See the unit learning plan form in Box 10.1.

Box 10.1 Early Childhood Backward Design Unit Planning Form

Title of unit
Age of children or learners
Description of unit
Unit rationale (Why this topic?)

Desired Results	
Standards that are being bundled for this unit	
Concepts or big ideas	
Enduring Understandings	Essential Questions
Topical enduring understandings	Topical essential questions
Knowledge—The child will be able to:	Approaches to Learning

Skills–The child will be able to:	Possible preconceptions or misconceptions
Assessments	
Pre-assessments	Formative assessments
Summative assessments or key final assessments	

Experiences		
Specific experiences	Learning context	Strategies
The children will:		The teacher will:
Provocation		

How will you supplement your learning centers to support the unit?
How will you involve families in the unit?
How will you culminate the unit?
Rubrics for key assessments.

Tips for Completing the Unit Plan Form

In developing your unit plan, it is critical that you continually consider the alignment between your desired results, assessments, and experiences. Some teachers find it helpful to use the alignment grid found in Box 10.2.

Box 10.2 Early Childhood Backward Design Alignment Grid

Desired result	How will the desired result be assessed?	What experiences allow children to develop the desired results?

As you complete the form it may be helpful to review the following information. Sections of the unit planning form and where to find the information.

- Choosing a topic—Chapter 9
- Standards to bundle—Chapter 3
- Concepts or big ideas—Chapter 3
- Enduring understandings and essential questions—Chapter 3
- Knowledge, skills, and approaches to learning—Chapter 2
- Preconceptions and misconceptions—Chapter 5
- Pre-assessments, formative assessments, and summative assessments—Chapter 4
- Experiences: Interactions and strategies—Chapters 7 and 8
- Experiences: Learning contexts—Chapter 6
- Learning centers—Chapter 6
- Involving families—Chapter 9
- Culminating projects—Chapter 9
- Designing rubrics—Chapter 4

Please also note the following as you complete the form.

- Enduring understandings and essential questions typically include both overarching and topical understandings and questions.
- Under knowledge and skills, the sentences begin with, "the child will be able to."
- When listing the experiences, remember to include a variety of different contexts and research-based strategies. Also, since your interactions are such a critical part of children's learning you may want to list specific interaction techniques that you will be using.
- Under the experiences the sentence stem is, "the children will."
- Under the strategies the sentence stem is, "the teacher will."

Because designing units is so challenging, it is helpful to use the unit plan rubric to self-assess your units. It is also very helpful to have peers review your unit. We will examine this next.

It looks like planning a backward design unit has a lot of benefits, but it is a lot of work. I wonder whether I'll have time as a new teacher to design backward design units?

It is a lot of work. However, units typically last for several weeks or even longer. As the unit unfolds, you will have less daily planning since you have invested time in planning the unit up-front. When you are just beginning with this approach you might want to start small, by just planning and implementing one unit per semester. You can use the typical curriculum approach for the rest of the curriculum. Additionally, this work is often not completed in isolation. Instead, designing units using backward design might be a project that you work on with other teachers in your school.

Early Childhood Backward Design Unit Rubric

The backward design unit rubric can be used to self-assess a unit. It can also be used for peer-assessment. See the rubric in Box 10.3.

Box 10.3 Early Childhood Backward Design Unit Rubric

	Novice	*Nearing Proficiency*	*Proficient*
Identifying desired results			
Standards	Desired results are identical to state and national standards. Many standards are listed that have superficial relevance to the unit.	Desired results are identical to state and national standards. Listed standards are directly relevant to the unit.	Desired results are based upon bundled, unpacked, and prioritized national and state standards. Listed standards are directly relevant to the unit.
Desired results	Desired results are developmentally inappropriate.	Most of the desired results are appropriate for the audience (engaging, worthy, challenging, relevant, developmentally appropriate).	All desired results are appropriate for the audience (engaging, worthy, challenging, relevant, developmentally appropriate).
Enduring Understandings	The focus is on knowledge, skills, or topics of study rather than enduring understandings.	Enduring understandings are stated in a sentence format but are not clearly connected to transferrable big ideas.	The identified understandings reflect important, transferrable big ideas that need to be "uncovered" They are clearly stated in a sentence format.
Essential Questions	The questions are closed-ended (have a right or automatic answer).	The questions are open-ended but may not require much inquiry.	The questions are open-ended and require inquiry rather than recall.
	The questions relate to the enduring understandings but are not essential (not thought-provoking and not related to transferrable ideas within and across disciplines).	The questions relate to the enduring understandings and are somewhat essential but may not be the most essential questions (thought-provoking, can be revisited again and again, encourages active meaning-making, related to important, transferrable ideas within and across disciplines).	The questions relate to the enduring understandings and are essential (thought-provoking, can be revisited again and again, encourages active meaning-making, points toward important, related to transferrable ideas within and across disciplines).

	Novice	*Nearing Proficiency*	*Proficient*
Assessing desired results			
Align with desired results	The assessment tasks are not aligned to the desired results AND/OR They do not provide the correct level of complexity.	**Most** assessment tasks are aligned with the desired results and match the complexity found in the desired results.	**All** assessment tasks are aligned with the desired results and match the complexity found in the desired results.
Authentic tasks	Many of the tasks are inauthentic.	**Most** tasks are highly authentic, involving a direct or simulated application of the targeted understanding, knowledge, and skills.	**All** tasks are highly authentic, involving a direct or simulated application of the targeted understanding, knowledge, and skills.
Validity	The assessments are limited or incomplete and so do not provide evidence that the desired results have been met.	The assessments provide some evidence but are not in-depth enough to determine if the desired results have been met.	The assessments provide sufficient evidence to determine if the desired results have been met. Pre-assessments, formative assessments, and summative assessments are used
Rubric	The rubric focuses primarily on quantitative indicators rather than quality indicators AND/OR The focus is on a particular assignment rather than the desired results.	The rubric is clearly aligned in content and depth to the desired results. The performance criteria and descriptors are clearly defined, distinct, observable, and provide a clear and logical developmental progression. The descriptors primarily focus on descriptive, qualitative indicators.	The rubric is clearly aligned in content and depth to the desired results. The performance criteria and descriptors are clearly defined, distinct, observable, and provide a clear and logical developmental progression. The descriptors focus primarily on descriptive, qualitative indicators. The descriptors state what is present rather than what is missing.
Planning learning experiences			
"Rich" unit topic	The topic is superficial or is based on a distinct skill making it difficult to engage in meaningful learning (e.g. the letter A, the color red)	The topic is worthy of the children's effort and time in studying it.	The topic is worthy of the children's effort and time in studying it.

	Novice	Nearing Proficiency	Proficient
	AND/OR The topic is unrelated to children's geographic area making it difficult to engage in hands-on and inquiry-based experiences. AND/OR This topic is unlikely to allow the children to achieve the desired result.	The topic is likely to interest the learners, be relevant to them, and applicable to their lives. The topic allows for in-depth study and first-hand, active engagement in meaningful learning experiences. The topic will allow children to achieve the desired results.	The topic is likely to interest the learners, be relevant to them, and applicable to their lives. The topic allows for in-depth study and first-hand, active engagement in meaningful learning experiences. The topic will allow children to achieve the desired results. The topic will allow meaningful integration of different curricular areas.
Provocations	The teacher designs a unit without considering the children's interests. AND/OR The unit begins without a provocation.	An attempt is made to follow learners' interests or to provide a provocation, but the provocation is only superficially related to the unit.	The unit is designed around the current group of learners' interests or it has a powerful provocation.
Developmentally appropriate	**Several** of the learning activities and experiences are developmentally or culturally inappropriate. AND/OR Learning experiences are not based upon pre-assessment and do not offer a range of developmental levels.	**Most** of the learning activities and experiences are developmentally appropriate and based upon either pre-assessments or they offer a range of opportunities to meet all learners' needs. Learning activities and experiences are culturally relevant and appropriate.	**All** the learning activities and opportunities are developmentally appropriate and based upon either pre-assessments or they offer a range of opportunities to meet all learners' needs. Learning activities and experiences are culturally relevant and appropriate.
Depth	Experiences are superficial or are too few to make it likely the learners will achieve the desired outcomes.	Enough rich experiences are provided to allow learners to meet some of the desired outcomes. However, some outcomes are covered superficially.	Enough rich experiences, aligned with each of the desired outcomes, are provided to allow learners the opportunity to gain in-depth knowledge and understandings.

	Novice	Nearing Proficiency	Proficient
Varied instructional contexts and research-based strategies	The unit activities primarily occur within groups that are teacher-directed with few opportunities for engagement in learning centers. AND/OR Most teaching strategies are the same and are not based on best practice. AND/OR Experiences are a series of unrelated activities.	The unit includes a balance of instructional contexts (child-initiated and teacher-directed activities, whole group and small group activities, and learning centers). The teacher uses a variety of different strategies. **Most** techniques and methods are effective, based on research and best practice. Experiences are connected and flow together.	The unit includes a balance of instructional contexts The teacher uses a variety of different strategies. **All** techniques and methods chosen are effective, based on research and best practice. The experiences are connected and flow together with the teacher assisting learners to see the relationship to past and future learning.
Active learning	Children are primarily involved in passive activities such as listening to the teacher and completing worksheets. AND/OR There are limited opportunities for child choice and child initiation.	Some learning activities and experiences involve learners in active, engaged learning through inquiry, research, problem-solving, experimentation, and other hands-on activities. There are some opportunities for child choice and child initiation.	Most learning activities and experiences involve learners in active, engaged learning through inquiry, research, problem-solving, experimentation, and other hands-on activities. There are many opportunities for child choice and child initiation.

Peer Review

The purpose of the peer review is as a formative assessment allowing the author to gain feedback that will strengthen the unit. Feedback consists of:

- pointing out praiseworthy sections of the plan, those areas that meet the rubric criteria.
- Asking questions where the plan is unclear.
- pointing out items that are missing or do not meet the criteria. For example, the peer reviewer might state, "I see that the essential question can be answered with a yes or no rather than being open-ended."
- offering tentative suggestions. For example, a peer reviewer might state, "I have found that using the alignment grid has been helpful in ensuring my desired results and assessments align."

Early
Childhood
Education

> I can see that completing the rubrics on the peer's units would help the peer. It seems like it would also help the reviewer by further clarifying the important aspects of the backward design process.

Yes, I agree. To successfully implement peer feedback, I have found that it is important to provide expectations that feedback will be specific and address both strengths and areas that need work. You may also need to provide instruction and support to help the reviewers in giving clear, honest feedback in a non-threatening way.

Backward Design Examples

Following are three unit examples; a ball investigation for infants and toddlers (Box 10.4), a butterfly project for preschoolers (Box 10.5), and a heroes unit for second grade (Box 10.6). You will note that each teacher develops the unit in a slightly different way based upon the teacher's beliefs and the development of children the unit is being designed for.

Box 10.4 Balls Investigation

Title: Balls Investigation

Age of children or learners: 12 months to 36 months

Overview of investigation: This investigation will focus on exploring the properties and the motion of balls. Children will have many hands-on opportunities to explore the different properties of balls such as size, texture, shape, color, and weight. They will investigate how the property of the ball affects what you can do with it. For example, how well the ball rolls or bounces. They will also explore how balls move and how their actions affect the ball's movements. Since the children in the classroom are a variety of ages and developmental levels, they will have choices of participating in experiences based upon their interests and development.

Investigation rationale (Why this topic?) Balls are readily available, interesting objects that promote physical activity and play. The children in my classroom are physically active and challenging their new-found physical skills by rolling and kicking balls. As children play with the balls, they can see an immediate result of their action.

Desired Results
Standards that are being bundled for this unit
Scientific Thinking and Use of the Scientific Method Standard
As children seek to understand their environment and test new knowledge, they engage in scientific investigations using their senses to observe, manipulate objects, ask questions, make predictions, and develop conclusions and generalizations.

- Identify similarities and differences among objects
- Participate in simple teacher-initiated investigations to test observations, discuss and draw conclusions, and form generalizations

Physical Science Standard
Children develop an understanding of the physical world (the nature and properties of energy, non-living matter, and the forces that give order to the natural world).

- Explore how objects move
- Explore cause and effect

Data Analysis Standard
Children apply mathematical skills in data analysis, such as counting, sorting, and comparing objects.

- Group a few objects by similarity

Algebraic Thinking Standard
Children learn to identify, describe, produce, and create patterns using mathematical language and materials.

- Classify, label, and sort familiar objects into a known group.

Standards are from the Montana Early Learning Standards (O'Dell & Montana Early Childhood Project, 2014).

Concept or big idea Classification	
Enduring Understandings Objects have properties that can be observed, described, compared, classified, and investigated. The property of an object affects the way it is used. In investigating objects, we can observe the object, pose a question, form a hypothesis, and test our hypothesis to see if we were accurate. Topical understandings Balls are objects that have some similar and some dissimilar properties. The properties of the ball affect the way it moves. We can make balls move differently based upon our actions.˙	Essential Questions How do the properties of an object affect its use? What are ways that we can investigate objects? Topical questions What are the properties of a ball? How do the properties of the ball affect the way it moves? What are the ways we change the way the ball moves?
Knowledge The child will: use vocabulary for different properties of balls and types of movement of balls determine attributes of balls that make them easier to throw, catch, roll, and bounce	Approaches to Learning Curiosity Perseverance
Skills The child will: experiment with different ways to change the movement of balls classify balls by attributes	Possible preconceptions or misconceptions All balls roll All round items are balls

Assessments

Pre-assessments	Formative assessments
Describe the properties of a ball (Tell me about the ball? Can you tell me more?) Given a collection of four balls, the child is able to determine which will roll best The child will demonstrate how you make a ball roll further The child will demonstrate how you change the direction of a ball	Interviews with children after conducting investigations to see if they understand why they are engaging in the activity and if they know the outcome.

Summative assessments or key final assessments
The pre-assessment and summative assessments will be the same so that we can determine how much the children have learned.

- Describe the properties of a ball (Tell me about the ball? Can you tell me more?)
- Classifies balls
- Given a collection of four balls, the child is able to determine which will roll furthest
- The child will demonstrate strategies to make a ball roll further
- The child will demonstrate strategies to change the direction of a ball's movement

The context column has been removed from this grid. Consistent with our beliefs about developmentally appropriate curriculum for infants and toddlers, all activities except for the field site visits will be conducted individually or in spontaneous small groups.

Specific experiences The child will:	Strategies The teacher will:
Provocation: The circle area will be filled with balls when the children enter the classroom.	provide balls that are different types, sizes, colors, and shapes.
explore the properties of the balls and classify balls by the properties.	talk about the properties of balls as she is interacting with children. provide hula hoops to classify balls and help children to classify.
conduct investigations that will help determine properties.	design investigations that will explore the balls' properties: • Do all balls float? • Do all balls bounce? • Do all balls roll? • Which balls are easier to throw? • Which balls are easier to catch?
	assist children to synthesize what they are learning by making posters with photos of the balls and the actions. For example, the ball that children determine is the easiest to catch will have a photo of the ball and a photo of a child catching the ball.
listen to stories about balls.	read books about balls to individuals or small groups of children.

use materials for interacting with the ball's properties.	add props that will further the investigations into properties such as basketball hoops and baskets for throwing and items to knock down for rolling.
see people using balls in different sports.	plan walking trips to see teams or individuals using balls. We are on a college campus so will visit basketball practice, soccer practice, and the bowling alley. Let children handle the balls. Talk about the properties of the ball. Talk about how the ball is being used such as basketball being dribbled. provide vocabulary and parallel talk.
draw and paint representations of different types of balls and create balls from three-dimensional materials.	provide art media and balls that children can observe as they draw and paint. provide newspaper and tape to create three dimensional balls.
explore how balls move.	provide ramps and tubes for exploring ball movement.
change the movement of a ball.	create challenges such as: How can we make the ball roll further? How do we change the path of a ball?

How will you supplement your learning centers to support the unit or project? I will:

- provide a variety of different types of balls, footballs, soccer balls, beach balls, waffle balls, nerf balls, cloth balls, Koosh balls, and large exercise balls. Also, I will include a variety of round items that are not balls such as cotton balls, an ice cream ball, and a plastic orange
- provide accessories for the balls, small basketball hoops, laundry baskets, inclined planes, hula hoops, tubes
- provide the following books on balls

    o *My first book of motion* by Eric Carle
    o *Where is baby's beach ball* by Karen Katz
    o *Ball board book* by Mary Sullivan
    o *A ball for Daisy* by Chris Raschka
    o *Ball: Baby unplugged* by John Hutton
    o *How far will it bounce? My blue ball* by DC Swain
    o *ABC's of balls* by Nina Snyder
    o *Stop that ball* by Mike McClintock

- stress the following vocabulary

    o experiment
    o property
    o movement
    o names of props such as inclined plane, hula hoop, basket
    o names of types of balls
    o colors
    o different textural words

o   different shape words such as round and sphere
o   words for actions with balls roll, dribble, kick

How will you involve families in the unit or project?

- Families will be invited to share balls and books on balls.
- Families will be invited to show children ball skills and attend walking field site visits.
- Daily documentation will be shown on a digital screen when families pick up children.
- The families will be invited to a culminating event.
- The families will each receive a digital book on the ball investigation.

How will you culminate the project or unit?

- Families will be invited to a picnic with numerous ball activities that children and families can partake in together. The digital book will be running on an outdoor projection screen so that families and children can watch it together if they wish.

Rubric for Ball Investigation Pre-Assessment and Summative Assessment

	Emerging	*Progressing*	*Well-developed*

Describe the properties of a ball
  The teacher might ask, "Tell me about the ball? Can you tell me more? What can you do with the ball? What is this type of ball called?"
	Names one or two properties of the ball.	Names a few properties of the ball.
		  Describes one thing that they might do with the ball.
		  Is unable to identify the type of ball.
			Names several different properties of the ball.
			  Names several things they can do with the ball.
			  Identifies the type of ball.

Classifies balls	Classifies by color when the teacher suggests this.	Classifies by a self-chosen attribute.
		  Can sort by another attribute when asked.
			Classifies by a self-chosen attribute.
			  Can sort by another attribute when asked.
			  Can describe the attributes.

Identifies which ball will roll furthest	Chooses the incorrect ball.	Identifies which ball will roll further.	Can identify which ball will roll further and can tell why.
Uses strategies to make a ball roll further	Uses no strategy or an unsuccessful strategy.	Can use at least one strategy to make the ball move further.	Can use at least one strategy to make the ball move further and can explain the strategy.
Uses strategies to change the direction of a ball	Uses no strategy or an unsuccessful strategy.	Can use at least one strategy to change the direction of the ball.	Can use at least one strategy to change the direction of the ball and can explain the strategy.

Wow, I had never thought about this type of in-depth project with children so young. Is it ever okay to use someone else's unit?

Using a unit designed by someone else may be a way to begin the backward design process. However, there are several caveats. You will want a high-quality unit. Make sure that you assess any unit you find using the backward design rubric. The backward design units that you find through searches on the Internet often do not meet these criteria. It is critical that the unit is relevant and appropriate for your group of children. That sometimes makes it challenging to use units that others have designed. Most likely you will want to make changes in the plan based upon such things as your children's skill levels, interests, and available resources. When you do so, it is helpful to complete the alignment grid to ensure that all the elements are still aligned. You might consider designing your own unit but using work from others as a starting point. I'm excited to hear that you are thinking about creating backward design units.

Box 10.5 Butterfly Project

Age of children or learners: 3–5 years old

Description of project: This project will be a study of butterflies. Here are some of the tentative plans. Children will witness the butterflies in the wild, hatch butterflies, study and build butterfly habitats, observe and study the butterfly metamorphosis using technology tools and representational art, study the differences and similarities between butterflies and moths, and conduct simple experiments. As they study the butterfly, they will learn about life cycles and the interdependence of butterflies and the environment. Previously, children have studied the life cycle of plants during a plant project and have studied the life cycle of humans during a project on babies. They will revisit what they've learned in these units. Since we are using the project approach, we will also be focusing on investigating children's questions. The project will continue until children's questions get answered or they lose interest.

Unit rationale (Why this topic?) Children found many caterpillars in the school play yard and were interested in learning more about these "funny worms." This unit allowed us to bundle many different standards in science, literacy, social science, technology, and the arts. It also allowed us to focus on conceptual learning while providing many hands-on experiences.

Desired Results
Standards that are being bundled for this unit
Science 4.15.d. Identify similarities and differences among objects 4.15.e. Participate in simple teacher-initiated investigations to test observations, discuss and draw conclusions, and form generalizations

4.15.f. Collect, describe, and record information through a variety of means
4.16.g. Describe the relationship between living things and their habitat
4.16.h. Observe and describe plants, insects, and animals as they go through predictable life cycles

Literacy
3.1.k. Focus on the meaning of words to enhance understanding and build vocabulary
3.5.l. Use books, magazines, and other printed materials to enhance play

Social Studies
4.22.g. Take responsibility for caring for living things

Technology
4.23.g. Demonstrate appropriate use and care of technological tools
4.23.h. Use technology as a tool for learning new information

Visual Arts
4.9.g. Use different colors, surface textures, and shapes to create form and meaning
Standards are from Montana Early Learning Standards (O'Dell & Montana Early Childhood Project, 2014).

Concepts or big ideas
Change, interdependence, cycles

Enduring Understandings All living things have predictable life cycles, but this varies by the organism. Living things change their form and behaviors as they go through the life cycle. Organisms and their environment are interdependent. Organisms have physical, structural, and behavioral adaptations that help them to survive, get food, and protect themselves from predators. **Topical enduring understandings** Butterflies change form and behaviors as they go through a predictable life cycle that involves metamorphosis. Some other living things grow and change but their basic form stays the same. Butterflies and the environment they are in are interdependent. Butterflies have physical, structural, and behavioral characteristics that allow them to survive, get food, and protect themselves.	**Essential Questions** How do different organisms change as they go through their life cycles? How are organisms and their environments interdependent? How do organisms adapt to their environments? **Topical essential questions** How are different organisms' life cycles the same and different? How are butterflies and their environments interdependent? How do the butterfly's physical characteristics, structural characteristics, and behaviors help it to survive, get food, and protect itself?
Knowledge The child will be able to: • describe the process of metamorphosis. • use new vocabulary such as metamorphosis, larva, pupa, cocoon, chrysalis, herbicide, insecticide.	Approaches to Learning Curiosity

Skills	Possible preconceptions or misconceptions
The child will be able to: • observe and compare butterflies and moths. • communicate their thinking through visual representation. • correctly use technological tools such as digital microscopes and magnifying glasses to observe.	Children might think that caterpillars are worms or that butterflies are caterpillars with wings.

Assessments

Pre-assessments	Formative assessments
KWHL chart prepared by small groups of children. Names are listed so that the teacher knows which children are responsible for which comments.	Science journal specifically Venn diagrams, representational drawing, diagram of metamorphosis and life cycles of plants and humans

Summative assessments or key final assessments
Individual interview Science journal

Experiences

Specific interactions and experiences The children will:	Learning context	Strategies The teacher will:
Provocation—the appearance of many caterpillars in the outdoor play yard.		
complete a KWHL	Small group	
listen to stories about butterflies and complete a T chart, "What I already knew and What I learned from this book."	Small group	read stories to small groups. assist children to complete the T chart, "What I already knew and What I learned." emphasize new words using the word wizard (a large stuffed wizard who introduces all new words in the classroom).
determine what caterpillars, pupa, and butterflies need in their environment to survive.	Whole group	lead a discussion about similarities between what butterflies need and what plants, animals and humans need using compare and contrast charts.
design a habitat for the caterpillars.	Small groups design two habitats one for butterflies and the other for moths	lead a discussion about the needs of the caterpillars, pupa, and butterflies and moths. assist children to brainstorm a list of needs. beside each need determine how this will be met within the habitat. work with small groups of children to develop the habitat.

collect caterpillars outside.	Small groups outdoor time	help children to carefully collect caterpillars to place in their habitats.
participate in a simple experiment determining what caterpillars like to eat.	Whole group Learning center	discuss with children how to conduct the experiment, what to offer the caterpillars. set up the experiment with interested children during learning center time. each day at whole group discuss and record how many caterpillars are eating what foods.
investigate their own questions from KWHL chart.	Small group	regularly revisit children's questions and update the KWHL chart. set up experiences to assist with answering children's questions.
interview an entomologist.	Whole group	invite an entomologist to visit the classroom. prepare the children for the visit by helping them plan questions. prepare the entomologist for the children's developmental level, the desire for interaction, and ask if he can bring tools and if any of these can be left for children to explore.
use new vocabulary words.	Whole group Small group Individual	post new vocabulary words. introduce words with the word wizard. use new vocabulary words during whole group, small group, and when working with children individually.
use materials in learning centers to learn more about butterflies.	Learning centers	introduce and build interest in materials.
observe the caterpillars, pupas, and butterflies using magnifying glasses and the digital microscope.	Whole group Learning center	conduct mini-lessons on using the tools. demonstrate the digital microscope and encourage children to notice each of the parts of the butterfly and to discuss the function. use I see, I notice, I wonder routine.
create representations by drawing each part of the metamorphosis.	Learning centers	provide journals for each child and encourage them to revisit their drawings.
create representations in other art media such as painting and clay.	Learning centers	post photos and pictures of butterflies by artists in the art area.

keep a science journal.	Routine time Learning centers	prepare journals with pages for: • drawing each part of the metamorphosis • drawing the life cycle of humans and plants • collecting data on the time and number of butterflies that hatch • representational drawing • Venn diagram comparing moths and butterflies Introduce journals during a small group time.
contribute to counting and tracking how many caterpillars become pupas (chrysalis) on the class calendar and create a data chart.	Whole group	prepare a large wall calendar. help children count how many caterpillars become pupas each day.
continue to visit the play yard and surrounding community looking for where caterpillars and butterflies are found.	Small group outdoor	take digital photos and help children to analyze the photos to determine differences and similarities in the environment.
compare how the moth and butterfly are alike and different.	Small group	help children to examine the moth and butterfly using the digital microscope. Record the similarities and the differences on a Venn diagram.
plan the culminating butterfly release.	Whole group	have children determine the criteria for the event (e.g. show families what they have learned, make it fun, have food, let the butterflies live). assist children to brainstorm how they will meet each criterion. help children to choose what they will include in the event and to make more detailed plans. choose a time that will be conducive for the families but will also allow for the safety of the butterflies.
create invitations.	Whole group Learning centers	present a mini-lesson on writing invitations. help the class determine what should be on the invitations. provide materials for invitations.
revisit documentation and reflect upon what they learned.	Small group	assist children to reflect upon what they learned by using the protocol I used to think____but now I think.

Alignment Grid

Desired result	How will the desired result be assessed?	What experiences allow children to develop the desired results?
How are different organisms' life cycles the same and different?	Science journal rubric (life cycle)	Read books Discussion Compare and contrast chart for butterfly, person, plant Draw cycles in journal
How are butterflies and their environments interdependent?	Scenario rubric (needs and contributions)	Books Discussion and development of habitat Compare and contrast chart for butterfly, person, plant Visits to play yard and community to see butterflies in their natural habitat Guest speaker Discussions
How do the butterfly's physical characteristics, structural characteristics, and behaviors help it to survive, get food, and protect itself?	Scenario rubric (describe specific characteristics)	Close examination of butterfly characteristics with magnifying glasses and digital microscope Discussion Books Representational art and discussion about the art
Describe the process of metamorphosis	Science journal rubric (life cycle)	Observations Representational drawings Books
Use new vocabulary such as metamorphosis, larva, pupa, cocoon, chrysalis, herbicide, insecticide	Scenario rubric (terminology)	Teachers post words, introduce words with the word wizard, and use words during whole group, small group, and when working with children individually
Observe and compare butterflies and moths	Science journal rubric (compare butterflies and moths)	Observe using digital microscope and record findings on Venn diagram
Communicate their thinking through visual representation	Science journal rubric (representational drawings)	Several representational drawings, paintings, and clay models
Correctly use technological tools such as digital microscopes and magnifying glasses to observe	Observation	Mini-lecture Using tools throughout the project

How will you supplement your learning centers to support the unit or project?

Manipulative

- Games such as match the butterfly lotto game, butterfly metamorphism seriation, plant life cycle seriation, and human life cycle seriation. For more advanced children, I will provide a matching game of butterflies and their host plants.

Science area

- The butterflies and the moths in their habitats
- Journals
- Vocabulary words posted so that all adults in the environment remember to use them when interacting with children
- Butterfly facts posted
- Class generated KWHL's posted
- Investigative tools such as magnifying glasses and digital microscope
- Calendar with the number of caterpillars that become pupas each day
- Items supplied by the entomologist

Writing area

- Word wall with words such as metamorphosis, chrysalis, larva, nectar, host plant. Additional words added upon child request.

Art area

- Photos and artists drawings and paintings of butterflies to provide information and inspiration.
- Clay and wire for creating caterpillars

Dramatic play

- Add dress-up butterfly wings and put a transparency on the overhead projector of butterflies flying.

Reading area

- Include books on butterflies

  o *Caterpillar Diary* by David Drew
  o *Caterpillar to Butterfly* by Melvin and Gilda Berger
  o *A Butterfly Grows Up* by Melvin and Gilda Berger
  o *Butterfly* by Marie Canizares
  o *Monarch Butterfly* by David M. Schwartz
  o *The Monarch: Saving Our Most-Loved Butterfly* by Kylee Baumle
  o *National Geographic Kids Look and Learn: Caterpillar to Butterfly*
  o *Face to Face with Caterpillars* by Darlyne A. Murawski
  o *National Geographic Readers: Great Migrations Butterflies* by Laura Marsh
  o *Fly with a Butterfly*—National Geographic Young Explorer

Literature Selections:

  o *The Very Hungry Caterpillar* by Eric Carle
  o *Munch, Munch, Munch* by Norma L. Gentner

- Bookmark short videos of butterflies on the tablets such as Life Cycle of a Butterfly by Smart Learning for All; Butterfly, Butterfly Song by Harry Kindergarten; The Life Cycle of a Butterfly Song by Silly Schools Songs

During center time teachers:

- Use targeted vocabulary words

    o   Metamorphosis
    o   Stages of metamorphosis Larva (Caterpillar) Pupa (Chrysalis, Cocoon), Caterpillar
    o   Interdependence
    o   Habitat
    o   Host plant
    o   Nectar plant
    o   Herbicide
    o   Insecticide
    o   Pollination
    o   Puddling
    o   Parts of the butterfly-head, thorax, abdomen, antennae, wing, proboscis

- Encourage children to participate in close observation
- Assist children with any needed art techniques in creating representations
- Provide butterfly facts for children when appropriate
- Read stories to children about butterflies
- Ask open-ended questions such as, "Why do you think some caterpillars become butterflies sooner than others? What type of foods do you think the butterfly will eat? What would happen if the sticks were removed from the habitat?"

How will you involve families in the unit or project?

- Inform families of the unit and ask for ideas and input, assistance, and resources
- Invite families to the butterfly release

How will you culminate the project or unit?

- The culmination will be a celebration where the butterflies are released and the families get an opportunity to see children's documentation. The rest of the celebration will be planned by the children.

Summative assessment
I will interview children individually using the following scenario.

> A girl named Tabatha wants to create a butterfly garden. Her parents have said that Tabatha can create a garden, but they want her to explain why the butterflies would be helpful in their yard. She needs your help in explaining why butterflies are helpful. Tabatha also needs your help in deciding what she will need in the garden so that the butterflies can survive and what to avoid in the garden so that she doesn't hurt the butterflies? Here is a picture of a butterfly. How do the different butterfly body parts help the butterfly?

To make the scenario more lifelike, I will provide photos of Tabatha, Tabatha's parents, a butterfly garden, and a butterfly as the story is told.

Rubric: *Butterfly Scenario Summative Assessment*

	Beginning	*Developing*	*Accomplished*
Characteristics Describes specific characteristics (physical, structural, and behavior) that help the butterfly survive, get food, and protect itself?	Information is inaccurate and superficial.	Information is accurate but not in-depth. Can describe some characteristics of butterflies and how this relates to their survival, ability to get food, and to protect themselves. Does not use terminology learned in the unit.	Information is accurate and in-depth. Mentions such things as camouflage, roosting behavior, hibernation, and migration. Discusses specific physical characteristics and how they help the butterfly survive.
Needs	Describes a need of the butterfly	Describes the needs of butterflies for habitat, protection against predators, and a suitable food source.	Describes the needs of butterflies for habitat, protection against predators, and a suitable food source. Describes things that might hurt butterflies such as herbicides and pesticides.
Contributions	Describes how butterflies are beautiful or fun to watch.	Describes the butterfly as being beautiful and as a pollinator.	Describes how butterflies are a part of the food chain, pollinators, and are beautiful.
Terminology	Uses one or two new terms as discusses butterflies.	Uses a few new terms in their discussion about butterflies.	Uses several correct terms as they discuss butterflies such as metamorphism, larva, caterpillar, pupa, cocoon, chrysalis, herbicide, and insecticide.

Rubric: *Science Journal Summative Assessment*

	Beginning	*Developing*	*Accomplished*
Life cycle	Only part of the life cycle of plants, humans, and butterflies are shown.	Includes each part of the life cycle for a plant, human, and butterfly.	Includes each part of the life cycle for a plant, human, and butterfly. Can describe the similarities and differences between them.
Compare butterflies and moths Uses a digital pen to record or adult transcribes	Venn diagrams are inaccurate.	Venn diagrams are accurate but provide limited detail.	Venn diagrams comparing moths and butterflies are accurate and provide detailed information.
Representational drawings	Limited representational art is available. AND/OR Little detail is included making it difficult to determine the child's knowledge.	Several forms of representational art are included that demonstrate children's ideas and knowledge of butterflies.	Several forms of representational art are included that demonstrate children's ideas and knowledge of butterflies. Art shows increasing detail demonstrating a deepening understanding of butterflies.

I've conducted several projects focused on life science in the past, but I've never emphasized the "big picture." I'm excited to work toward engaging children in this type of deeper learning.

Yes, it is challenging to contemplate what enduring understandings and essential questions are appropriate for young children. However, it becomes easier with practice and it is exciting to see the deeper learning that can occur as a result.

Box 10.6 Heroes Unit

Heroes unit (Heroes in this unit apply to all genders).

Age of children: second grade

Description of unit: This is a multi-week unit, that integrates social studies, language arts, technology, visual arts, and health. There are three distinct segments to the unit beginning with, "What is a hero?" where the children read stories of modern-day and past heroes, analyze the attributes of the heroes they are reading about, and ultimately develop a definition of a hero and list qualities that heroes have. During this segment, there will be discussions about how the characteristics of a hero are culturally based. The next segment is, "Who is a hero?" where children will explore heroes around them, choose a hero to research, and will type a story about their hero. The third segment is, "Becoming a hero" where children analyze their qualities against those of a hero. They examine heroic actions and plan and implement a class hero project.

Unit rationale (Why this topic?) There have been several bullying incidents in the school. The teachers have met and created an action plan to eliminate bullying using several strategies. One is to focus on positive attributes. Another is to plan more cooperative group activities. This unit addresses both of these. Additionally, it meets several standards, allows for hands-on investigation and in-depth learning. Finally, there is a national heroes project, called MyHero that I think the children will be interested in.

Desired Results
Standards that are being bundled for this unit
Social studies (DoDEA, 2016). Students understand how the actions and integrity of individuals change the ways in which people in society work and live together
• 2SS4.a: Explain how the actions of heroes from long ago and the recent past have made a difference in others' lives.
• 2SS4.b: Identify real people and fictional characters who are good leaders and responsible citizens, and explain the qualities that make them admirable, such as honesty and trustworthiness.

2SSK2: Use print and non-print reference sources to locate information.

Language arts (National Governors Association Center for Best Practices, Council of Chief State School Officers, 2010)

- Demonstrate command of the conventions of standard English capitalization, punctuation, and spelling when writing.
- Describe how characters in a story respond to major events and challenges.
- Describe how reasons support specific points the author makes in a text.
- Write informative/explanatory texts in which they introduce a topic, use facts and definitions to develop points, and provide a concluding statement or section.
- With guidance and support from adults, use a variety of digital tools to produce and publish writing, including in collaboration with peers.
- Ask and answer questions about what a speaker says in order to clarify comprehension, gather additional information, or deepen understanding of a topic or issue.

Technology

- Use keyboarding to create a document.
- Add graphics to a document.
- Use the Internet to find credible information.

Health

- Develop a positive self-esteem focused on individual strengths

21st-century skills

- Engage in collaborative discussions and projects

Concept or big idea Cultures shape values	
Enduring Understandings Admirable attributes are culturally determined. Most people have both admirable and non-admirable attributes. **Topical Enduring Understandings** Heroes are people who have admirable attributes, as defined by the culture. We can each develop attributes that make us a hero.	**Essential Questions** What attributes does your culture admire? How do your personal attributes align with the attributes considered admirable by your culture? **Topical Essential Questions** What are the attributes of a hero in your culture? Who is a hero? How can I become my own hero?
Knowledge The child will be able to: define the qualities of a hero and provide a rationale for their description. identify and describe the characteristics of historical and modern heroes. understand the influences of culture on what is viewed as heroic.	Approaches to Learning Initiative in developing the projects Attentiveness to other group members and visiting experts
Skills including meta-cognitive skills The child will be able to: present information with supporting evidence justify information based upon reasons. write a well-developed paper that considers the audience.	Possible preconceptions or misconceptions. Heroes are always warriors or fighters. Celebrities are heroes.

work collaboratively with a group to develop and implement a project. locate information using various sources such as books, the Internet, and interviews. assess their own attributes.	Heroes have supernatural powers like having X-ray vision, super-human strength, or the ability to change to another form.
Assessments	
Pre-assessments Children answer the following questions. What is a hero? Who is a hero? Are you a hero? Why or why not?	Formative assessments Writing workshop rubrics
Summative assessments or key final assessments • Hero story rubric • Hero project rubric	

Specific interactions and experiences The children will:	Learning context	Teaching and learning strategies The teacher will:
Provocation: Wonder Woman and Batman arrive and introduce the unit. They also discuss a real-life hero, Hannah Taylor by talking about her and playing a story tape describing her actions.	Whole group	Lead a discussion of the difference between superheroes and real-life heroes.
What is a hero?		
read several books and stories about heroes and make a class grid of hero characteristics.	Whole and small group	have children compare likenesses and differences between different hero's characteristics using a compare and contrast grid.
learn more about modern-day heroes through newspaper clippings and articles about heroes.	Morning meeting	tell a brief story of a hero from the newspaper or from magazine articles. These will be articles I find or ones that are posted on the MyHero website.
listen to stories about heroes, watch videos of heroes, and read books about heroes.	Learning centers	bookmark audio and video about heroes from MyHero website. provide a variety of books. scaffold children's learning as they listen or read books.
watch the virtual reality video of The Crow.	Whole group	obtain The Crow video from MyHero website. discuss the attributes that made the crow a hero. lead a discussion about whether animals can be heroes.
interview families about "What is a hero?"	Individual Small group	conduct mini-lesson on how to interview. teach children how to ask good questions by reviewing open and closed-questions. help children to develop interview questions.

share what they learned in their interviews with the group.	Whole group	have two or three children each day share what they have learned with the group. lead discussion about similarities and differences in answers. have children review the characteristics of heroes and make changes. lead a discussion about how culture affects our view of a hero.
determine the difference between a hero and an idol.	Whole group	bring photos of some of the children's idols. lead a discussion on whether they meet the criteria for heroes.
create a definition of a hero and a list of rules for heroes.	Small groups	help children synthesize what they have learned by creating a definition of heroes and by creating a list of rules for heroes. begin with the prompts, "A hero is ..." and "To be a hero you must..."
Who is a hero?		
identify local school heroes and give them badges.	Individual Whole group	encourage children to closely observe those in the school for heroic attributes. encourage children to nominate a potential person. lead the group in using the thinking routine, Claim, Support, and Question. have the children come to a consensus on whether the person should receive a hero award.
interview a visiting expert.	Whole group	help children determine who to have visit and the questions to ask the expert. prepare the expert with information on the project and the developmental characteristics of the children. encourage the expert to bring props if possible.
choose a hero to learn more about. This could be a historic or a modern-day hero. It could be someone the child personally knows.	Share the chosen hero with a small group	assist children in using Claim, Support, and Question to defend their choice of hero.
investigate their hero.	Learning centers	individually interact with children providing suggestions for books, assisting with Internet searches, and helping develop interview questions.

write a story about his or her hero using multiple drafts. participate in writing workshops with small groups. provide feedback on each other's stories using Warm and Cool Feedback, a protocol that they have been using all year.	Individual during learning center time. Small group sharing.	have children share drafts with their writing workshop group. provide mini-workshops on skills as needed based upon formative assessments. during writing
create an image of their hero through drawing or photography.	Whole group introduction. Individual during learning center time	review some images on MyHero, using I See, I Think, I Wonder to explore the image. discuss the media used. have children provide advantages and disadvantages of different media. teach a mini-lesson on how to insert the photo or artwork into their story.
share the story of the hero with the class.	Whole group	have a few children share their story each day. encourage children to ask questions of the presenter.
reflect on their learning.	Individual	introduce children to Two Stars and a Wish and have them use this technique for their reflections
Becoming a hero.		
discuss heroic actions.	Whole group	develop and read scenarios to children. This could be about local issues such as bullying. assist children to brainstorm how a hero would act.
determine a hero project.	Whole group	help children determine the criteria for the project. have children brainstorm possible projects. help children to rate the projects against the criteria. have children vote on the project.
develop an action plan.	Whole group	help children develop steps to implement the project. determine who will complete which steps.
implement the action plan.	Individual and small group	use cooperative learning groups to complete the project, if appropriate.
reflect on what they have learned about heroes.	Small group	assist children to brainstorm a list of what they now know about heroes.
develop and implement a culminating event.	Whole and small groups	assist children in planning an event to share information on their hero unit.

How will you supplement your learning centers to support the unit?

- Books of heroes will be added to the literacy center, such as *The story of Ruby Bridges* by Robert Cole, *26 big things small hands can do* by Colleen Paratore, *A bus called heaven* by Bob Graham, *Nobody knew what to do* by Albert Whitman, *Superheroes are everywhere* by Kamala Harris, *Heroes for all times* by Mary Pope Osborne, *Ordinary people change the world* series by Brad Meltzer.
- Specific stories about heroes from the MyHero website will be bookmarked on computers and tablets for children to explore, such as Alexandra Scott, Vivienne Harr, John Tacket, and Caine Monroe. The Rebel Girls podcasts will also be bookmarked.
- Individual hero folders for each child will be created and stored in the cloud so children can work on reports from multiple computers.
- A class MyHero website will be created to post and share the children's stories.
- Digital cameras and old phones that children can use to take photos will be added to the technology center
- Drawings and paintings of heroes from the MyHero website will be posted in the art area. Media will be available so children can create an image of their hero.
- Bulletin boards will contain the on-going class characteristics of hero's grid.
- The MyHero story rubric will be posted in the writing center.

How will you involve families in the unit?

- We will share MyHero's website link and the link to the class website on heroes.
- I will send a letter about the hero's unit to ask for ideas and to describe ways that families can assist with the unit.
- Children will interview family members to determine who the family considers heroes.
- Families will be invited to the culminating event.

How will you culminate the unit?

The culminating event will be a MyHero Fest. It will be planned by the children using materials from the MyHero website. It might include such things as a display of the children's stories, a video recording of each child discussing why they are a hero, recognition of their local heroes, and a discussion of their final project.

Rubric: MyHero Story Summative Assessment

	Novice	Developing	Proficient
Describes a hero	Describes a hero that conflicts with what the class has studied. For example, describes superheroes.	Lists one or two characteristics that make their chosen person a hero.	Lists several characteristics that make their chosen person a hero.
Justifies the choice of the hero	Justifies the choice of a hero using characteristics that are not consistent with the definition.	Justifies the choice of a hero with an example that matches the characteristics listed.	Justifies the choice of a hero with specific, well-described examples that match the characteristics listed.

	Novice	*Developing*	*Proficient*
Uses effective writing	Some sentences are punctuated and capitalized appropriately. Some subjects and verbs agree. Beginning paragraph and an ending paragraph might not be obvious. Some of the writing makes sense. Most of the writing is on topic. Little variety is evident in sentences.	Most sentences are punctuated and capitalized appropriately. Most subjects and verbs agree. Includes a beginning paragraph and an ending paragraph. Most of the writing makes sense. Most of the writing is on topic. Includes some varied sentences.	All sentences are punctuated and capitalized appropriately. Subjects and verbs agree. Includes a beginning paragraph and an ending paragraph. Writing makes sense and is on topic. Uses a variety of types of sentences. Uses interesting words.
Uses technology skills	Typing contains many mistakes. AND/OR Needs extensive support with typing and adding the photo.	Accurately types the report. Needs support typing or adding the photo or artwork.	Accurately and independently types the report and independently adds the photo.

Rubric: Hero Project Summative Assessment

Describes heroes (interview)	Defines a hero in relation to the current project only.	Can define a hero including historic, modern-day figures, and themselves. Lists 3-4 characteristics of heroes. Provides an example of how heroes make life better.	Can define a hero including historic, modern-day figures, and themselves. Lists 5-6 characteristics of heroes. Describes several examples of how heroes make life better. Able to discuss how heroes are different in different cultures.
Actively participates in planning a hero project	Does not participate. OR Provides information that is not relevant to the topic.	Participates but ideas might not show a deep understanding of heroes. Listens to other's ideas.	Provides relevant ideas that show a deep understanding of heroes. Builds upon other's ideas.
Collaborates effectively with others	Shares ideas but has difficulty making compromises and valuing other's ideas.	Listens respectfully, shares ideas, makes compromises, and values other's ideas.	Listens respectfully, shares ideas, makes compromises, values other's ideas, and assists the group to arrive at a consensus.

Follows through with hero activities	Completes limited activities for the hero project.	Completes activities for the project.	Completes activities for the project and supports others with their work.

These rubrics are for my assessment. I will create separate rubrics for the children to use. For example, I will have a child-friendly rubric that children can use in their writing workshops.

In Summary

Creating units using backward design helps to ensure that children meet standards and that they also gain concepts that will transfer to new learning situations. This method of planning allows for flexibility to meet the needs of each unique group of learners while also providing a structure that helps to ensure that we meet desired outcomes.

As you begin to design units, it is advisable to start small. This is very cognitively demanding work especially since this is not the way most of us have planned curriculum in the past. Choosing the right topic is very important. Begin with a topic that is interesting to you and the children and provides for in-depth, hands-on learning. If possible, work with peers. As you work on your design keep alignment in the forefront of your mind. Very often different parts of a unit do not align and therefore either the learners do not meet the desired results, or it is not possible to know if they have. The alignment grid can be a helpful tool. Designing your unit is an iterative process. For example, as you design assessments, it is likely that you will clarify your enduring understandings and essential questions. This will often occur again as you design your rubrics. Finally, remember that there is rarely, if ever, a perfect unit. Even with a thorough and well-designed unit, you may discover hidden flaws as you implement it. However, you will be able to make changes as you go.

Embarking on planning using backward design can be challenging, but will create more aligned, conceptually based units leading to enhanced learning. Well-designed units can also be extremely engaging. As a teacher, there are few things more rewarding than seeing learners excitedly partaking in deep, challenging learning experiences and witnessing their joy as they learn a new skill, acquire new knowledge, or gain a deeper understanding. Through backward design, we can facilitate this type of deep thinking and learning. As Confucius states, "Learning without thinking is fruitless" (Huang, 1997, p. 55).

Apply Your Knowledge

1. What are the similarities you see between the three sample units in the chapter? What are the differences between the units?
2. Critique at least one of the sample units using the backward design rubric. How could the unit be changed to make it more effective?
3. Design your own unit using the unit plan template. Critique your unit with the backward design rubric.
4. Complete an Internet search for a backward design unit. Use the backward design rubric to critique the unit. How could the unit be improved?
5. Think of a provocation for each of the following units; a study of crickets, a project called our campus trees, and a unit on our neighborhood.

References

Department of Defense Education Activity (DoDEA). (2016). *Social studies grade two: People who make a difference: Social studies content standards*. Retrieved from https://www.dodea.edu/Curriculum/social-Studies/upload/2009stn_SS_grd2.pdf

Huang, C. (ed.). (1997). *The analects of Confucius*. New York: Oxford University Press.

National Governors Association Center for Best Practices, Council of Chief State School Officers. (2010). *Common core state standards English language arts*. Washington, DC: National Governors Association Center for Best Practices, Council of Chief State School Officers.

O'Dell, C., & Montana Early Childhood Project. (2014). *Montana early learning standards*. Retrieved from https://opi.mt.gov/Portals/182/Page%20Files/Early%20Childhood/Docs/14EarlyLearningStandards.pdf

Index

CPSIA information can be obtained
at www.ICGtesting.com
Printed in the USA
BVHW011300220721
612643BV00011B/131

9 781138 570139